Bat Boy

Doubleday

New York   London   Toronto   Sydney   Auckland

Matthew McGough

Bat Boy

*My true life adventures coming of age
with the New York Yankees*

PUBLISHED BY DOUBLEDAY
a division of Random House, Inc.

DOUBLEDAY and the portrayal of an anchor with a dolphin are
registered trademarks of Random House, Inc.

While all of the incidents in this book are true, some of the
names and personal characteristics of the individuals involved
have been changed in order to protect their privacy. Any
resulting resemblance to persons living or dead is entirely
coincidental and unintentional.

Book design by Maria Carella

Photo of baseball bats courtesy of Photodisc
Collection / Getty Images

Library of Congress Cataloging-in-Publication Data
McGough, Matthew.
Bat Boy : my true life adventures coming of age with the New York Yankees /
Matthew McGough.—1st ed.
    p. cm.
1. McGough, Matthew. 2. Bat boys—United States—Biography.
3. New York Yankees (Baseball team) I. Title.
GV865.M294A3 2005
796.357'092—dc22
[B]   2004061756

ISBN 0-385-51020-9

PRINTED IN THE UNITED STATES OF AMERICA

May 2005

First Edition

1 3 5 7 9 10 8 6 4 2

in memory of my friend Greg Trost

Contents

1 · The Best Seat in the House · *1*

2 · Are You the Yankees Bat Boy? · *31*

3 · The Rookie · *56*

4 · Road Trip · *93*

5 · Should We Tell the Kid? · *113*

6 · Spring Training · *148*

7 · The Veteran · *191*

8 · Spider's Web · *218*

9 · Retiring from Baseball · *251*

10 · Extra Innings · *261*

Acknowledgments · *271*

Aesthetics of Being a Baseball

Go as fast as you can
In whatever direction.

Kenneth Koch, from *On Aesthetics*

Bat Boy

The Best Seat in the House

The game of baseball frames many of my sweetest childhood memories.

I made my first friendships playing Little League, and these friendships were shaped by countless hours of team batting and fielding practice on our neighborhood diamond. I consider our coach, a burly police officer named Mr. Ferguson, to have been my first great teacher. He drilled us in baseball fundamentals until they became second nature, but also allowed us time to practice acrobatic catches and double plays, feats we dreamt ourselves capable of but had little chance of ever actually executing in a game. Practices were focused but fun, a solid foundation for a lifelong love of baseball.

As a fan, I grew up rooting for the New York Yankees, and the team's players became my earliest heroes. I looked forward to visiting Yankee Stadium at least as eagerly as I anticipated the first day of summer vacation, Halloween night, or Christmas morning. I was still too young to realize that I might lack major league talent, and the handful of games I'd seen in person just fueled the dream that I too might play someday at the Stadium.

As momentous as any trip to see the Yankees seemed at the time, there was one particular game that made an impression so vivid and powerful that I can hardly imagine my childhood without it. In fact, it's hard not to wonder how my adolescence might have unfolded had I been anywhere else but Yankee Stadium that day.

The game, against the Kansas City Royals, was played on a sweltering Sunday afternoon in late July 1983. I had just turned eight. Personally speaking, it had been a banner summer for baseball.

I was halfway through my second season of Little League, starting at shortstop and leading off for my team, the legendary, perennially pennant-contending Brunt & Brooks Pharmacy. Being sponsored by a pharmacy didn't yield the tangible rewards enjoyed by some of our rival teams—namely, Tony's Pizzeria or the Ice Cream Villa—but one through nine, B&B had the best third-grade ballplayers in town. My team won many games that summer.

After the school year ended that June, my bedtime had been pushed back late enough that, if the pitchers worked fast and kept the score down, I could watch Yankees night games on television right up to the last out. Summer days peaked with Little League practice, then dinner in front of the TV listening to Phil Rizzuto call that night's Yankees game until Mom or Dad sent me to my room. That Fourth of July, I sat on the living room floor and watched every pitch of Dave Righetti's no-hitter against the Boston Red Sox. It was one of the most exciting things I'd ever seen; the fireworks show broadcast later that night from over the East River seemed dim in comparison. A few nights later, tuning in to another game, I saw Dave Winfield reach up and over the outfield wall to pull a game-winning home run back into play. I was awestruck by his catch. For weeks afterward, I imitated it so tirelessly against the four-foot-tall chain-link fence surrounding our Little League field that I came home from baseball practice every night with scrapes and bruises up and down my left arm.

Then came the game against the Royals. Since the night my dad brought home the tickets—one each for him, my little brother Damien, and me—I'd been able to think and speak of little else. We arrived at Yankee Stadium in time for the national anthem, and our seats in the upper deck had an expansive view of the field and the Bronx beyond it. Once the game started, though, I had trouble keeping my eye on the ball.

A friend had recently taught me how to keep score, the system of shorthand by which the details of any baseball game can be recorded for posterity. In my eagerness to correctly make note of each at bat on the scorecard, I spent a good share of the afternoon with my head in the program, half a step behind what was happening in the game.

Also competing for my attention were a trio of belligerent beer-swilling Yankees fans in the row directly behind us, huge men, unshaven and foul-mouthed. I stole quick glances at them over my shoulder between pitches, fascinated but terrified they might catch me staring.

The Yankees took a 4–3 lead into the ninth inning. Damien and I joined the crowd in a lusty chant of "We Want the Goose," a reference to Goose Gossage, the Yankees' celebrated relief pitcher warming up in the bullpen. It was my favorite ballpark huzzah, excepting the bugle call that always ended with a spirited "Charge!" After a two-out Royals single put the tying run on first base, Yankees manager Billy Martin acquiesced to the crowd and brought Gossage in to close out the victory. My brother and I retook our seats, satisfied at having influenced the course of the ball-game. I noted the pitching change on my scorecard and, while the Goose warmed up, double-checked my earlier handiwork.

"Wait, is the shortstop number 5 or number 6 if you're keeping score?" I asked my dad.

"Number 6," my dad answered.

"So when the shortstop throws to the first baseman, it's 6–3, right?"

"That's right," he said. The crowd cheered Gossage's first pitch, a strike.

"And a called strike three is a backward K or a regular K?"

"Matt, get your head out of the program. You're missing the game."

"But which one is it?"

"Backwards. But you're missing all the action. George Brett's up. Watch the game. You can do that when we get—"

He was cut off in midsentence by the crack of the bat. By the time I located the ball, it had begun its descent; it came down far beyond any Yankee's reach, over the outfield wall. With two outs in the top of the ninth inning, Brett's homer had put the Royals ahead by a run. One of the men in the row behind us cursed and tossed his half-full beer cup over my head, over the upper-deck railing, and down onto the fans in the box seats below. More than a few drops splattered my scorecard; long streaks of inky beer ran down the page into my lap. I looked to my dad, who had somewhat miraculously been spared the shower. Unaware, he still faced the field, watching Brett circle the bases. I blotted fruitlessly at the scorecard with my T-shirt.

"Here comes Billy!" screamed the beer-thrower over my shoulder.

I craned my neck and could see that the Yankees manager had indeed left the home dugout. Martin walked out toward the home plate umpire, gesturing animatedly at the bat Brett had just used to hit his home run.

"What's he saying?" I asked my dad.

"I don't know," he said.

All four umpires huddled around home plate. The home plate ump emerged from the conference and turned to the Royals dugout, then extended his thumb and swung his arm, throwing Brett out of the game.

Brett, the Royals' best player, didn't take the ejection very well. He burst out of the Royals dugout and onto the field, charging straight at the umpire. The Yankee Stadium crowd went bananas. In half a second, thirty-five thousand fans, including the tall ones in the row in front of me, were on their feet. Another cup of beer sailed over my head.

"I can't see the field!" I shouted. "I can't see anything!"

My dad lifted Damien onto his shoulders and helped me up onto my seat. In the middle of a huge scrum at home plate, Brett was being forcibly separated from the ump by three of his teammates. A fan to our right with a transistor radio reported that Brett's bat had been ruled illegal—"something about too much pine tar"—and the home run nullified. The game was over; the Yankees had won. The first few lyrics of Frank Sinatra's "New York, New York" blared from the Stadium's public address system.

My last glimpse of the Yankee Stadium field that day had Brett, still livid, being escorted up a tunnel from the Royals dugout. Up a tunnel to what, I didn't know.

A twenty-two-year-old Yankees first baseman, Don Mattingly, was also at the Stadium that afternoon. Though it was his rookie season, Mattingly had already established himself in the Yankees lineup; he had in fact had a hit in each of New York's nine previous games.

Without a doubt, he had watched the Brett spectacle unfold

from a better seat than mine. But at that point in his career, he'd been in the big leagues only a few months, and I'd like to think he was just as thrilled as I was to be at Yankee Stadium that afternoon. I imagine he watched that game from the Yankees dugout with the same sense of wonder I felt myself, way up in the upper deck.

At breakfast the next day, my mom spread the morning's sports page on the kitchen table and pointed out the article about what was already being called "the pine tar game." I had never been present at a newsworthy scene before, and I pored over the story and photos; I grasped for the first time that what happens in the world one day is what shows up in the paper the next.

After reading the story and studying the box score of the pine tar game, I moved on to the accounts of all the other major league games that had been played that Sunday. In those box scores and recaps, I recognized one or two players' names from the few dozen baseball cards in my collection. I made the connection between the names and the faces, and that connection made a big impression on me. I understood: you could follow the game this way.

When I started receiving an allowance of a few dollars a week that fall, it passed nearly instantaneously from my dad's pocket, through my hands, into the pocket of the five-and-dime-store owner who sold me more of these cardboard portraits. As my collection developed, I learned more teams, and players' names, and early eighties baseball history. I stored the cards in shoe boxes, like my dad told me he'd done growing up in Brooklyn forty years before, and swapped doubles with Damien and friends at school. I studied the ballplayers' faces and statistical histories, and became a reader by returning to the sports page to look for those same names in more box scores and game stories.

I coveted my Mattingly cards over all the others. Through the mid-eighties, when Mets fans owned bragging rights at school and on the playground, I kept my faith in the Yankees.

Mattingly made this possible. He won the American League batting title in 1984, when I was nine, and its Most Valuable Player Award in 1985. In 1986 Mattingly had 238 hits, more in one season than any Yankee had ever hit before. In 1987 he set an American League record by hitting six grand slams and tied the record for consecutive games with a home run with eight. I watched them all. Defensively, every year from 1985 to 1989, Mattingly was awarded the Gold Glove as the league's best-fielding first baseman. By the fall of 1989, when I entered high school, the wallpaper in my bedroom was fully obscured by Don Mattingly posters and photos, pictures that I'd carefully clipped from sports magazines over the previous half decade.

Though my family lived in North Tarrytown, a suburb about twenty miles north of New York City, I enrolled as a freshman at Regis High School, an all-boys, all-scholarship Jesuit school on the Upper East Side of Manhattan. It was the same high school my dad had graduated from thirty-seven years before. At age fourteen, I began taking the train and subway to and from school, an hour each way.

The tracks ran along the Hudson River, through the Bronx, into Manhattan; as the train passed through the South Bronx, it was possible to catch a glimpse out the window, just for a second or two, of the Yankee Stadium facade. During baseball season I tried to sit on the side of the train—the left side on the way to school, the right side on the way home—that gave me a look at the Stadium and the sign that announced when the Yankees would next play at home.

On game days, a wholly different energy emanated from the ballpark than on those days when the Yankees were on the road. Knots of cars and tailgaters softened the usually harsh landscape of vast, empty asphalt parking lots; the sidewalks around the Stadium bustled with cops, vendors, and early-arriving fans. Behind the facade, you knew preparations were being made for a baseball game to be played. Even passing the Stadium at forty miles per hour, with the sounds of the ballpark muted by the train's half-inch-thick glass windows, you could feel the place buzz: the Yankees are home and playing tonight.

One morning a few weeks into my junior year at Regis, I was on my way to school when I saw that the Stadium sign read BOSTON TONIGHT 7:05. It was late in the 1991 baseball season, and though the Yankees were already well on their way to a fifth-place finish in the American League East, the Red Sox were still within reach of the pennant. It's always a big game when the Red Sox visit Yankee Stadium; in this one, the Yankees could play the spoilers. I also knew there wouldn't be too many more chances to see a baseball game that season. I picked up a newspaper on the seat next to me and checked the starting pitchers. By the time the train crossed into Manhattan, I'd decided I was going to the ballgame.

I took the subway up to the Bronx right after school let out, paid five dollars for a walk-up bleacher ticket, and entered the

Stadium as soon as the gates opened. For a year or two already, I'd been convinced there was no better seat at Yankee Stadium than in the back row of the right-field bleachers. Only from the bleachers did you watch the game from the same perspective as the players in the field, facing the batter, which heightened the feeling of being in the game. I also believed that from my seat at the base of the Stadium facade, I could see more of the park than from anywhere else in the house. Every other view lacked the panorama available from the cheap seats. Fans sitting in the upper deck couldn't see those in the box seats down below, and vice versa; most fans in the park had to lean forward and crane their necks to see into one corner of the outfield or the other. From the back row of the bleachers, though, I could take it all in: the roiling mass of bleacher fans immediately before me, the expanse of grass patrolled by the right fielder, the infield in front of him, and finally, framing my view, the three tiers of seats that sat tens of thousands. The only sight I missed was of the scoreboard directly overhead, but I already knew the score and had all the stats in my head anyway. I was close enough to watch visiting outfielders feign ignorance or grimace at the taunts from the bleachers. Close enough to have developed, by close observation, an authoritative impersonation of the Yankee outfielders' between-pitch fielding stances. Close enough to have a fighting chance at leaving the ballpark with a home run ball. Closer than I'd ever been or imagined I'd ever be to the game of baseball and to the New York Yankees.

But there was a better seat at Yankee Stadium. Sitting alone in the bleachers that night watching the Yankees and Red Sox, I noticed for the first time a kid my age, dressed in pinstripes, down the right-field line: a Yankees bat boy. He sat on a stool and watched the game a long throw from where I was sitting in the bleachers. I must have known that the Yankees employed bat boys, but until that night I'd always looked right past them. Each inning I watched him walk out to the outfield grass to play catch with Jesse Barfield, the Yankees right fielder. I wondered how he'd earned the right to walk on such hallowed ground.

He clearly hadn't earned it by virtue of his athletic ability; the bat boy who was out there that night couldn't throw and could barely catch. He one-hopped the ball to Barfield on one throw and then sent the next over his head, it rolling all the way to the outfield wall. I was sixteen years old and scrawny, but sure of at least one thing: however this kid got his job, I could play catch better than he could.

Before leaving the Stadium, I found a discarded program and tore out the page that listed all the executives in the Yankees organization. On the train ride home that night, I circled names and job titles that I thought might be responsible for bat boy hiring.

I didn't tell friends, or my brother or sister, or ask my parents' permission. It seemed premature to do so, given how improbable it was that the experiment might be successful. Or maybe it was the early independent streak that had been tapped and nurtured by my daily train and subway rides to and from Manhattan. In any case, I pursued the position secretly.

Over the following week, I composed a job application letter as best as I knew how. Once I was satisfied with it, I wrote out twelve copies by hand, one to each of the dozen executives whose names I'd circled on my list, including Gene Michael, the Yankees general manager; Stump Merrill, the field manager; and George Steinbrenner, the then-unpopular owner of the Yankees.

"Dear Mr. Steinbrenner," I wrote in my most businesslike penmanship:

I have been an avid Yankees fan since I attended the "Pine Tar Game" in 1983.

I am a sixteen-year-old Junior at Regis High School, in Manhattan. A number of my articles have been published in our school's sports magazine. I am hard working and dependable, having held the same weekend job for the past two years.

The Yankee Tradition has fascinated me since I was able to read about it, and I am knowledgeable about this team, and the game of baseball.

I would very much like to work as batboy during the 1992 season. This will give me a great opportunity to be closer to the Yankees and baseball (and, of course, to see some terrific games!).

I am so interested in being batboy that if I don't hear from you soon, then I would appreciate being able to telephone you to see if my request can be accepted. I would be happy to meet with you, or the appropriate people in the organization, for a personal interview.

Thank you very much for your consideration.

Sincerely,

Matthew McGough

Matthew McGough

With a naive faith and earnestness, I mailed them off.

After a long week passed without a reply, I barricaded myself inside my bedroom with the phone and dialed the number listed on the roster of team executives.

"New York Yankees," a woman answered.

"Hi, this is Matt McGough," I said into the telephone.

The operator who manned the Yankees switchboard evidently had neither heard of me nor seen my letter.

"I sent a letter in last week inquiring about a bat boy position for next season," I reminded her as professionally and politely as possible.

"Okay," she said.

"And I haven't heard anything back," I said.

"Okay?" she said.

"Okay," I said, hoping to confirm that we were both on the same page.

"Okay," she repeated again.

In my bedroom at home, confused at the stalemate we seemed to have reached, I cocked my head to the side.

"Hello?" she said.

"I'm here," I stammered. "I'm just following up like I said I would."

"Well, I'm sorry," she said. "I don't know anything about it. But I'll have someone get back to you."

"Great," I said. "Thanks."

She had hung up the phone before I realized she hadn't even asked me for my phone number or address.

I dialed the same number again a week later. I repeated my introduction and explained why I was calling.

"Didn't we speak last week?" she asked me. She seemed amused to hear from me again. She wanted to know how old I was and laughed when I told her. At the end of our conversation, she took down my name and address.

Days later, three weeks after the '91 season ended, the mailman delivered me a letter on Yankees letterhead. It was signed by Brian Cashman, then the Yankees "Major League Administrative Assistant" (and within a few years, the team's general manager himself). Cashman's letter instructed me to call Nick Priore, the Yankees equipment manager, to schedule an interview.

My friend the switchboard operator put me through to

Nick the next day. Nick didn't make much conversation but told me to come up to the Stadium Friday after school.

I broke the news to my parents the night before the interview, sitting around the kitchen table over dinner.

"A bad boy?" my mom asked.

"Bat boy, Mom," I said. "Yankees B-A-T boy."

My brother and sister smirked. I slid the Yankees letter across the table to my father.

"How many games do bat boys work?" he asked, looking it over. "All of them?"

"I think," I said.

"That's a lot of games," he said.

My mom finished his thought. "What about school?" she said. "It's your junior year. You have to get your grades up this year for college."

I had anticipated this question. "There's no weekday day games until school lets out for the summer," I said. "Besides Opening Day," I added quietly. "Just that one day."

"But night games end after ten o'clock," my dad said. "And then travel time, getting home from the Bronx. How late do you have to stay at the Stadium after games?"

"I don't know," I pleaded. "I don't even have the job yet. Can I at least get through the interview first?"

My dad smiled.

"Well," he said. "Good luck on your interview."

I dressed the next morning in my jacket and tie, and hopped on the 4 train up to the Bronx as soon as classes let out.

I didn't know whether to expect a conversation or a cross-examination; I'd never been on a job interview before. On the ride uptown, I rehearsed answers to questions I considered likely.

My favorite subject in school was English. I didn't play baseball at Regis but had made my Little League all-star team the last two years I'd played. I mentally paired retired jersey numbers with the Hall of Famers who'd worn them: Ruth 3, DiMaggio 5, Mantle 7. I reviewed my thoughts on the current Yankees lineup, ready to explain to Nick why we needed another lefty in the bullpen and a slugger behind Mattingly in the batting order.

In the early nineties, the Yankees were not a perennial playoff contender, and the off-season came earlier then to Yankee Stadium than it would in the second half of the decade. Walking from the subway station to the ballpark, the familiar landscape seemed unnaturally lifeless.

I circled the Stadium, past shuttered gates and ticket kiosks, until I reached the double glass doors of the Yankees lobby. The security guard behind the desk told me to take a seat while he called Nick. I passed ten minutes in the pin-striped lobby, my schoolbag at my feet and my hands folded on my lap to prevent myself from fidgeting. A bell chimed from one of the two elevators that opened onto the lobby.

The elevator doors parted to reveal a man whose age could have been anywhere from forty to eighty. Nick's black hair was combed back and run through with grease. Between a handful of teeth he held the nub of a soggy, half-smoked cigar. He wore a ribbed, sleeveless white undershirt tucked into his Yankees gym shorts; a half dozen Sharpie markers dangled from the elastic waistband. White athletic socks were hiked up to his knees above black high-tops that looked to have been thoroughly and frequently worked over with shoe polish.

Without shifting his stance or moving forward from the back of the elevator, Nick turned his head in my direction and flicked his chin up and back. I took this as a signal to approach. I grabbed my books and joined him in the elevator. No handshake, no nice to meet you. No conversation at all. No eye contact whatsoever.

We rode the elevator down one level in silence and emerged at the mouth of a series of long underground tunnels. I scrambled to keep up with Nick, who stayed two steps ahead of me. He turned left at one corner and right at the next before stopping at a heavy steel door in the concrete hallway. A plaque mounted on the wall announced that here, right in front of me, was the Yankees clubhouse.

I followed Nick into a room about eighty feet long and forty feet wide, thinly carpeted and ringed by open-faced lockers. The stalls along the walls had been emptied for the off-season by then, but each was still topped with its tenant's nameplate. Some names—Mattingly, Bernie Williams, Jim Leyritz—remain familiar today. Others—Pascual Perez, Matt Nokes, Mel Hall, Hensley "Bam-Bam" Meulens—were familiar then but resonate today only with real fans. The floor was littered with cardboard boxes and open trunks that spilled their contents: hats, T-shirts, stirrup socks, the famous pin-striped uniforms, and dozens of pairs of the same Yankees shorts that Nick sported.

He signaled me to take a seat at an old wooden picnic table squarely in the center of the clubhouse. Nick sat opposite me and began to rearrange the paraphernalia within arm's reach: Sharpie markers, an ashtray, invoices, a toppled stack of baseball cards, two autographed baseballs, and a roll of large-denomination bills bigger than my fist. He took the wet cigar out of his mouth and rested it on the lip of the ashtray. As I watched him and timidly waited for the interview to begin, I noticed for the first time his hugely bulging right cheek. He tongued the inside of his mouth, which I thought maybe held a big chaw of chewing tobacco.

Even from two feet away, though, I couldn't discount the possibility that Nick was harboring an abscess the size of a Spaldeen. It could have gone either way. Both possibilities had me feeling queasy.

Nick finally lifted his eyes from the table to me in my Easter Sunday blazer and tie. I tensed for the questions to come. I readied myself to talk about school, about my favorite book, about my respect for the tradition of the Yankees, about my range behind second base and deep in the hole.

Nick cleared his throat, or grunted, and looked me up and down, sizing me up. "Your parents," he snarled. "They going to mind you taking the train home late at night?"

I wasn't sure I'd heard him right.

"I, uh, I take the subway to school every day. I'm fine on the train at night," I answered. Unsatisfied, he waited.

"I'm sure my parents won't mind," I added tentatively.

Nick stood up. "Come back Opening Day," he decided. He produced a tape measure and measured me from armpit to belt, then belt to ankle, and sent me back out into the hallway alone.

I found my way back to the lobby and out of the park, and took the subway downtown to Grand Central, where my dad was waiting to meet me. It was rush hour, and the train home was packed with dark-suited businessmen, men dressed as my dad was, no one less than a dozen years my senior. We found two seats across from each other in an otherwise packed car. People around us turned the pages of novels or shuffled papers. After the train pulled out, I spoke quietly about the interview and how it had ended.

"I think I'm hired," I concluded, sotto voce.

"Sure sounds like you're hired," he said. "Nick said come back Opening Day, right?"

"Yeah," I said.

The train shot out of the tunnel and onto the elevated tracks of Harlem, then into the Bronx. As we came up on the Stadium in fading sunlight, we both turned to the window. THANKS FANS, the sign announced. SEE YOU ON OPENING DAY.

My dad broke our silence. "Should be fun," he said, grinning broadly.

"Yeah," I grinned back, unable to hide my own excitement any longer.

Still, I couldn't believe it was really going to happen. I waited a month to tell my friends that I thought I had the job. It wasn't until I'd worked at the Stadium half a season that someone told me I was the first bat boy in memory to be hired without having had a connection.

I heard nothing from Nick or the front office in November or December.

In January, I saw a report on the six o'clock news, live from Yankee Stadium, on the team packing up and leaving for spring training. In the corner of the screen, over the reporter's shoulder, I spotted Nick and three big guys surrounded by dozens of stacked equipment trunks. Nick was scowling and kept jabbing his finger into the air and at his assistants.

Two more months passed.

In mid-March, I called the Stadium and asked to speak to Nick. The operator told me that he was still in Florida with the rest of the club. She also mentioned that Nick didn't keep a hotel room or apartment during the two months he spent at spring training: he slept at the Yankees' spring training ballpark. She gave me the number of the pay phone in the Yankees clubhouse in Fort Lauderdale.

When I finally reached him on the phone late one night, I asked him what time he wanted me to come in Opening Day.

"We'll be seeing you around 9:00 A.M., Matty," he answered reassuringly.

The night before Opening Day, I pulled the last page from a calendar I'd fashioned from a pack of Post-it notes counting down the days to the Yankees' home opener. I laid out my clothes for the next morning alongside the letter I'd secured from school excusing me for the day.

I'd had conversations both with my parents and with the headmaster at Regis, and understood the conditions under which I'd been allowed to take the job: after Opening Day, no missed classes; no excuses or blaming the Yankees for any schoolwork I failed to complete or if my grades suffered. I promised them I wouldn't let them down.

When I woke the next morning I discovered that my dad, before leaving for work, had slipped a note under my bedroom door. I read it on the train on my way to the Bronx.

"Matt," he wrote:

Happily, you embark on your Yankees adventures this afternoon! I am very excited about that prospect, most particularly for you but also for the family. I have some reflections that I would like to share with you—

1. Enjoy your time in the Clubhouse—there will probably be more to see and savor there than in the dugout;

2. Keep your antennae tuned; be cautious in sizing up your surroundings both in and around the Stadium, particularly the subway station;

3. Enjoy the "Star Stuff," but be mindful of the human side of the players as well;

4. Enjoy the players—and the practical jokes and ribbing they'll no doubt inflict on you;

5. If you chew tobacco, don't let the juice stain your uniform or your teeth;

6. If you meet Steinbrenner, resist the temptation to kick him in the shins;

7. Keep a running diary, but keep it at home (that way no one can confiscate it from you);

8. Do the favors that the players ask—but don't become beholden to anyone;

9. Get your time frames down pat, particularly from the Stadium to Grand Central (if you miss your train, you'll quickly learn how boring it is to hang out in G.C. Terminal);

10. Get your studies done <u>before</u> reaching the Stadium; you won't be in the mood coming home on the subway or train;

11. Watch out for the crowd after the games—they've done a lot of drinking and may, at times, be unruly at the 161st Street subway station.

I hope to share a number of games with you this season. I won't sit with the "real fans" in the Bleachers, though. If I did, I'd only see you through my binoculars. Maybe the "Boss" box—if it's available! In any event, we love you and want you to have a great summer.

Enjoy,
Dad

I walked into Yankee Stadium the morning of Opening Day again dressed for a holiday dinner and with my book bag over my shoulder.

The security guard in the Yankees lobby checked my name off a list and pointed me through a door just inside the Stadium press gate.

"Down the stairs and follow the blue stripe on the floor," he said.

I recognized the tunnel from my interview in October and soon found myself standing before the heavy clubhouse door. I took a deep breath, pulled the door open, and walked inside.

The last time I'd seen the clubhouse it had been empty, save for the trunks and boxes of clothes that Nick had strewn across the clubhouse floor. Now, the sight and sound of at least a hundred people hit me head-on.

A leading sign that spring has arrived in New York, Opening Day at Yankee Stadium has always been among the most newsworthy of the City's annual sports events. That year was no exception, and the fact that the Yankees were opening the season against the Boston Red Sox only heightened the already significant fan and media interest in the game.

Dozens of reporters rushed around the room, camera crews in tow. Carpenters, electricians, and painters hurriedly put final touches on different parts of the clubhouse. An entourage from Mayor Dinkins's office milled around, mixing with uniformed cops and security men in dark suits. And weaving through the mob, in various states of dress, were the ballplayers, most of whom I recognized from TV, but none of whom I'd ever seen except across rows and rows of Stadium seats. One with a barrel chest and huge biceps strutted past me across the room. Another sat at his locker doing a crossword puzzle. Two younger guys in pinstriped uniform pants and blue Yankees T-shirts—rookies, I guessed—stood to the side and spoke quietly while they too eyed the crowd. Veterans joked loudly and looked very much at home. And on the far right, in the corner locker twice the size of any other, sat Don Mattingly, Yankees captain. Donnie Baseball. The guy in midswing on the poster in my room at home. I swung my book bag off my shoulder, inadvertently bumping a camera and drawing a midinterview scowl from the cameraman. I thought I'd better go find Nick.

I approached him at his picnic table, where he stood with a black marker, purposefully printing players' names in big block letters on the collars of baseball undershirts.

"What do you want me to do, Nick?" I asked.

"Stay the fuck out of the way," he answered. Two players walked over a second later and impatiently began listing their grievances: Nick, I can't find the bag I packed in spring training; Old man, I need Nike batting gloves, I can't wear Adidas; Nicky, you have four AA batteries?

I must have looked as lost as I felt. I backed away and stumbled toward a distant corner, next to the trainers' room, that seemed slightly less chaotic than the rest of the clubhouse. I found myself in front of one locker, unlike all the others, that bore not a nameplate but a number: 15. Save for a catcher's mask and pair of shin guards that hung from a hook on the side of the cubby, it was forlornly empty.

I realized suddenly whose locker it had been, whose locker it still was. "Thurman Munson," I said to myself in wonder. "Wow."

Munson, a catcher, was a beloved Yankee, the captain of their championship teams in the late seventies. His career had ended near its peak when he was killed in a midseason airplane crash. The Yankees had evidently preserved his locker as a monument and memorial. I reached out to run my fingers across the gashes in Munson's battered shin guards when I felt a tap on my shoulder.

I turned and was suddenly face-to-face with the team's

current captain, Mattingly, the man himself. He extended his right hand to me.

"Hey, I'm Don Mattingly," he said. "You going to be working with us this year?"

It took me a moment to process my hero's simple question. I realized that Mattingly could have introduced himself with any number of other less generous but still thrilling questions: Are you the new bat boy? Who are you? What's your name? Are you going to be working *for* us this year? But he hadn't. Of all that I had imagined in the days before the season opener, I'd never thought about my new job in these terms: working *with* the Yankees, in common pursuit of a common goal.

"Uh, I know who you are, Mr. Mattingly," I managed to stammer. "I'm Matt, the new bat boy."

"Nice to meet you," Mattingly said with a firm handshake.

"Thanks," I replied instinctively. "I mean, nice to meet you, too."

"Listen, Matt," he said, as if I could have done anything else. "I've got an important job for you. I just unpacked all my bats from spring training. I don't know if it was the humidity in Florida or the altitude of the flight or what, but they're all coming up short. The game starts in a couple of hours. I need you to get me a bat stretcher."

I nodded, trying to keep cool and project competence. Get a bat stretcher.

After Mattingly returned to his locker, I ran a lap around the clubhouse looking for Nick. I found him a minute later, digging through a trunk of underwear over by the coaches' room.

"Nick," I said, "I need a bat stretcher for Don Mattingly."

I'd barely gotten the words out of my mouth when Nick hit my virgin ears with a stream of expletives terrifying in their intensity and earnestness. Spittle hit my cheek as he screamed at me. I'd never heard such a tirade before, not even in the movies, let alone one directed at me. I scurried away, leaving Nick over my shoulder cursing loudly into his pile of underwear. Nick's assistant, Rob Cucuzza, sat at the picnic table, and I blurted out the mission with which I'd been entrusted.

"Don Mattingly asked me to get him a bat stretcher, and Nick, uh, Nick told me not to bother him."

Rob put his hand on my shoulder and smiled.

"Try Tartabull, Matty," he told me kindly. "I think I saw him using one earlier this morning."

Danny Tartabull, the Yankees' new high-priced, power-hitting right fielder, was getting dressed at his locker all the way on the other side of the clubhouse. He had just pulled his jersey over his head when I summoned up the courage to approach and ask if I could borrow his bat stretcher.

"Uh, Mr. Tartabull," I offered. "I'm Matt, the new bat boy. Don Mattingly just unpacked his bats from spring training, and they're all too short. I heard you were using the bat stretcher earlier this morning."

Tartabull kicked at some boxes and baseball spikes at the foot of his locker before turning to face me.

"It's Matt?" he asked. "I was using it earlier, Matt, but I must have left it in the manager's office. Try in there."

I thanked him, checking my watch as I took off in the direction of the office. Time was short, and I felt a heavy burden of responsibility. First pitch wasn't more than a couple of hours away, and more than fifty-six thousand fans were coming from all over New York City, on Opening Day, to see Don Mattingly lead the Yankees against the hated Red Sox. I didn't need anyone to explain to me that Mattingly wouldn't be able to do much against Roger Clemens, then Boston's hard-throwing ace, with a shrunken piece of wood in his hands. He had asked me to help him, and I couldn't fathom what it might mean—for him, for the team, and for my job prospects—to let him down.

Yankees manager Buck Showalter sat behind his desk surrounded by a half dozen reporters, holding what appeared to be an impromptu press conference. I entered and waited patiently, a few feet inside the door, until the conversation fell silent. All eyes turned to the nervous kid in the blue blazer and the baseball-themed tie standing in the middle of the Yankees manager's office, in the heart of the Yankees clubhouse, on the morning of Opening Day.

"I'm, uh, really sorry to interrupt, Mr. Showalter," I began. "I'm Matt, the new bat boy. Don Mattingly needs a bat stretcher because his bats shrunk on the way up from Fort Lauderdale, and Danny Tartabull had it before but, uh, he says he left it in here with you this morning." Everyone was listening intently. Showalter scanned the floor at the feet of the beat writers and peered for a second around his desk.

"He left it in here?" he mused aloud. "It's possible, I guess. But do you need a right-handed one or a left-handed one?"

I knew that Mattingly was one of the best left-handed hitters in baseball.

"I need a left-handed bat stretcher," I answered confidently.

"Well, Tartabull's isn't going to do Mattingly any good at all then, is it, Matt? You better try down at the Red Sox clubhouse." I grinned weakly at the writers and excused myself from the room.

The Boston clubhouse was a lot less crowded than the Yankees', and thankfully I was able to find the Red Sox equipment manager right away. I recounted for him what I'd been through that morning—from Mattingly, to Nick Priore, to Tartabull, and now Showalter, who I thought maybe had a right-handed bat stretcher but not the lefty one that Mattingly needed immediately. He patiently heard me out, and given the traditional enmity between the two teams, I was relieved that he seemed willing to help. He checked his watch.

"You don't have much time," he said. "We didn't bring any bat stretchers at all with us, but we could use one, too." He dug into his pocket and produced a twenty-dollar bill. "Go to the sporting goods store on 161st Street and buy two, a left-handed one for Mattingly and a right-handed one for us."

By the time I got up to street level, fans had begun to descend on the Stadium en masse, and it took me a good ten minutes walking against the human tide to make it to the corner of 161st and River Avenue. I was about to cross the street when the thought crossed my mind that, for someone about to pick two up at the store, I didn't even know what a bat stretcher looked like. I crossed under the elevated tracks, then stopped dumb at the door of Stan's Sporting Goods. I'd played and followed baseball my whole life, but before that morning, I was pretty sure, I had never even heard of a bat stretcher.

The possibility that this might be a joke scared me even more than the thought of failing in my first assignment as Yankees bat boy. If there were bat stretchers for sale in the sporting goods stores around Yankee Stadium, there could be only one outcome worse than failing to produce one for Don Mattingly in his time of need.

What if I rolled back into the clubhouse and told Mattingly I was too smart to fall for his BS about stretching shrunken bats— and was wrong? I'd be ostracized at school. I'd be back in the bleachers, permanently. I mulled over my prospects during three full laps around Yankee Stadium, convincing myself that it had to be a prank, before I worked up enough courage to walk back into the clubhouse and confront the ballplayers.

The room erupted into laughter. Mattingly smirked at me from his corner locker. I tried to smirk back, trying hard to let him know: Yeah, you got me. But that's cool, I can take it.

Working in the clubhouse the next two seasons, I watched other intensely naive and naively intense new kids learn the ropes their first day the same way I did.

During long rain delays, bat boys have been sent out onto the field with a roll of toilet paper and instructions to protect the chalk baselines and batter's box from washing away in the downpour. Twenty or thirty thousand bored fans will watch the bat boy run a thin layer of toilet paper up and down the baselines and lay a neat box around home plate.

Pitchers have presented a bat boy with two dozen brand-new baseballs and a hammer, explaining that "these are fastballs, but I need two dozen curveballs." Right away, of course. Getting back a bewildered and terrified look, the pitcher will explain (correctly) that a thrown ball curves because the air catches the raised red thread that holds the baseball's leather together. See how little the stitches protrude from the surface of these two dozen baseballs? See that? Good, go to it. For the next hour or two, the initiate will lie on the floor of the clubhouse, pounding the ball's white leather with the hammer, trying to perceptibly raise the seams to the pitcher's satisfaction.

On other nights, the pitching coach has approached a half hour before game time, barking about the stiff arm the starting pitcher just developed warming up in the bullpen and the need for a "bucket of steam" to be brought out to the pen right away.

Someone will have already taken the time to affix to an empty Gatorade bucket a piece of athletic tape hand-labeled STEAM. Someone else—a trusted, more experienced friend on the clubhouse staff, usually—will gently explain how to accomplish the cryptic assignment. By way of instructions: "Go into the shower room and turn on all the showers as hot as they will go. After the room fills completely with steam"—here demonstrating with the empty Gatorade container—"clap the bucket shut and hustle it out to the bullpen. Make sure you fill it up completely." After being scolded by the pitching coach for bringing out a bucket with condensed water on the lid—"Son, did you *walk* this bucket of steam out here?!?"—this rite usually ends with the fully uniformed bat boy standing again in the middle of the steam-filled shower room, giving it another go. Or two or three.

An hour before first pitch, Nick issued me a uniform— identical to the ballplayers', but with BB on the back in place of a number—and a pair of brand-new baseball spikes. It took me a few minutes to figure out the proper way to put on my stirrups; I'd never used a garter to hold up my socks before. After I dressed, Nick caught me admiring myself in pinstripes in the mirror, bending the bill of my Yankees cap just right.

"For chrissakes, it's not a beauty pageant," he growled. "Get out there."

I walked down the tunnel to the Yankees dugout and took a hesitant first step up onto the immaculately manicured field of my dreams. I thought back to the time when, as an eight-year-old Little League ballplayer, back before anyone pointed out to me or I realized myself that it was an unrealistic dream, I fully expected that I would grow up to wear Yankees pinstripes and walk on the Yankee Stadium field. I averted my eyes from the handful of security men ringing the dugout, half expecting that one of them might challenge whether I belonged here. But the uniform I wore was an apparently unassailable credential, and people I encountered on the field or in the dugout only nodded or smiled as we crossed paths. I couldn't believe my luck. It was almost too much.

Before the game, watching warm-ups from the grass near the on-deck circle, I learned that big league curveballs really do curve, three or more feet, side to side or top to bottom, before swerving over the plate. Joe DiMaggio threw out the first pitch and brushed my arm as he came back through the dugout. During the national anthem, I stood with the team on the top step of the dugout between Frank Howard and Clete Boyer, first and third base coaches. All three tiers of seats ringing the field, from the foul pole in left to the foul pole in right, were packed with people. From here I could also see that the bleachers were full as well, from the first seats behind the right-field wall all the way back to my old row. Every seat in the Stadium was taken.

During today's game, the head bat boy Jamie told me, it would be my job to collect balls that skittered past the catcher to the backstop and to run fresh balls out to the home plate umpire, three at a time. In the bleachers, I'd pined for an authentic major league baseball or some lesser souvenir. Now, within sight of my old seat four hundred feet away, I sat on the dugout bench with a canvas bag of balls at arm's reach.

Using one of his spring training bats, Mattingly singled in the bottom of the first inning, the Yankees' first hit of the season; he would go three-for-four off Clemens that afternoon. In the second inning, Nick came down from the clubhouse to see if I was cold and wanted a jacket. In the bottom of the third, I tentatively walked down to the communal cooler at the far end of the dugout and poured myself a cup of Gatorade. Nobody flinched. I took a handful of sunflower seeds from a bag identical

to one I'd bought on the street the day before. There was no indication on the packaging that these seeds were better than those
sold to the general public, but I believed it true: these seeds, after
all, had been produced and earmarked for big league consump-
tion. In the top of the sixth, the attendance was announced as
56,572; it was the largest crowd at the Stadium in twelve years.
A fifteen-minute subway ride away, school was just letting out for
the day when the Yankees put the Red Sox down in the top of
the ninth and secured their first win of the season, the home
opener, my first game in pinstripes.

After the last out, I stood at the mouth of the dugout, waiting for the team to file off the field and back into the clubhouse.
Sinatra boomed from the oversized speakers in center field.
"Wow," I thought. "I'm going to be hearing 'New York, New
York' a lot from now on." Showalter and the Yankees coaching
staff stood just in front of me, offering congratulations to the
ballplayers. I'd unwittingly placed myself at the tail end of the receiving line.

"All right, all right," Showalter said over and over, patting
each Yankee on the butt or shoulder as he passed him.

As Mattingly approached, I impulsively offered my own
high five.

"Nice game," I blurted, as if I were back in a Little League
postgame handshake line.

"Attababy," he said as our palms made contact. "Attaboy."

Looking back, it's hard to say exactly what changed for me
on Opening Day. I went home that night to the same parents and
curfew and litany of chores, to the same bunk bed that I would
share with Damien until my sister Sarina left for college. I still had
homework to do. I hung out after school with the same neigh-

borhood crew I'd grown up with. I watched no less bad television and spent no less time at night on the phone with my friends, at that time talking more about girls than actually talking with them. I was no older, no more self-assured, and not really any wiser for having stumbled my way through Mattingly's pregame initiation rite.

But I no longer felt like the fan I'd been before. I'd seen some things that I'd never dreamed of seeing and that no one else I knew was wise to, and I had the sense that I was going to see more, as close to the action as if I'd been named to the Yankees roster itself.

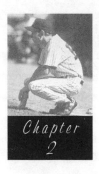

Chapter
2

Are You the Yankees Bat Boy?

The rationale behind the single question that Nick had put to me during my job interview quickly became apparent. It was a good thing my parents didn't mind me taking the train home late at night. At least under Nick, Yankees bat boy was not a ceremonial position.

The clubhouse routine when the Yankees were in town, well honed over the course of dozens of seasons, called for bat boys to report for work no later than three-thirty or four o'clock for night games, nine o'clock in the morning for day games. Given a three-hour ballgame and the time it took to complete our work afterward, it was often as late as one or two o'clock in the morning before we finished up in the clubhouse and could go home for the night.

Compared with the army of ticket-takers, ushers, security guards, and the precinct's worth of cops it takes to preserve order in the Stadium on any game day, Nick ran the Yankees clubhouse with a skeleton crew: two assistants and a trio of moonlighting high school students.

The clubhouse seemed to have been run in this fashion since time immemorial. Nick had worked in the clubhouse for almost three decades, and he had inherited the top job directly from Pete Sheehy, the legendary Yankees equipment manager. Sheehy had helmed the clubhouse from 1927 until his death in 1985, a tenure that spanned the playing careers of Yankees greats from Babe Ruth to Reggie Jackson. He oversaw twenty-one World Championship teams; the pallbearers at his funeral included both Yogi Berra and Don Mattingly. Decades after it happened, people still told the story about the time in the clubhouse that Sheehy had teased Joe DiMaggio in front of his teammates. DiMaggio, notoriously prim and considered above even good-natured razzing, had asked Sheehy to take a look at a red mark he'd found on his backside after a game.

"Is there a bruise there?" DiMaggio asked him.

"Sure looks like it," Sheehy answered. "Probably from all those people kissing your ass."

Witnesses to the exchange couldn't say what was more shocking: that Sheehy had made the joke, or that DiMaggio laughed along with the rest of the clubhouse. When Yankee Stadium was renovated in 1976, the home clubhouse was named for Sheehy, and a metal plaque on the door still announces the room behind it as the PETE SHEEHY CLUBHOUSE.

In the mid-sixties, Nick was hired off the Yankee Stadium grounds crew to be Sheehy's assistant. He had worked in the clubhouse ever since. Though Nick was never one to hold forth on his life story, some of its contours had been illuminated, if dimly, by word of mouth. Nick had served in the navy in Korea, and had a son in his thirties who came around the Stadium from time to time, but no one ever spoke of a Mrs. Priore. Nick's friends seemed to come exclusively from among the handful of men of his own generation who passed through the clubhouse on a daily basis: the older Yankees coaches; the Italian tailor who patched the holes in the players' uniforms; one or two of the more wizened Yankees groundskeepers; the Walter Winchell–era newspaperman whom the Yankees had brought on board as a part-time public relations adviser. There were unsubstantiated rumors that Nick kept an apartment deep in Queens, but from April to October he slept in the clubhouse at the Stadium, on a leather couch in the manager's office.

It was a running joke in the clubhouse that the United States government had no record of his existence. Nick seemed to leave Yankee Stadium only every few months, and when he did he dealt solely in cash, peeling twenties off a fist-sized roll of high-denomination bills. Because he never learned to drive, he held no government-issued identification. He was enough of a fixture at the Stadium to have earned exemption from the pic-ture ID rules that regulated other Yankees employees' passage through the ballpark. On a road trip a few years before, though, Nick had lost his room key and was unable to definitively prove to the hotel clerk that he was who he said he was. He waited hours, fuming in the lobby, until a passing ballplayer vouched for him so he could get back into his room.

Nick perennially rejected invitations to appear in the Yan-kees' annual team photo. In fact, as best as we could tell, in his entire life Nick had posed for only a single photograph: a head shot, standing against a cinder-block wall, mug-shot style, from twenty or more years before. It appeared every year in the Yan-kees yearbook above the following caption: "Nick Priore heads the Yankee clubhouse and has been with the team for over 25 years . . . Was Pete Sheehy's assistant."

Below Nick in the chain of command were two clubhouse

attendants, Rob Cucuzza and the Mule. As befits two guys in their mid-twenties who shared not only the same demanding work schedule but also a very crotchety boss, Robby and the Mule were inseparable friends. Unlike Nick, whose capacity for amusement may have been exhausted around the time Mickey Mantle retired, they still saw their jobs in the Yankees clubhouse as providing not only a paycheck but also a reliable avenue for adventure and comedy. They laughed off the verbal abuse that Nick sporadically hurled at them and carried themselves in the clubhouse with a nonchalance borne of deep familiarity; both had worked in baseball and around ballplayers since they were teenagers.

Close in age to the Yankees players, they had their trust and joked with them as easily as the players did among themselves. The ballplayers often approached Rob and the Mule with the day-to-day concerns that Nick wasn't so well suited to handle, like recommending a romantic restaurant in Manhattan or securing a VIP table at the nightclub-of-the-moment; Nick might have sent them to the Stork Club or Toots Shor's.

Rob had first worked for the Yankees as a bat boy himself. After college, he returned to the Stadium as Nick's assistant equipment manager. Cucuzza had been a familiar name around Yankee Stadium for decades. Lou Cucuzza, Rob's father, ran the visiting clubhouse at Yankee Stadium for many years. All three of his sons worked for him at the ballpark as teenagers, and when Lou retired, his eldest son, Lou Jr., inherited the visiting clubhouse job. Because Rob was already working for Nick on the home side, Lou Jr. hired as his assistant equipment manager the other Cucuzza brother, John. Lou Sr. himself still occasionally came around the ballpark to lend his sons a hand.

When Steve Sax, a Yankees veteran traded away near the end of his career, returned to the Stadium for his first game as a member of another ballclub, he walked to the Yankees clubhouse out of habit before realizing he'd lost his way.

"Where's the visiting clubhouse, Nick?" he shouted through the open door.

"Down the hall, turn left at the third Cucuzza," Nick answered.

The Mule's journey to Yankee Stadium was more elliptical. He'd grown up in Seattle and gotten his start in baseball as a bat boy for the Mariners. After graduating from that role, the Mariners equipment manager had called Nick to see if the Yankees could use an extra clubhouse attendant; Nick agreed to hire him.

Though the Mule was white and came from one of the least soulful cities in America, he had an overriding fascination with black culture. He was into hip-hop music and fashion long before they became mainstream or even fashionable. You could sense that his interest was genuine, not for show, and it made the Mule particularly popular with the Yankees' black ballplayers. When shipments came in from the apparel companies the ballplayers were sponsored by, the Mule was showered with so many Nike and Adidas track suits and sneakers, you'd have thought he had his own endorsement contract. Part of their affection for him was also rooted in his diminutive stature: the Mule was just about five feet tall, and, even with the thick, gold-plated chains he usually wore around his neck, couldn't have weighed more than a hundred pounds. His nickname was also an allusion to size: back when he was still with the Mariners, one of the ballplayers had seen him coming out of the shower and called out, loud enough to be heard across the clubhouse: "Jesus Christ, Pete, you're hung like a goddamn mule!"

The Mule neither trumpeted the etymology behind his nickname nor tried to dissuade people from using it. It was never clear to me whether the Yankees brass, let alone the sweet old ladies working in the Stadium ticket office, knew the meaning behind their words when they greeted him passing through the clubhouse or front office.

"Hiya, Mule," they'd say. He'd nod back, smiling shyly.

Below Rob and the Mule in the clubhouse hierarchy were the three Yankees bat boys. Hector was a rookie, like me; Jamie had worked in the clubhouse the season before, and as the lone bat boy retained by Nick for the '92 season, had assumed the mantle of head bat boy. Though Jamie had only a single year of big league experience under his belt—which left him maybe forty years short of Nick and a decade or more short of Rob or the Mule—you would never have known it from the way he ordered his subordinates around. Nick's hands-off management style—our mentoring sessions at his picnic table of an office frequently began with "Christ, if this isn't important, you're gonna be sorry," or the shorter, sweeter "What the fuck is it now?"—left lots of room for Jamie to assert his seniority at our expense.

Jamie also had a stock answer he used to dismiss every question Hector and I ever asked him.

"Jamie, how'd you get Tartabull to leave tickets for your friends?"

"Don't worry about it."

"Jamie, did you really meet Mickey Mantle at Old Timers' Day last year? What was he like?"

"Don't worry about it."

"Did Nick really tell you to tell me to clean all these toilets myself?"

"Don't worry about it."

"I'm just asking you a question. Why are you being an asshole?"

"Don't worry about it."

. . .

On game days, getting to work on time meant leaving Regis as soon as the final class bell rang. Locker to locker, it took me about thirty minutes to get from the Upper East Side of Manhattan up to the Bronx. Bat boys who showed up after the players started arriving, around three-thirty, could expect to be publicly chewed out by Nick upon walking into the clubhouse.

We ran errands until batting practice—BP—started at five. These tasks were varied, the most prized "runs" being those that earned us tips of ten or twenty dollars from the ballplayers. Jamie steered the more lucrative runs to himself, errands like filling up the players' cars with gas or picking up the manager's wife at the airport. "Food runs" fell to Hector and me, and we made endless trips to the fast-food restaurants on the Grand Concourse— the American-born ballplayers were partial to Wendy's or McDonald's, the Latin ballplayers to Cuchifritos, a Puerto Rican luncheonette—for late lunches or early dinners. Returning to the Stadium from my first food run, I handed the first baseman Kevin Maas his Extra Value Meal along with the three dollars and coins left over from the ten-dollar bill he'd given me. I'd kept his change carefully sequestered from my own money and thought I was demonstrating trustworthiness and honesty; Maas smirked and told me to keep it. It was weeks before I understood that I was allowed to buy myself lunch as well if I wanted it, and learned the tipping protocol practiced by savvy waiters and bartenders: a player was more likely to tell you to keep a ten than ask you to break it. It was an important lesson to learn. Given a good day of food runs, I could sometimes match my daily wage of thirty-five dollars a game.

By the time batting practice started, two of the three bat boys had to be in uniform and on the field, shagging flies and keeping the BP pitcher supplied with baseballs. As was Jamie's prerogative as head bat boy, he always dressed for batting practice. Hector and I took turns staying in the clubhouse to help prepare the pregame spread of cold-cut sandwiches and run whatever additional errands Nick might send us on. These ranged from picking up a gallon of milk to placing a bet at the neighborhood OTB. My favorite Nick errand involved restocking the small refrigerator in Mattingly's corner locker with beer. Mattingly enjoyed having a cold one at his locker after a game, and preferred bottles of Coors Light to the cans of Budweiser that Nick provided in the players' lounge. I liked having a role in my favorite player's postgame relaxation regimen and took secret pleasure in the fact that in South Bronx bodegas, unlike Westchester 7-Elevens, proving you were of age wasn't necessarily part of the transaction. I was carded only once. "It's for Don Mattingly," I said, proffering my Yankees identification, and walked out of the store with a pair of six-packs.

Nothing compared, though, to going out for batting practice. Dressing for BP, you put your uniform on at the same time as the ballplayers and took part in the team's short commute from clubhouse to dugout, en masse, at precisely five to five. You took the field as the clock turned five, your own glove in hand, as surely as a businessman carries his briefcase. You heard the late-afternoon quiet of a Yankee Stadium not yet open to fans, the only audible sounds being bat against ball or ball against glove. It really felt like you were going to work.

Per Jamie's own directive, his job in batting practice was to roam around the outfield, shagging fly balls and throwing them in toward a mesh screen set on the grass just behind second base. Also per Jamie's directive, it was my job to stand behind the screen and receive his throws, filling a plastic bucket with the baseballs he'd just fielded, sometimes acrobatically. Why did I have my job and Jamie his? I was told not to worry about it.

When I had a few dozen balls, or at the batting practice pitcher's signal, I ran the bucket in from my station in shallow center field to the pitcher's mound, also protected by a mesh screen. I ducked behind the pitcher and emptied the bucket, then sprinted back across the infield toward second base.

One of my first days out on the field for BP, returning from one of these trips to the mound, I was met at the screen behind second base by an older man wearing Yankees pinstripes. He must have been in his sixties, but stocky and still muscular, he was built like one of the ballplayers. He was about the right age to be a coach, but I couldn't remember seeing him in the dugout during games.

"You ever been hit in the back of the head by a baseball?" he asked me sternly.

I shook my head side to side. On cue, a line drive whistled past us a few feet over our heads.

"It hurts like hell," he said. "Never turn your back to the plate during batting practice." He concluded his lecture with the same advice my Little League coach had given me a few years before, in a very different context: "Always keep your eye on the ball."

I thanked him but felt bashful, as if I'd exposed my lack of experience on the baseball diamond. With renewed vigor, grateful to have something to do, I turned back to filling the bucket.

"I'm Nick Testa," he said, extending his hand.

"Are you a coach?" I asked, careful to keep myself behind the screen.

"I throw batting practice here," he said. "At Shea, too, when the Mets are in town." I'd had a friend who sold peanuts at both Shea and Yankee Stadiums, and knew from him that the New York teams rarely both play at home at the same time. Vendors, security guards, and batting practice pitchers, too, apparently, moonlight at both ballparks.

We watched Jamie make a nice over-the-shoulder catch in deep right field.

"Wow," I said, fielding Jamie's throw on one hop. "How'd you get that gig?"

Nick laughed. "Oh, I've been around for a while," he said. "A long time."

"Did you play in the majors?" I asked.

"I had a cup of coffee with the Giants back in the fifties," he said, using baseball slang for a brief stint in the big leagues.

"In New York or San Francisco?" I asked.

"San Francisco," he said. "Their first year there." Then after a pause: "Just one game."

"Oh," I said, unsure whether it might be impolite to ask him the circumstances surrounding a one-game big league career.

"I'll tell you the story sometime," he said, as if reading my mind. A few weeks later, standing out in center field with the bucket between our feet, he did. It was the most implausible and heartrending baseball story I'd ever heard.

Nick was born and raised in the Bronx and signed with the New York Giants as a catcher at age nineteen. He spent the next ten years in the minor leagues, bouncing around from farm team to farm team, never once getting called up to the major league club. In 1958 he was invited for the first time to the Giants' big league spring training camp and made the team as its third-string catcher. He was nearly thirty years old, a rookie teammate of Willie Mays. He wasn't called upon to play until a home game, late in May, against the St. Louis Cardinals. The Giants, down

6–2 in the bottom of the eighth inning, rallied for two runs; Nick was sent into the game as a pinch runner but was stranded without scoring. He caught the top of the ninth. The Cardinals scored another run, and the Giants came to bat in the bottom of the ninth down 7–4. Given where he'd come into the lineup the previous inning, Nick's turn to hit was down deep in the Giants batting order; it would take an uncanny sequence of hits and outs for him to even get to the plate.

But the stars were aligned that night: with two outs, the Giants loaded the bases, and Nick found himself on deck, bat in hand, a teammate's base hit away from making his major league debut. Any base hit but one: Nick stood in the on-deck circle and watched his teammate hit a ball over the fence for a game-winning, game-ending grand slam. The Giants released him a few weeks later; it was the only major league game he ever played.

After his baseball career, Nick earned a master's degree from New York University; when he wasn't pitching BP to the Yankees or Mets, he was a schoolteacher in the Bronx. "Baseball took me a lot of places," Nick concluded, not a trace of bitterness in his voice. "Japan, Canada, all over Latin America. The money I made playing paid for my education."

The world of baseball has always been rich enough to accommodate both young boys' dreams and grown men's nostalgia. Nick and I occupied opposite ends of the time line, with the present-day players at the center. I thought, though, that if you went back far enough into Nick's childhood and compared his baseball dreams to mine at the same age, they'd be fairly identical. And while I'd never bet that I might be pitching BP for the Yankees half a century from now, I expect my perspective on baseball then will share a good deal with Nick Testa's.

Neither of us would ever play major league baseball, we

both knew. But back on that April afternoon when we first met, standing in brilliant spring sunshine on the lip of the Yankee Stadium infield, it felt like we were pretty close.

Mattingly, taking his turn in the batting cage, was spraying balls across the right side of the outfield. Nick and I watched Jamie backhand a sinking line drive in the gap. He looked to be having a field day.

"You want to go out there?" Nick asked me.

"Yeah," I said quickly. "But I think I'm supposed to—"

"I'll man the fort," he said, shooing me away with his glove. "Go ahead."

I ran across the outfield grass in short bursts, ten or twenty feet at a time, pausing for pitches, turning to face the batter in time for the next delivery.

I hadn't caught a fly ball since Little League, and these balls were hit hundreds of feet farther than the meek ones I'd corralled as a twelve-year-old shortstop. I found it hard to read the trajectory of the ball off the bat; even considering how high they hung in the air, they came at me hard and fast. I got late jumps on the first two or three catchable ones and, though hustling, watched them land out of reach.

Just as they opened the gates and fans began to file into the Stadium, I started to get the hang of it. Slightly less awkwardly than before, I ranged right and left, in and back, judging the ball before settling under it. When one came down cleanly, with a small pop, in the pocket of my glove, I felt a little jolt of excitement: my first catch in Yankee Stadium. I tossed the ball back in to Nick Testa on one hop, trying to hide my pride at having made a quintessentially routine catch, and readied myself for the next batting practice pitch to be hit my way.

. . .

Hector and I jealously guarded our respective turns in the batting practice rotation. Staying in during batting practice did offer a thin silver lining, though: if I ran Nick's errands quickly and took a pragmatic rather than an artistic approach to making the cold-cut platter, it was usually possible to squeeze in a few minutes of schoolwork. Homework I'd otherwise have to complete late that night on my early-morning train ride home.

Despite poker-faced assertions to the contrary made to Mom, Dad, and any number of skeptical high school teachers, there are few worse places to study than the home clubhouse at Yankee Stadium an hour before first pitch.

I'd already been struggling mightily since the beginning of the school year in math class. As confusing as I found calculus to begin with, doing problem sets in the midst of twenty-five pro baseball players, a dozen sportswriters, and an extremely irascible boss boosted neither my retention nor my grades. I knew it'd be an uphill fight to avoid summer school that July.

As an all-scholarship school, Regis is private but tuition-free; every student who is admitted and chooses to attend does so on a full scholarship. In return, the school expects a great deal from its students; like most of its graduates, I found everything after high school—college, graduate school—comparatively a breeze. If you failed a class at Regis, you were required to make up that work in a monthlong, five-morning-a-week summer session. If you failed in the summer session to satisfy the school's requirements, you were forced to relinquish your scholarship, which meant finding another high school to attend.

I'd already been through it once before, after failing Latin my freshman year. I'd managed in summer school to raise my F to a D, but came through the experience somewhat worse for wear.

The Latin teacher who had failed me that June and taught me that July had both high expectations and a short temper. His demeanor in the classroom was similar to what I'd expect from Nick Priore had he gone into teaching rather than equipment managing. Mistakes in class were not corrected calmly and gently; finding you unable to properly conjugate a given verb on his cue, he would place his fists on your desk on either side of the textbook, lean over you menacingly, and berate you until you complied. Whether it worked for other students or not, it was not a teaching method especially conducive to my learning process.

Or psyche. I managed to pass, barely, but the experience proved a psychological assault severe enough to not only resuscitate but exacerbate a stutter that I'd developed during a short— but not short enough—stint on Regis's much-heralded debate team. I'd joined the team with vague hopes of enhancing my future college applications; I left it not only terrified of public speaking but with a curious and embarrassing speech impediment. It manifested itself, inexplicably, only when I had to say my name: the "Matt" came easily enough, but "McGough" would invariably get caught in the back of my throat.

Failing summer school would mean leaving a school I loved, either for Sleepy Hollow High School in Tarrytown or, if I wanted to stay in the City, for a lesser school for which my parents would have to start paying tuition. I'd have to lower my hopes and expectations as to the colleges that I might attend. I'd be cut off from all my friends at Regis, the only close friends I felt I had since leaving my neighborhood middle school for a high school in the City. These were significant fears, but they paled in relation to the nightmare I imagined for myself during roll call my first morning at whatever other high school I might transfer to.

"We have a new student, class," I pictured the teacher saying kindly. "Why don't you tell us your name?"

"Matt Mc . . ." I imagined myself attempting. "Mc . . . McG . . ."

The thought was unbearable. It had provided motivation enough for me to pull my act together and manage a passing grade in summer school two years before. Now, with two months left in my junior year, my math grade was somewhere in the neighborhood of a D. Maybe a D-plus, if such a mark existed. My math teacher was a Jesuit priest, ancient and not notably a baseball fan. I could feel my old fears stirring, my tongue growing uncooperative.

Now I had not one but two full-time jobs: one at Regis High School and one at Yankee Stadium. I knew I'd have to bust my ass to pull off both of them, but I kept my reservations to myself. If I shared them, I knew which job would be taken away from me first.

Before night games, batting practice ended at exactly 6:10 P.M., and by 6:11 everyone was back in the clubhouse to prepare for the game. One bat boy got to work wiping down and polishing each of the twenty-five pairs of baseball spikes that had been worn during batting practice. A second gathered the tools of the hitter's trade—pine-tar rags, lead weights for the bats, a rosin bag, and each position player's batting helmet (also polished after batting practice)—and began moving the equipment down to the dugout. The third picked up a stack of towels and two oversized tubs of Gatorade (one for the dugout, one for the bullpen) from the trainers' room, and scattered packs of sunflower seeds and Bazooka bubble gum around the dugout.

The incentive to finishing this work quickly was not insignificant—the leftovers from the players' pregame spread were whisked out of the clubhouse at game time, leaving a preciously small window of time for an all-you-could-eat dinner.

During games, there were always five bat boys in uniform and on the field. Along with the three of us from the Yankees clubhouse, the visiting clubhouse also employed a full staff of New York kids. Two of these visiting clubhouse bat boys were on the field each game, one of whom worked the visiting dugout and so had to wear that team's uniform. For this reason, major league baseball teams travel with bat boy uniforms in every conceivable size: the need might arise to outfit an overweight nineteen-year-old visiting clubhouse bat boy in Detroit and a skinny fifteen-year-old in Cleveland later that same road trip. The second visiting clubhouse bat boy and one from the Yankees "side" dressed in pinstripes and headed "down the line." Down the line, you sat all game on a stool in foul territory just past first or third base, fielding foul balls and playing catch to warm up the outfielders each inning. The other two bat boys worked in the Yankees dugout, one responsible for "bats," the other for "balls." The kid doing balls kept a running count of the number of baseballs that went into the stands, and ran three new baseballs out to the home plate umpire for every three that went out of play. The kid doing bats sat at the top step of the dugout or knelt at the batting circle and removed the bat from home plate after each Yankee made an out or reached base.

Each of these game-time tasks had its advantages and disadvantages.

"Bats" was most highly prized, and as was his privilege, Jamie most often chose this assignment. For the top half of each inning, the bat boy doing bats had nothing at all to do except sit on the bench and watch the game with the ballplayers who weren't out on the field. As a clubhouse veteran, he already knew most of the Yankees and so could coolly rap with the players on the bench while the visitors hit. When the Yankees were at the plate, Jamie was in an ideal position to greet scoring runners with a high five or, as was becoming the fashion, by holding a clenched fist up high for the ballplayer to tap, knuckles to knuckles, as he passed. After Yankees home runs, Jamie would linger at home plate, maximizing his television time; a few weeks into the season he made the back page of the *Daily News*, congratulating a Yankee after a game-winning homer.

"Balls" was least valued because it required your constant attention and because there was no glory in shuffling back and forth from the dugout to the umpire every five or ten minutes. Word had come down from the front office that balls fouled back behind the plate were to be used in batting practice the next day rather than given to fans. Fans' early-inning pleas for baseballs gave way to late-inning insults. You'd be surprised by the ferocity of the heckling inspired, even in the corporate seats, by fans disappointed at not being given a souvenir to take home from the ballpark. I ran the balls back to the dugout, head down, ignoring the taunts.

Going down the line was fun at first: you played catch with the right fielder every time the Yankees took the field, and during the game fielded foul grounders while thirty thousand fans waited for an error. But with ballgames averaging a little over three hours, and nighttime temperatures in April still in the forties, it got lonely and boring and cold sitting out there on a metal stool all night long.

Only occasionally would Jamie offer to go down the line. When he did, it was hard not to be impressed with the use he made of his time sitting in right field up against the box seats: Jamie usually returned to the dugout flaunting scraps of paper bearing phone numbers that he'd coaxed from girls sitting in the stands. It seemed way beyond my own fledgling social abilities, as I still found it harrowing to ask a strange girl for her number even when she might see the question coming, say at a school dance or a house party. How do you ask a girl you've never met for her number at a baseball game? I wanted to know how he pulled it off, but I settled for trying to be satisfied not worrying about it.

As head bat boy, Jamie also got the choicest postgame task—vacuuming the clubhouse—while Hector and I shined the players' game spikes (again, twenty-five pairs), wiped down the bathroom sinks, and emptied the clubhouse's six oversized trash cans. You couldn't really begin any of this work in earnest until all the players and reporters left for the night and the clubhouse was empty. About two hours after the game, this work complete, all the underclothes worn by the team that day—the "whites"— came out of the dryer. The night's work ended with the whole clubhouse staff standing around a shopping cart in the middle of the room sorting the laundry. Nick usually oversaw the crew while smoking a stogie at his picnic table.

This was the only time we ever really spoke critically about the ballplayers. In the empty clubhouse, names would come to mind as we pulled a given player's whites out of the shopping cart.

"Lee Guetterman," Jamie might say, his voice tinged with disgust, tossing the struggling left-handed reliever's T-shirt in the direction of his locker. "Horrible."

"He'll be in the minors by July," the Mule might add. "Out of baseball by August."

"Yeah," I might say, still tentatively, but trying to get into the flow. "He sucks."

Jamie would throw me a look, as if I hadn't yet earned the right to make such a pronouncement. Robby would shoot Jamie a look of his own, as if he hadn't yet earned the right to shoot me such a look.

Every once in a while, Nick would toss his two cents in from his picnic table. "You know who I like?" he'd say. Nick was notorious for butchering players' names; you could follow his thinking process by the long groans he'd emit trying to retrieve the name he was searching for. "Uhhhhhhhh, uhhhhhhh . . ."

"Uhhhhhhh," Robby would softly mimic.

"Uhhhhhhh," Nick would continue, lost in thought. "That Italian kid, on Seattle. First base. Uhhhhh . . . Tino Martino. Kid's got a great bat."

"Tino Martinez," the Mule would say. "But, uhhhhhhhh, he's not Italian. His last name's Martinez, Nick."

"You know what your problem is, Mule?"

"What, Nick?"

"You're hard to look at. You don't please the eye." Standing at the shopping cart, finishing up the whites, the five of us knew that a second, more specific insult would follow. "You're so goddamn skinny, you've got to run around in the shower to get wet."

The four of us, minus the Mule, would laugh hysterically. "Tino Martino," the Mule would mutter. "Nick's a frickin' illiterate."

Nick was consistent in his late-night banter: the Mule was always insulted as ugly; Robby as dumb; Jamie as a thief. For the first few months, at least, Nick took it easy on Hector and me.

In playing eighty-one home games a season, the Yankees sometimes played every day for as long as a week or ten days running. I spent so much time at the Stadium whenever the team was in New York that, the following season, my first girlfriend's father nicknamed her "the Yankee Widow."

Through April and May, the months that the baseball schedule overlapped with school, it became clear to me that it made little sense to travel home from the Bronx at one in the morning, only to head back into Manhattan for school at seven the next day. I eventually learned to bring a week's worth of clothes to work at the beginning of each homestand, and, rather than go home, sleep at the Stadium and take the subway between there and school every day until the team went on the road again. In the beginning, though, I didn't feel enough at home at the Stadium to consider sleeping in the clubhouse like Nick and the Mule normally did.

After work, I took the subway downtown to meet a northbound train heading home to North Tarrytown. I knew the schedule by heart: the last train left Grand Central at 1:20 in the morning, stopped at 125th Street (two downtown stops on the 4 train from the Stadium rather than five to Grand Central) at 1:31, and arrived in North Tarrytown at about 2:10. From the train station, our house was a short five-minute walk. I could leave Yankee Stadium as late as 1:10 or 1:15 in the morning and, if the timing was right, still catch the train at 125th Street to be home and in bed by 2:30.

I timed the commute perfectly one Thursday night early that May, sprinting down 125th Street with a bagful of books and meeting the train just as it pulled into the elevated station. I had a physics exam in school the next morning, and I hadn't cracked the book since mid–March. The game plan involved reading my textbook on the train ride home, then waking up at six the next morning to take an early train into school. I would study in the cafeteria, right up until the test began. The train wasn't ten minutes from 125th Street before I was fast asleep in my seat.

I was jarred awake by a woman shaking me by both shoulders, telling me in an urgent voice that I had to switch trains. Still half asleep, I rubbed the moisture off the window at my seat and peered out into foggy spring weather to see where we were. We had pulled up at a train platform, and I recognized the steel-and-concrete footbridge over the tracks as the Tarrytown train station, one stop before my own. Across the platform sat another train, lights blazing, doors open, and passengers filing in. I figured that our train must have broken down and, fearing that its replacement was about to depart, I grabbed my physics book, jacket, and bag, and hustled across the platform. The doors closed behind me just after I boarded. By the time I grabbed a seat, the train was already moving fast.

I was back into my physics book when the conductor made his way down the aisle to my row of seats, and I flashed my train pass at him. "Where are you going?" he asked. I told him the name of my stop. "This train just left Croton Harmon," he told me, referring to the last stop on the train line, three stops past my own, "and it's headed *way* north." I looked at my watch, which read 2:30. I'd slept straight through Tarrytown and my own stop and had mistaken the Croton train station for Tarrytown. I knew without asking that this was the last train of the night running north or south. I dug into my pocket and pulled out my wallet, which held eight one-dollar bills. There had been no lucrative food runs that day.

The woman who had pointed me across the platform was sitting across the aisle, and seeing the anguished look on my face, offered me a ten-dollar bill for a cab home from wherever the train next stopped. I knew that I was already at least a thirty or forty-dollar taxi ride from home, and the train was moving fifty miles an hour in the wrong direction. I didn't want to take her money. I gathered my books and prepared to get off at the next stop.

Peekskill. Thursday night, almost three o'clock in the morning. I swear I saw a tumbleweed as I walked down the middle of the street I thought might lead to town. I was looking for anyplace warm and safe, somewhere I could sit and wait for the trains to start running again, when a squad car turned the corner. I flagged down the cop, who slowed to a stop and rolled down the front passenger window.

"I fell asleep on the train and missed my stop," I told him. He leaned toward me slightly across his seat, impassively sizing me up. "I just need somewhere safe to sit until I can get a train to school in the morning. Can you give me a ride to the police station?" I asked. He reached over to open the backseat door, and I slid into the police cruiser. He didn't make any conversation, and we didn't pass any signs of life on the streets between the train station and the station house.

I dropped my bag on the wooden bench in the empty lobby of the police station and fished a quarter out of my pocket to call my parents. My dad was sound asleep when I called, and he didn't take the news too well when I let him know where I was and that I wasn't coming home that night. My father knew as well as I did that it was nearly impossible to end up in Peekskill by accident—you actually had to switch trains—and his agitation was growing as he came to his senses. He told me to wait where I was, that he'd come and pick me up. I knew that by the time he got out of bed and into the car, drove all the way to Peekskill and then back, it'd be time to get on a train to Regis anyway. I told him that I was safe where I was and would call him when I got to school in the morning. Dad insisted on speaking to the cop on duty, and I left the pay phone to go knock on the plexiglass window. The cop looked up at me from his chair behind the plastic.

"My dad wants to talk to you," I said sheepishly, pointing toward the pay phone.

The cop came out from behind the plexiglass and took the

receiver dangling from the wall. I sat down on the bench and tried to make myself somewhat comfortable. I could overhear my father telling the cop how I'd ended up on the last train of the night—"burning the candle at both ends"—and that he appreciated him keeping an eye on me until morning. The officer looked sidelong at me a couple of times while they spoke. "Oh, the Yankees . . . Really? . . . Well, don't worry about him, we'll make sure he's on his train in the morning." The cop finally hung up the phone, nodded reassuringly in my direction, and then walked back to his desk across the room. I took out my textbook again and began reading where I'd left off, still on the page I'd dog-eared back in March.

A few minutes passed quietly before the intercom suddenly crackled above my head. I heard the cop's voice in the lobby: "So you're really a bat boy for the Yankees?"

I told him I'd just gotten the job, and we spoke via intercom for a little while about the team and its chances that year.

"What's Don Mattingly like?" he asked.

I told him about my first day at work. The cop seemed impressed that I had met the players, and I told him a bit about the guys I'd found to be kind and generous, and the one or two who'd been cheap or surly. Our conversation lasted about ten minutes before we fell back into silence. My eyes were getting heavy again, and the physics I was reading wasn't making much sense. I began to doze.

The intercom came to life again. I looked over at the officer through the plexiglass. He was grinning at me. "Son," he said, leaning into the mike, "we're gonna get you home." He told me to pull my things together and go wait in front of the station house. Outside a minute later, a Peekskill squad car pulled up. The passenger window came down.

"Hey, you the Yankees bat boy?" the officer behind the

wheel shouted in my direction. He pushed the front passenger door open, and I hopped in to a handshake and a barrage of baseball questions.

"So you really know Don Mattingly?" he asked as we pulled onto the highway. I told him the bat stretcher story, my second time that night. I described the clubhouse, told him about Nick, and Robby, and the Mule, and Nick Testa.

As we drove, I was aware that I had no sense of where we were or even what roads we were taking. I'd heard of Peekskill growing up, but as far as I knew I'd never been there before. We drove for twenty minutes before pulling over just past an intersection. A tin WELCOME TO OSSINING sign stood at the side of the road, ten or so feet in front of us. We weren't stopped for more than a minute before the cop told me, "Hop out here." I knew Ossining was somewhere closer to home than Peekskill. I was also sure that I was still at least an hour's walk from my bed. I wasn't sure what to say, and so didn't say anything, but stepped out of the cruiser onto the shoulder of the road with my book bag.

Trees lined both sides of the road where I stood. I couldn't even tell in which direction I should walk to find a pay phone I could use to call and wake up Dad again. Or call a taxi. I wished I'd taken the lady's ten dollars.

A second later, coming from the opposite direction, another police car pulled up. It flicked on its high beams and its window came down. "Are you the Yankees bat boy?" the cop from the Ossining squad car shouted. I clambered into the front seat of the car. Ten minutes later the Ossining cop dropped me at the border of Ossining and North Tarrytown. A North Tarrytown cop, radioed ahead and on the lookout for a stranded Yankees bat boy, picked me up there. The relay ended when he dropped me at the doorstep of my parents' house, almost four o'clock in the morning. The next day, on three hours' sleep, I somehow managed a B on my exam.

The lengths that the cops went to to get me home made me understand for the first time the degree to which people were fascinated by the world to which I'd gained access and my own minor role in it.

Later that month, coming off the field after batting practice, I lingered at the top step of the dugout while one or two players signed autographs for a cluster of fans. They called out to the ballplayers by name, thrusting balls and programs and pens in their direction.

A young boy, not more than five or six years old, stood away from the fray jockeying for position. He held a baseball and pen of his own, and for a moment I made eye contact across the top of the dugout with his mother.

"Please sign his ball for him," his mom called out to me.

"I'm just a bat boy," I said.

"But you're wearing the uniform," she replied. "He doesn't know the difference. Just sign it for him, please. It'll make his day." Her son looked up sweetly and extended the ball in my direction.

"You're sure?" I asked.

"Please," she said. She turned to her son. "Go on," she told him. "Give him the ball, he'll autograph it for you."

I wasn't used to signing autographs. I took the ball and signed it, feeling self-conscious, but the boy smiled broadly when I handed it back to him. It was 6:15; first pitch was in less than an hour, and I went to join the rest of the team in the clubhouse.

The Rookie

The early nineties will never be remembered as a golden age of Yankees baseball. Following their Opening Day victory over the Red Sox, though, the 1992 Yankees won their next five in a row, their best start since 1933, and thirteen of their first nineteen games. They ended April in second place, just two games behind the Toronto Blue Jays, and the tabloid sports pages were full of hopeful stories about the team and its playoff chances.

As the season entered its second month, however, injuries began to expose a lack of team depth, and the Yankees starting pitching staff began performing as it had the previous few years: poorly. The two premier free agents the Yankees had signed in the off-season, Danny Tartabull and shortstop Mike Gallego, both languished on the disabled list with assorted injuries and were reduced to the same role that I embraced myself, if under very different circumstances: sitting on the bench, cheering. Injury rumors plagued Mattingly as well; the fact that he was a notoriously slow starter at the plate went only so far toward explaining a batting average that in mid-May was still only .217. The team's losses seemed to come in bunches: six in a row on a seven-game West Coast road trip, eight of their first ten games in June.

The Yankees' problems were not confined to the playing field. Outfielder Jesse Barfield suffered one of the more peculiar injuries of the young baseball season when he slipped and fell in his home sauna; he went on the disabled list with a bruised and burned left arm. The papers reported that George Steinbrenner, out of baseball since 1990 for paying a gambler for information to use against one of his players in contract negotiations, was being investigated by the commissioner's office for contacting Yankees employees; to have done so would have contravened his agreement with Major League Baseball to keep his distance from the team. A Yankees relief pitcher, Steve Howe, was suspended from baseball after pleading guilty in federal court to attempting to buy cocaine; it was the former Rookie of the Year's seventh and final drug-related suspension.

In early June, the first-place Blue Jays came to town and took three straight games at the Stadium, dropping the Yankees to fifth place. I was down the line for the last game of the series and watched Tartabull, off of injured reserve and back in the lineup, badly misplay an inning-ending fly ball. Just a few dozen feet in front of me, Tartabull staggered around a small patch of right field, unable to find the descending baseball in the Stadium's floodlights. The ball dropped at his feet and the Blue Jays followed with seven consecutive hits, breaking the game open.

Even the Yankee clubhouse seemed to be slumping. Hector, the other rookie bat boy, suddenly left the ballclub, and Nick let Jamie and me know that he would not be hiring a replacement. From that date forward, Jamie and I would split Hector's work between us. During games, one bat boy would go down the line; the other, in the dugout, would do both bats and balls. After games, I had not only my own usual postgame work to complete but also the share of Hector's that Jamie delegated to me: twice as many pairs of baseball spikes to polish, twice as many lockers to straighten, twice as many sinks to wipe down. Starting immediately, I would be working at the Stadium even later into the early morning.

Nor did the end of the school year provide the respite from my scholastic day job that I'd looked forward to after two months of sixteen-hour workdays. My math teacher informed me that my efforts to resurrect my failing grade had been insufficient. I would need to attend summer school. If I failed to raise my grade there, he reminded me, I would lose my Regis scholarship and be expelled from the school. My tongue tightened in memory of the contortions my Latin teacher's tirades had induced two summers before.

Given the promise I'd made to my parents at the beginning of the season, I couldn't expect much sympathy from them over my predicament. I broke the news at dinner, after my brother had left the room, by sliding my report card across the table. My mother, a high school English teacher for two decades, had no trouble spotting the subpar math grade. I didn't need to explain that I'd be back in school in July.

"Oh, Matthew," she said. "How could you let this happen?"

"Mom, don't worry," I tried to reassure her. "It'll be fine. It's just for a month."

"Maybe he should take a break from the Stadium," she addressed my father. "It's too important—"

"Mom," I started to protest, "there's only two bat boys—"

My dad put his hand up, momentarily quieting us.

"Do you understand why your mother's so upset?" he asked me. "Do you understand what's at stake here?"

"I do," I said. "Mom, really, I do. It's gonna be fine. I swear."

"Oh, Matthew," my mom repeated her lament. I lowered my head.

"When's summer school start?" my dad asked.

"Right after the Fourth of July."

"Are the Yankees home that whole time?"

"I don't know. Probably not."

"Well," he said, "you've been through summer school before."

I nodded gravely.

"And you know what's expected of you at the Stadium. Are you going to be able to do both?"

I nodded again.

"It's up to you," he said. "Don't let yourself down."

I still had to speak to Nick. I approached him late at night, after a game, as the remaining clubhouse staff sorted whites. Nick sat at his picnic table, reviewing invoices, smoking a cigar. Jamie, Robby, and the Mule stood in a circle around the shopping cart, maybe ten feet away, turning socks inside out.

"Uh, Nick," I said. "I have to tell you something."

He drew deeply on his cigar, then held it out at arm's length, examining the brightly glowing cherry.

"I, uh, failed math class," I said, "so I'm gonna have to go to summer school in July."

Nick cocked his head in my direction; his face showed surprise for a brief moment before melting into mild disgust.

"Don't worry, though," I said. "It's just in the morning, so it's not gonna conflict with work."

He paused, making sure the others were listening.

"I knew it all along, Matty," he said. "I always knew you weren't as bright as you looked."

Jamie cackled loudly behind me.

Nick motioned to me with the end of his cigar for the benefit of his audience.

"The kid's not too bright," he declared.

Up to that moment, Nick's mild insults had been directed solely toward Jamie, Robby, or the Mule; since Opening Day he had always held his fire on Hector and me. I took the slight, counterintuitively, as a hopeful sign: if Nick is insulting me, I may not be long for rookie status. The kid's not too bright? My stature in the clubhouse might actually be improving.

Notwithstanding the brief dip in my own fortunes, and the Yankees', a consensus still held at school and at home: I was the beneficiary of the ultimate lucky break. I had my own uniform in my own locker in the heart of the Yankees clubhouse. I had a paid job that amounted to watching every Yankees home game from a seat in the dugout. Teachers, neighbors, friends of my parents—grown, successful men, twenty or thirty years my senior—asked me if I knew, as they apparently did, that my future working life would be "all downhill from here." I would nod, idiotically, not knowing how else to respond. What else is a sixteen-year-old supposed to do or say in response to a declaration that thoughtlessly cruel?

Even so, I rarely dwelled on how lucky I was to have won my inside view. I was much more conscious of what I lacked and couldn't figure out how to acquire: the elusive ability to act like an insider amid the guys on the Yankees roster. The bat stretcher affair boosted my faith that, on a certain level, I'd been accepted as the new kid in the dugout. But I still spent most of the first few homestands sitting silently on the bench, intimidated and mute. With Hector gone, I was the lone freshman on the clubhouse staff; I felt it made my lack of guile stand out even more dramatically. Jamie, Robby, and the Mule exuded confidence in dealing with the players, but it took me a while to work up the courage to answer questions with more than a word or two, let alone initiate a conversation.

The gulf between myself on one hand and the ballplayers on the other seemed impossibly broad. I couldn't put out of my mind the thought that they lived on a plane wholly different from mine. Different, in fact, from that of anyone I'd ever met. I knew they all made more money in an hour than I would earn working all summer, and that pretty much any of them could have paid off my parents' mortgage or covered my college tuition without sacrifice. I saw their pictures on the back page of the papers every morning on my way to school and overheard their names in countless subway conversations. I saw how fans in the stands begged for a moment of their attention or stood outside the Stadium all afternoon, pressed against police sawhorses, waiting for a handshake or autograph.

A few months before, I couldn't have imagined a demographic more nerve-racking to talk to than pretty teenage girls, but now I found myself sitting on the bench next to Don Mattingly and the others, too scared to open my mouth and risk saying something stupid.

I marveled at the ease with which Jamie moved through the clubhouse, making deals like a teenage horse trader. Getting the players to leave tickets for his friends, hitting up the Nike representative for the newest model of Air Jordans, trading high fives up and down the bench after home runs or inning-ending double plays. Every interaction I had at the Stadium felt bumbling, frustratingly devoid of style and humor and grace.

So at first, the truly enjoyable moments at work came not during games, surprisingly, but late at night, long after all the players and fans had left the Stadium. Best of all were those weekend nights when the Yankees had an evening game followed the next afternoon by a day game—usually Friday into Saturday, or Saturday into Sunday. On these nights, when work ended after one and we needed to be back on duty before nine the next morning, the entire staffs of both clubhouses usually stayed overnight at the Stadium.

Two bat boys, Ray and Kenny, worked for Lou Cucuzza Jr. in the visiting clubhouse.

Ray was the senior bat boy on the visiting side, like Jamie a veteran of the season before, but the teenagers came from opposite ends of the City, literally and figuratively.

Jamie was a stocky, streetwise Dominican kid from 230th Street in the South Bronx; the fact that he was a pretty good ballplayer seemed to ease his interactions in the clubhouse. Ray, from Queens, was awkwardly cerebral and carried a good deal of baby fat under the bat boy uniform of whatever team was visiting Yankee Stadium; his bearing suggested a childhood more suburban Nassau County than inner-city Queensbridge.

Jamie was most notorious for his transparently apocryphal stories about major league scouts who had seen him down the line, playing catch with the Yankees outfielders, and returned to the Stadium to see him . . . bat boy. There was no point pressing Jamie on the details of these purported scouting sessions. Calling him out would have just provoked a stream of don't-worry-about-its.

Ray on the other hand was most notorious for his role in a game against the Oakland A's the season before: serving as ball boy down the third-base line, he had fielded a fair ball, arguably costing the Yankees the ballgame. The Yankees had come back from an early 8–1 deficit to tie the game when Oakland outfielder Jose Canseco came to bat in the eighth inning. At the time, Canseco was regarded as one of the most powerful hitters in baseball; he was also known as an occasional loafer on the base paths. In this at bat, Canseco hit a hard grounder that deflected off the third base bag—fair ball—and bounded into foul territory. Ray jogged over from the stool where he was sitting a few feet away and scooped up the ball, which was still in play. The umpires awarded Canseco a ground-rule double; it's unlikely that he would have made it to second base on his own had Ray left the ball alone for the left fielder or third baseman to corral. The Yankees manager was ejected for arguing the call. The next A's batter lined a double, scoring Canseco, which turned out to be the winning run. Before the bottom of the inning, Lou pulled Ray off the field, for his own protection, and hid him from reporters after the game behind the washing machine in the visiting clubhouse.

Kenny's personality was somewhere between Jamie's and Ray's. He was a childhood friend of Ray's but carried a slight chip on his shoulder. Kenny was also the most athletic and physically imposing of the four of us. Tall, wiry, and strong, he walked with a swagger that suggested he knew he could, in a tense moment, stare down most other guys our age, not to mention each of the three of us: me, Ray, even Jamie.

Notwithstanding our differences, it wasn't hard to find common ground, particularly on sleepover nights. Following the other bat boys' lead, I quickly learned that under Nick's indifferent supervision, very little of the ballpark was off-limits to us. Once we'd finished cleaning our respective clubhouses, we had the run of Yankee Stadium.

On sleepover nights Ray and Kenny usually came through the door of the Yankees clubhouse by 1:30 in the morning. Having just finished their own postgame work, they would seat themselves at Nick's table and attempt to regale us with stories about what various visiting players had said or done in their clubhouse before or after the game. Nick, when he acknowledged Ray and Kenny at all, would tease them by butchering their names or sometimes pretending to forget them altogether.

"Who the hell are you?" he'd demand of Ray, though he'd met him forty or fifty times before.

"Ray Fink," he'd answer.

"Fink," Nick might say, repeating the somewhat unfortunate last name. "Now I remember."

When the chatter grew too much for him to bear, Nick would shoo the four of us away, signaling that Jamie and I were now off duty, and we'd start rifling through the wooden bins near the clubhouse door where the players' bats were stored. Though we had our pick of game-used Mattinglys and Tartabulls, I would toss those aside for the shorter, lighter bats used by slap-single hitters like Andy Stankiewicz or Mike Gallego; these were the only bats I was strong enough to swing easily without choking up too much on the handle. In most of the players' lockers there were boxes full of brand-new calfskin batting gloves, and we took our choice of these as well. We collected the pine-tar rag, rosin bag, and weighted batting donuts that sat during games in the on-deck circle, the bucket of scuffed baseballs set aside for batting practice the next morning, and, from Nick's picnic table, the key to the Columbus Room.

The Columbus Room, presumably named for the Ohio home of the Yankees' AAA affiliate, was where the Yankees held batting practice on days with threatening weather. The room was located at the end of the long tunnel under the right-field seats and was impressively outfitted with a stereo system, artificial turf, and an oversized pitching machine. Black netting hung from the low ceiling to the green plastic carpet and created a long corridor equal in length to that between pitching mound and batter's box. One at a time, bad early-nineties hip-hop blaring from top-dollar stereo speakers, each of us stepped inside to take our hacks. Considering our ages and sizes, the surroundings felt appropriately big league.

The machine spat balls across the room at one speed only, maybe eighty-five or ninety miles per hour; thankfully, it lacked the breaking ball technology that would have sent balls veering through the strike zone on unexpected trajectories. For me, at least, a mix of ninety-mile-an-hour fastballs, curveballs, and sliders in on the hands would have felt not just baffling but life-threatening. As it was, the pitches were reassuringly never more than an inch or two off the corners of the plastic home plate that sat on the turf. The height of the pitches was equally consistent but personally a little troublesome, as at that time I was close to a full foot shorter than the average Yankees ballplayer. I had to chase fastball after fastball up at armpit level. Jamie and Ken were decent hitters, and slapped line drive after line drive into the mesh screen protecting the front of the machine. I swung just to make contact, choking up more and more on the bat, but usually still ended up swinging through or under pitches, popping them straight up into the net over my head. It didn't matter to me. The batting practice raised blisters on my hands that lasted for days, but I hardly noticed those, either. I was deep inside Yankee Stadium, wide-awake at 3:30 in the morning, free to hit off the Yankees' pitching machine until I felt like going to sleep. Some nights we never got to sleep at all.

Even better were those nights when we completed our work in the clubhouse before the cleaning crew had finished sweeping the stands. The Yankees' electricians left the Stadium's lights on for the sweepers to see by, and for those few hours the empty ballpark was lit as brightly as during any game. Though the grounds crew draped the diamond with a tarp, the outfield was always left uncovered—and irresistible to the four of us. We roamed the outfield not in our uniforms but in baseball spikes and clubhouse-issue T-shirts and shorts, carrying the bucket of beat-up balls and a bat or two each. From the lip of the infield grass behind first base, it wasn't more than 175 feet to the outfield wall and the legendary "short porch" that had over the decades so tempted Ruth and Gehrig, Mantle and Maris, Jackson and Winfield. In front of a heckling and hooting audience of sweepers, we played home run derby from the grass at the edge of the infield, self-tossing balls into the air and driving them toward the right-field wall, deep into the outfield and occasionally into the seats. Home runs rebounded off the hard plastic seats with a satisfying *thwock* that would echo once or twice around the empty Stadium.

When we ran out of balls—we left our home run balls in the stands for the next day's fans—or the Stadium floodlights went off, we'd adjourn to the visiting clubhouse.

We played a card game called acey-deucey, for money, wagering the cash we'd earned as tips that a third card, turned down, would fall between the previous two cards, showing.

We invented an indoor baseball game in which the pitcher skipped a tightly rolled ball of athletic tape off a long table in the center of the clubhouse. The batter hit using a fungo bat—the elongated type of bat used by coaches to hit fly balls during outfield practice—and runs were scored stickball-style, depending on where in the room you were able to place the ball.

Some nights we'd chip in for a case of Budweiser from the local bodega and smuggle it back into the Stadium. I had my first beer in the visiting clubhouse of Yankee Stadium, and, the same night, the second, third, fourth, and fifth beers of my life. My first-ever fistfight took place there as well: judgment clouded and sensitivities inflamed one night by too much Budweiser and not enough cathartic indoor baseball, Kenny and I ended a game of acey-deucey by throwing punches at each other across the card table. The stakes that night were higher than usual—we'd been playing with twenty-dollar bills, I remember—and Kenny had lost much more than he'd won. We'd all been teasing him as his luck went bad, but I hadn't yet learned when to quit.

"How much you down now, Kenny?" I badgered him.

"Fuck off, Matt," he said.

I felt offended that he'd singled me out by name, and the resentment simmered while I nursed another beer. When Kenny lost his next big hand, I chimed in again, amusing myself and trying to amuse Ray and Jamie.

"Ha," I laughed. "Sucks for you."

Kenny stared me down across the table. I laughed again.

"Shut the fuck up," he said.

"You shut the fuck up," I said. Given the time of night and our mutual inexperience with alcohol, it was not shaping up to be much of a battle of wits. Ray and Jamie looked on, probably incredulous that, half his size, I wasn't backing down.

"Crybaby," I fatefully mumbled.

The word was barely out of my mouth before Kenny lunged across the table at me, pushing me and my seat backward. As the chair went down, my feet came up, kicking the underside of the table and scattering cards and aluminum empties. I scrambled to my feet and shoved him back with both hands.

"What the fuck?" I yelled, my arms spread wide, posturing. Kenny inched toward me wordlessly.

I'd found growing up that raising your voice was a pretty surefire way of ending an impending fistfight before it got serious; not by any faint hope of intimidation, but by drawing attention to the ruckus and prompting an intervention by whatever adult happened to be nearby. For someone as scrawny as I was as a kid, it was a vital if ignoble tactic.

"Let's go," I hollered, raising my voice even louder. "You wanna fight?"

"Yeah," Kenny answered me, enraged.

It was at that moment that I realized no one was going to step between us this time; there was no one there to do so. Jamie and Ray had no interest in stopping the fight; in fact, given teenage boys' innate attraction to fistfights, the opposite was probably true. We were in Yankee Stadium's visiting clubhouse, an underground room with five-foot-thick concrete walls, at 4:30 on a Sunday morning. I was about as well-off as Piggy in *The Lord of the Flies* after he lost his glasses. There were no teachers around, no athletic coaches or referees, no bus monitors or school security guards, no adults or authority figures of any kind. I would not be able to posture my way out of this one.

The fight wasn't a close one but mercifully, it ended quickly, the way most slugfests do: both of us on the floor, gracelessly grappling, arms too intertwined to throw anything resembling a clean punch. We smacked at each other for a few minutes before I wrestled myself away from Kenny. My chest was heaving, and I could taste a little blood from where he'd evidently cut the inside of my upper lip. I had bought a thin gold chain for myself with one of my first paychecks and now saw it on the ground, its cheap clasp broken. I snatched it off the floor and sulked away.

Nick was folding towels when I walked back into the Yankees clubhouse.

"What happened to you?" he asked.

"Nothing," I said, trying to walk past him to the players' lounge. That was where, using postgame-spread tablecloths as makeshift bedsheets, Jamie and I usually slept on couches. Nick stepped in front of me. He took a look at my fat lip and har-rumphed.

"Kenny broke my chain," I complained, displaying the gold necklace in the palm of my hand.

"Well," he said, "maybe you shouldn't pick on guys bigger than you are."

Nick cuffed me on the back of my head.

"Sleep it off," he said. "Go on."

I retired from fighting with an oh-and-one record, and Kenny and I exchanged apologies the next homestand. Late-night home run derby and Columbus Room conversations returned to more mild ground, and in particular to the one question the bat boys had habitually debated since the beginning of the season: which side, home or visiting, had it better?

Kenny and Ray claimed that, given the contact they had with every other American League team, they would never trade their jobs for ones in the Yankees clubhouse. They took pride that many of the league's best players knew them by name. They cited the fact that they made more money during the season than we did, as they received tips from visiting players at the conclusion of each and every series at the Stadium. They had autographed balls from every all-star and future Hall of Famer who passed through the visiting clubhouse.

Jamie and I were not swayed by their arguments. To us, nothing compared with the one thing we knew our jobs in the Yankees clubhouse gave us: a full season to get to know one group of ballplayers. Not to mention the clincher, as I was slowly beginning to understand: the full season I had for that one group of ballplayers to get to know me.

It had taken only a few games to begin to grasp the personalities of the different Yankees—who was friendly, who was a loner, which guys were the leaders on and off the field. Mattingly was hands down the most generous player on the roster, giving both of his time and—as the best tipper on the team—his wallet. The pitcher Melido Perez was probably the funniest Yankee; a native of the Dominican Republic, his apparently tenuous grasp of the English language was belied by unexpectedly fluent one-liners. Center fielder Bernie Williams was the kindest and most cerebral ballplayer; I admired him for how he relaxed before games by strumming the acoustic guitar he kept in his locker.

Figuring out how to make use of these insights so that I felt more at ease amidst all the varied personalities took longer. You might blame Nick's short fuse or Jamie's dismissive mantra, but part of the problem was that no one who worked in the clubhouse learned anything by asking directly. What I learned I gathered by observation, watching how the guys ahead of me— namely Jamie, Robby, and the Mule—comported themselves, before, during, and after games.

Following this fundamental law of clubhouse dynamics, I gradually intuited how to carry myself around the ballplayers. The first lesson was that I didn't necessarily need to walk on eggshells all the time: it was okay to joke around with the ballplayers on the bench and in the clubhouse, but, just like in school, nobody likes a kiss-ass. I learned that pitchers were more laid-back than position players, probably because they had so much more time to kill than everyday players and so sat around all game amusing themselves and each other. This made them easier to talk to, and the first guys on the Yankees roster who I considered friends were pitchers: Scott Kamieniecki, John Habyan, Bob Wickman, Tim Leary.

From my very first day at work, people were curious to know which Yankees I'd found to be jerks or assholes; after "What's Mattingly like?" it may have been the question I most frequently fielded. In truth, there were only one or two, and I understood even then that without them my Yankee Stadium education in human nature would have been incomplete. It's instructive to discover at age sixteen that someone unimaginably wealthy could and would stiff you for twenty bucks after you'd picked up and paid for their lunch or dry cleaning. Or that you could work for two years with someone who never bothered to learn your first name. The better lessons came from the guys who reached out to me in small but meaningful ways—greeting me by name on the bench, asking about school, playfully inquiring about how I was getting along with the ladies.

I began to see that the ballplayers, despite their extraordinary athletic abilities, possessed the personalities of otherwise ordinary people—people I'd met before and knew from school or around the neighborhood. It was possible to relate to the players individually and personally rather than only as a baseball fan or as the kid who shined their baseball spikes and straightened their lockers. After all, I realized, most of them weren't more than a few years older than I was at the time. I remember well the day that summer when the Yankees' recently signed top draft pick, a high school shortstop from Kalamazoo, Michigan, arrived at the Stadium for his first workout with the big league club. Derek Jeter was eighteen years old, barely older than the bat boys working in the clubhouse. He seemed as awed as I had been on my first day of work. Politely reticent, he hung close by the clubhouse staff, making us laugh when he addressed Nick as "Mr. Priore," watching TV with us in the players' lounge until batting practice started.

Having learned firsthand that a player's performance on the field often has little connection to his character off it, in the dugout and outside of baseball, I knew I'd never again boo at a sporting event. I vividly remember the shock and sadness I felt later in the season when I heard in the clubhouse that Tim Leary—a veteran pitcher who was having a miserable season for the Yankees, booed mercilessly nearly every time he took the mound—had been traded to the Seattle Mariners. Though he'd lost the affection of the fans, I knew Leary was a first-rate guy, smart, friendly, and funny. It's hard to tell what he thought of the timid high school junior with whom he'd had a handful of conversations, but I thought of Leary as a friend of mine. I approached him nervously while he emptied his locker the afternoon the trade was announced. With as much earnestness as I had ever mustered in a conversation with an adult, I shook his hand and wished him well in Seattle.

The fact that I was the sole rookie bat boy, initially a source of anxiety, served in reality to quicken the pace at which I formed friendships with the ballplayers. After Hector left, Jamie preferred going down the line to doing both bats and balls in the dugout, so those game-time duties fell to me. I was spending every game in the Yankees dugout, and though handling both bats and balls seemed at first to be a feat of great concentration, I quickly got the hang of it. I was now the only kid on the bench during games, and mutual familiarity with the ballplayers developed swiftly.

I noted with pride that more and more of the players knew me by name. I feared less that guys were humoring me when we spoke, and for the first time, dugout conversations seemed not to dead-end but carry on naturally, and to more interesting places. Summer school had started just after the Fourth of July, but even two hours of remedial math classes a day couldn't dampen my excitement at finally feeling at home in the dugout and clubhouse.

Every game held the promise of a new exchange or adventure that might bring me deeper into the fold. I found common interests with a couple of players and grounds for conversation with others. I remember an early conversation with Bernie Williams about jazz and New York jazz clubs. I settled an argument between Kevin Maas, the Yankees backup first baseman, and Gary Weil, the strength and conditioning coach. Maas, who had graduated from UC-Berkeley with a degree in mechanical engineering, was probably the smartest and doubtless the best-educated person on the Yankees roster. Weil, whom everyone called "Troll," had a master's degree in education and before coming to the Yankees had served on the coaching staff of Notre Dame's football team. Maas and Troll were inexplicably debating the significance of Avogadro's number in chemical science, and the two of them turned to me to resolve their disagreement. I had studied chemistry the year before, and remembered both the number and what it meant: 6.02×10^{23}, the number of atoms or molecules in a mole of any chemical substance. Maas grudgingly conceded the bet. Troll threw me an enthusiastic high five, punctuating what was surely the most peculiar dugout exchange I had during my tenure with the Yankees.

A few days later, sitting on the bench with Troll waiting out a long rain delay, I asked him a couple of questions about the new equipment recently installed in the Yankee Stadium weight room. Troll invited me on a tour, which he concluded by offering to put me on a weight-lifting program. He designed a workout regimen for me as he would for any of the ballplayers: sets and repetitions of bench presses, shoulder presses, lateral pulldowns, bicep curls, tricep extensions. Never mind that the weight notations that I made on my workout chart were all in the mid-two-digits; I faithfully performed the routine he prescribed for me three days a week and carefully charted my progress on the same type of chart that the ballplayers used themselves.

I usually got my workouts in between summer school and batting practice. Occasionally one of the players would come into the weight room while I was still finishing up. I would hustle to get out of his way, but more often than not he'd insist that I keep going, reassuring me that I wasn't in his way. I felt bashful about struggling with weights that the players would have considered trifling, but took their encouragement to heart. "You've got to start somewhere," I was told more than once.

I flirted briefly with a more malevolent habit, chewing tobacco, amusing myself during a boring game by breaking open a pouch of Red Man that one of the players had left lying on the dugout bench. I pulled a plug's worth of leaves from the pouch and stuffed them inside my cheek; thank God I knew enough not to swallow the juice. Already feeling a little light-headed, I was promptly scolded by one of the Yankees' rookie pitchers: not for tobacco use per se, but for my amateurish chewing technique.

"Like this," he said, teaching me how to roll the pinch of tobacco in a skin of Bazooka bubble gum before tucking the tobacco-gum ball inside my mouth; the Bazooka bound the loose tobacco leaves together so that the chaw was neater and stayed intact longer. My dad's warning in his Opening Day letter proved correct—tobacco juice does stain your uniform—but for a few weeks I performed my game-time duties in something of a nicotine fog.

It took a swelteringly hot Sunday afternoon to break the habit. The Yankees were playing the Seattle Mariners, and Jamie had sent me down the line for the game. I sat out there all afternoon baking, my cheek grotesquely bulging, my head growing ever more light as the sun and tobacco worked over my faculties.

Two couples in their thirties sat in the first row of the box seats, a few feet from my stool, and by the third or fourth inning they couldn't help but notice the brown juice that I spat with gusto into the dirt between my feet. The women were particularly horrified.

"Oh," one of them said, her voice full of disgust. "Are you chewing tobacco?"

I spit a long stream into the dirt.

"That's revolting," the woman declared. "How old are you?"

I shrugged, suddenly bashful.

"I should tell your mother," she said. As the Yankees took the field, I left my seat to warm up the right fielder with a game of catch. I tossed the ball easily, enjoying the buzz, believing I looked the part of a big leaguer, or at least feeling like one. As the first Mariner came to the plate to lead off the top of the inning, I flicked my glove in the direction of Bernie Williams, giving him the customary signal that I was ready to receive the ball he'd been using to play catch with the Yankees left fielder. Bernie threw a strike from where he stood in center field, 150 feet away. I saw the ball clearly and raised my glove to meet its trajectory. In the last few feet, though, the baseball passed against the backdrop of the crowded right-field bleachers, and whether due to my impaired state of mind or the unfortunate location of a knot of white-T-shirt-clad fans, I lost sight of it for a moment. The ball sailed an inch or two over the pocket of my glove and ricocheted hard off my forehead. It rolled to a stop on the grass ten feet in front of me; my chaw of tobacco rested at my feet.

My first thought was disbelief that the impact hadn't knocked me out cold. The second, on regaining my already diminished senses, was sheer amazement that no one seemed to have noticed what had happened—neither Bernie nor the other players, the first base umpire, or any of the forty thousand fans in attendance. I retrieved the ball and retreated to my stool, my face flush with embarrassment. I spent the half inning running my fingers across the bump that already protruded just below the bill of my cap; it was pocked by slight indentations made by the seams of the baseball. The ball had rung my head like a bell, thoroughly routing the mild tobacco high I'd been enjoying a few minutes before. When the Mariners made their third out, I trotted off the field to run some cold water over my face. A few of the players were waiting for me on the top step of the dugout, laughing.

"Nice catch," Mattingly said, lifting my cap off my head. "Lemme see."

I tilted my head back slightly as he examined the bruise.

"Gino," he called to Gene Monahan, the Yankees' medical trainer. "You want to take a look at this?"

"I'm fine," I mumbled.

"At least you kept the ball in front of you," Mattingly joked. Tobacco always tasted sour after that.

Not all the lessons I learned at Yankee Stadium that summer came as painfully as that one. As the season entered July, my Yankee Stadium learning curve continued to soar.

I'd been mystified since Opening Day as to how Jamie regularly scored tickets to leave for his friends, how he filled his locker with free sneakers, girls' phone numbers, and autographed baseballs. Largely by observation, one by one, I taught myself these tricks of the trade.

How to get friends into the ballpark for free: inspect the players' ticket list around four-thirty or five o'clock, just before the Yankees traveling secretary took the list upstairs to the Stadium ticket office. Each Yankee was entitled to six tickets per game for his family and friends. Figure out which guys hadn't used their full ticket allotment, then approach and ask discreetly if you could "use their extras." Once you'd secured the two or three or four passes you needed, you'd add your buddy's name to the list under that player's name. With some trial and error, I learned to use nondescript block letters: scanning the list for unfamiliar penmanship was the traveling secretary's most potent countermeasure against having a Yankees family section full of bat boys' high school classmates and their girlfriends.

How to get the latest styles for free from sneaker company reps: understand that the reason they came to the Stadium was to recruit players to endorse their products and to manage the stable of clients they'd already cultivated. Remember that, unlike you, they were barred from entering the clubhouse. Seeing the Nike Guy or the Adidas Guy in the hallway outside the clubhouse door, introduce yourself and tell him you work with the ballplayers. Ask him if there's anyone he wants to see or get a message to. Let that ballplayer know that the Nike Guy wants to see him in the hallway. When they're done talking, ask the Nike Guy if he has any samples of those new Air Jordans in size eleven.

I even finally divined the art of collecting phone numbers from girls in the stands. I'm not sure whether the method I hit upon was the same one that Jamie so successfully employed, but with enough practice, it proved sufficiently effective. Sitting down the line, two or three sections of box seats were close enough to the field to allow the possibility of eye contact. Innings one through three were devoted to surveying the crowd for a pretty teenage girl. Ideally, the girl you were interested in would be at the game with a few of her girlfriends; less ideally, she'd be sitting next to her dad. In innings four through six you'd try to catch her eye, make her smile or giggle, which is when who she'd come to the game with became important. If she was at the Stadium with her girlfriends, they could be counted on to egg her on, convincing her: Yeah, see, I told you he's looking at you! By the late innings, after the fans in the box seats right up against the field had left to get a head start on the drive back home, you could signal for the girl to come down to the better seats, closer to where you were sitting. If she was agreeable, you had an inning or two to talk, find out where she lived and went to school, ask if she wanted to come to another ballgame or meet up and walk around the Village some night. If all those pieces fell into place, you'd exchange numbers right after the last out of the game, Frank Sinatra blaring from the center-field speakers as the Yankees filed back into their dugout.

I started to build a small collection of autographed baseballs to rival Jamie's. Like asking for a number down the line, getting a ball signed was a challenge involving multiple steps. The first was getting a clean American League baseball without paying eight dollars for it at the store. The second was getting the signature, sometimes of a guy who you knew didn't like to sign or would flat-out refuse. The bat boy assigned balls duty during a game picked up six dozen baseballs from the umpires' room before each game, but these were always already "rubbed up" with the thick Delaware River mud that is used to turn new balls into game balls. Since the 1930s, every baseball used in the major leagues has been slathered with soupy dirt harvested from the same secret mud hole in southern New Jersey. It's not just for the sake of tradition: the mud turns the ball dull brown, reducing the glare of the white leather, and a rubbed-up ball is easier for a pitcher to grip than an untreated one. Though you might want to get a game ball signed under rare circumstances—for example, having a pitcher sign a game ball from his no-hitter—for autographs it was almost always better to use a clean ball, so the signature wouldn't get lost in the muddy leather. The problem was that new baseballs were stored under lock and key and guarded zealously by Nick, who bitched and cursed at players, let alone bat boys, who asked for balls for signing purposes. Besides those delivered to the umpires' room, new baseballs came out only once every couple of weeks, when the team ran through the recycled game balls normally used for batting practice. If the BP pitcher was running low, to keep things moving he might add a few dozen brand-new baseballs to the bucket on the pitching mound. The trick, then, was to be in the outfield shagging flies during BP on those lucky days when the clean baseballs came out. Ground balls and line drives that skipped along the infield dirt or the outfield grass were scuffed or stained by the time I got to them. But if I was able to catch one of these new balls on the fly—one that had gone from its box into the BP pitcher's bucket, and then off the barrel of the player's bat directly into my glove— I had a "pearl," a pristine ball, suitable for signing.

Acting on a tip from Nick Testa, the batting practice pitcher, I stockpiled a dozen pearls in anticipation of Old Timers' Day.

A list of the Yankees legends who would be participating had come down to the clubhouse from the front office a month or so before the game. Three Hall of Famers would be in attendance: Joe DiMaggio, Mickey Mantle, and Whitey Ford. Phil Rizzuto, who would enter the Hall a few years later but whom I knew best as the voice of a childhood's worth of Yankees telecasts, was also on the list, along with a handful of more recent legendary Yankees, household names themselves: Joe Pepitone, Sparky Lyle, Catfish Hunter.

Sometime that spring I'd borrowed from the library a book, *Summer of '49*, that David Halberstam had written a few years before. The book recounts that year's Yankees–Red Sox pennant race; Boston came to New York with two games left in the season and a one-game lead over the Yankees. Needing to win only one game to advance to the World Series, the Red Sox lost both.

I thought it was the best book I'd ever read. The stars of *Summer of '49* are the stars of the two teams, DiMaggio and Boston's Ted Williams, but I was captivated by Halberstam's vivid portraits of the less-renowned players on the Yankees and Red Sox rosters. These men had been celebrities in postwar New York and Boston, but most of their names had faded with time. The book ends with an epilogue that runs down the rosters of the two teams and accounts for the players' lives after their baseball careers ended; many hadn't survived the four decades since that season.

Looking down Nick's list of old-timers, I was astonished to recognize a number of names from Halberstam's book. I shouldn't have been so shocked—members of the 1949 Yankees were certainly of age to participate—but I had read *Summer of '49* as a work of history. I hadn't suspected that, outside of DiMaggio, any of those ballplayers would be in attendance and that I might have a chance to meet them.

The names popped off the page at me. Dr. Bobby Brown, the Yankees third baseman in 1949, would be there; he became a heart surgeon after his baseball career ended and later the president of the American League. So would Allie Reynolds, a hard-throwing right-hander who went 17–6 that year and was recognized as one of the best pitchers in the league; Reynolds was part Native American, which accounts for the nickname "the Chief," by which he was known in those less-sensitive times. Outfielder Tommy Henrich was also on the list; he had been a famously regarded clutch hitter for the Yankees, a hero that summer for carrying the team through the first few months of the season while DiMaggio nursed an injured heel. I would meet Hank Bauer, the right-handed outfielder who had bristled at the then-innovative "platoon" system, instituted by Yankees manager Casey Stengel, by which Bauer alternated starts with a left-handed teammate. I even thrilled at seeing the names of Cliff Mapes and Spec Shea, two lesser-known players on the '49 team. The excitement prompted me to go back to Halberstam's book, which I reread on my train rides to and from the Stadium in the weeks before Old Timers' Day. One night at dinner, I asked my dad if he remembered any of the names himself.

"Of course," he said, thinking back to his Brooklyn childhood as a Dodgers fan. "I hated those guys."

"Yeah?" I grinned.

"Yeah," he said. "Not so much during the summer. During the season, the Giants were the big rivals. The Bronx was the other side of the world from Bay Ridge. But come October, it was the Yankees, and those guys just killed us. What year were you reading about?"

"Nineteen forty-nine."

"Forty-nine . . . They played the Dodgers in the Series that year, right?"

"Yeah," I said. "Beat 'em four games to one."

"That's right," he said, reminiscing. "I remember that Series. Henrich hit a home run in the bottom of the ninth inning to beat Brooklyn in Game One. I turned fifteen that summer. I was a sophomore at Regis." He paused. "God, I hated those guys."

One morning a few weeks before Old Timers' Day, I came downstairs to an obituary that my dad had clipped from the newspaper and left for me on the kitchen table. It reported the death of Eddie Lopat, a pitcher who, along with Reynolds and Vic Raschi, had formed the backbone of the Yankees' 1949 staff. I remembered Lopat well from *Summer of '49*. As a pitcher, he lacked the speed of either Reynolds or Raschi, but he was notoriously crafty, and Ted Williams considered him one of the five best he ever faced. His sluggish if baffling repertoire of pitches earned him the nickname "the Junk Man" from his Yankees teammates, but according to Halberstam, Williams never referred to him as anything but "that fucking Lopat."

"One of the best," my dad had written across the top of the obituary. "If you can get the time on Old Timers' Day, be sure to talk with his teammates when you see them."

Everybody slept at the clubhouse the night before Old Timers' Day. Jamie had given me the word that Old Timers' was, second only to the home opener, the busiest day of the season; it was apparently also the earliest morning.

"No playing around tonight," Nick warned us. "You finish the whites and you go to bed."

Nick had assigned each old-timer a current Yankee's locker to share, and Jamie and I walked around the clubhouse posting makeshift name tags according to Nick's list. It felt a little like hanging stockings the night before Christmas.

Hank Bauer was the first old-timer through the clubhouse door, not long after seven in the morning, a full five hours before the on-field festivities were scheduled to begin. He was accompanied by Bill "Moose" Skowron, his Yankees teammate from the Mantle-Ford-Martin days. Both looked the part of old-time ballplayers. Bauer, who had spent World War II in the Marine Corps, strode across the clubhouse with an authority he'd clearly learned either in Yankee Stadium or on Parris Island. Skowron still wore the buzz cut he'd had in his playing days; he'd earned his nickname not for the animal but when a teammate teased him that, with his tight haircut, he resembled Benito Mussolini.

Following shortly after Bauer and Skowron was Joe Pepitone, in a hairpiece the size and shape of a lion's mane. Sparky Lyle came next. Wearing the same familiar handlebar mustache he'd had as a Yankee, Lyle looked fit, as if he still had a few major league innings left in his pitching arm. Showalter arrived and circled the room greeting the Yankees legends, thanking them for coming. Even Nick seemed ebullient, laughing loudly at jokes and old memories, taking in stride the old-timers' playful demands for different size pinstripes and better locker assignments. The present-day Yankees arrived one by one and introduced themselves to the older men with whom they'd be sharing their lockers for the afternoon. I didn't recognize Allie Reynolds and Tommy Henrich until after they'd taken a seat in front of their temporary lockers. By 9:00 A.M., most of the old-timers had reported. With the overcrowding and loud teasing and handshakes and the cases of beer the old-timers went through before ten o'clock in the morning, it was the most chaotic I had seen the clubhouse since my first day of work.

Mickey Mantle and Whitey Ford arrived late, walking into the clubhouse together sometime after eleven. They were ushered directly into the coaches' room, where their teammate Clete Boyer, third baseman on the 1961 championship team and the 1992 Yankees third base coach, had his everyday locker. Boyer greeted Ford and Mantle with hugs, then closed the door behind them, sending the clear message that for the rest of the day the coaches' room was effectively off-limits to everyone but Nick; Clete, Whitey, and The Mick wanted to be able to catch up away from the fray. Word filtered down to the clubhouse that DiMaggio had also arrived at the ballpark, but as was his custom, he remained in Steinbrenner's box until the last possible moment before his introduction on the field.

I was glad Nick had enforced a curfew the night before; it would have been tough to make it through the day on less than a full night's sleep. All morning long, players handed Jamie and me baseballs to get autographed: today's Yankees wanted the old-timers to sign for them, and vice versa. The most popular Yankees—new and old—were each surrounded by a knot of people, and I spent an hour or two filling autograph requests, diving into the crush around Mattingly and Tartabull, Pepitone and Lyle. Just before noon, I noticed Henrich and Reynolds sitting in front of their lockers, talking quietly and nursing beers; they were not being bothered for autographs. I pulled a pair of pearls from the stash in my locker and made my way over to where they were sitting.

"Mr. Henrich," I said, extending the ball to him. "Would you sign this for me?"

He autographed the ball and handed it back to me. Reynolds signed one for me as well. I wanted to explain the connection I felt to them, how excited I was to meet them, but I wasn't sure how to put it. I feared "I'm a big fan of yours" might sound phony coming from someone born twenty years after their baseball careers had ended.

"I read a book about you," I said.

"Yeah?" Reynolds said.

"Yeah. *Summer of '49.*"

"Sure," he said. "Any good?"

"Really good. You read it?"

"Nah."

Long pause. Our six-decade age differential seemed to weigh heavily on the conversation.

"My dad was a Dodgers fan," I blurted. "In Brooklyn."

"They had good teams back then," Henrich said sagely.

"Yeah," I said, nodding my head knowingly, as if I'd been through those Yankees–Dodgers battles myself. A pair of middle-aged Yankees walked past where I was standing to head out to the field. The short three-inning game that is the centerpiece of the Old Timers' festivities was about to begin.

"You guys playing today?" I asked Reynolds and Henrich. They laughed.

"No," Henrich said. "We haven't played in years. A little too old for that."

"Oh," I said. "Well, thanks for signing for me."

"You're welcome," they said.

I extended my hand to Henrich and then Reynolds. The two legendary Yankees may have been pushing eighty, but their hands were steady, their handshakes firm.

I was determined to get balls signed by both DiMaggio and Mantle but had been warned that both were prickly about autographs. DiMaggio had an exclusive contract with a memorabilia company and signed only at events arranged pursuant to the lucrative deal. Mantle's reluctance was apparently just temperamental, rooted in the fact that The Mick had not yet given up drinking. In an uncharacteristically generous mentoring moment, Jamie had explained to me how he'd overcome the same predicament on Old Timers' Day the year before. I planned on following his approach to a tee.

Precious little time was left before the old-timers would take the field for introductions. Swallowing my natural timidity, I told myself to go for it. What's the worst that could happen?

Another pearl from my locker in hand, I gingerly pushed open the door to the coaches' room. Four-ninths of the 1961 Yankees lineup—Mickey Mantle, Clete Boyer, Moose Skowron, and Bobby Richardson—and Ford, the ace of the pitching staff, sat in a circle in the middle of the small room, laughing. A dozen or more empty beer cans littered the floor; only Richardson, a born-again Christian, and Boyer, who would coach third base in a meaningful game in a few hours, weren't drinking. Whitey Ford was telling a story, and Mantle and the others were listening, waiting for the punch line.

"Excuse me, Mr. Mantle," I said quietly, leaning in as unobtrusively as possible and presenting him with the ball and a pen. "Don Mattingly asked me to ask you to please sign this." According to Jamie, such a request, phrased this way, could not be refused.

Mantle refused.

"But—" I started to say.

"I said no," Mantle said.

My eyes met Boyer's, the Yankees coach I'd gotten to know best since Opening Day, but he just shrugged apologetically. I stood frozen with the ball and pen still thrust out in front of me. Ford's story was going nowhere with me in the room, and Mantle shot me a look clearly intended to send me on my way. As he glared at me, a foot away, I somewhat instinctively extended the ball another inch in his direction.

"For fuck's sake!" Mantle exploded. "Get out of here! Can't you see you're bothering us?"

I apologized meekly and fled the room. Slightly stunned, I decided to head down to the field to see whether the Old Timers' festivities had begun. In the hallway between the clubhouse door and the tunnel to the dugout stood DiMaggio; he was waiting for the adulatory public address introduction that would begin in a moment and culminate in his being announced as America's greatest living ballplayer. Unlike every other oldtimer, Joe D. wore not a Yankees uniform but a dark three-button suit. He was surrounded by a phalanx of a dozen men, bodyguards and Yankees executives. I slipped between two of his handlers and sidled up next to him.

"Excuse me, Joe," I said. "I work in the clubhouse. Would you please sign this ball for me?"

DiMaggio turned to me in my pin-striped uniform. One of the front office executives looked irritated at my audacity.

"I can't sign balls," DiMaggio told me. He nudged a member of his entourage. "Gimme something to sign for the kid."

Someone produced one of the eight-by-eleven-inch Old Timers' Day commemorative lithographs that were being handed out to fans upstairs at the Stadium turnstiles. The greatest living ballplayer, Marilyn Monroe's ex-husband, Hemingway's "great DiMaggio," asked me my name and signed a big sweeping autograph across the back of the card.

Jamie had reminded me numerous times in the weeks leading up to that morning that he would bat boy the Old Timers' game. Once Bob Sheppard, the Yankees' senatorial public address announcer, started the pregame introductions, I had little to do but sit in the dugout and watch the exhibition. Five decades of Yankees heroes took the field one by one, lining up along the first- and third-base lines, tipping their caps repeatedly until the cheering crowd was sated or the next name announced. The biggest heroes (and ovations) were saved for last: Phil Rizzuto, Whitey Ford, Mantle, and finally DiMaggio.

I caught Ford and Rizzuto coming off the field and got them to add their signatures to my lithograph as well. That left only Mantle; I still carried the pearl and a ballpoint pen in the back pocket of my uniform pants. The bench and dugout steps were crowded with both old-timers and present-day Yankees, press, handlers, and team executives. Rizzuto, who no longer did color commentary for every Yankees game, was working as a special Old Timers' Day correspondent to his successors in the broadcast booth. Rizzuto wore a small microphone clipped to the front of his jersey and roamed the dugout interviewing the most senior of the Yankees old-timers. I squeezed into a seat a few feet down from Mantle.

"Hey Scooter," Mantle called out to Rizzuto. "C'mere."

Rizzuto seemed even smaller than I'd imagined. His playing height and weight as the Yankees shortstop of the forties and fifties had been five-foot-six and 160 pounds. In the summer of

1992 he'd turned seventy-four, and his size seemed even further diminished by age. But he'd lost none of his good-natured Old New York folksiness.

"All right, Seaver," Rizzuto said into his microphone, addressing not only his old broadcasting partner up in the booth behind home plate but also tens of thousands of Yankees fans watching at home. "I'm gonna go see what Mr. Mantle has to say for himself. How ya doin', Mick?"

"Is that thing on?" Mantle slurred, leaning in toward Rizzuto's chest and tapping at the small microphone.

"Sure is, Mickey," Rizzuto said.

"Fuck, fuck, cocksucker," Mantle barked into the microphone, grinning wildly. "Cocksucker shitbag fuck!"

"Mary Mother of God!" Rizzuto cried out, reeling backward. "Holy cow, Mick!"

The old-timers in earshot—mostly teammates of Mantle, guys in their late sixties—burst into laughter. Rizzuto hurried down to the other end of the dugout, shielding the microphone with a cupped hand.

When the laughter quieted down, I decided to try once more for Mantle's autograph; I thought his Tourettesque joke might be a signal that a brief window of cheerfulness had opened.

I had read the signal wrong. Mantle was not yet tapped out of expletives.

"What the fuck did I tell you an hour ago?" he scolded me. Heads turned in our direction.

"But it's for Mattingly," I lied, meekly and probably transparently.

"Jesus Fucking Christ," he said, snatching the ball out of my hand. "Gimme a pen," he snapped to the Yankees intern who was acting as his handler. Mantle signed the ball and thrust it back into my hands.

He'd signed it hurriedly and in a very sour mood, but when I looked at the autograph, his penmanship was flawless. The signature was identical to the one on the vintage Mantle photograph framed and hanging in Buck Showalter's office. He'd clearly had tens of thousands of opportunities for practice. For Mickey Mantle—probably for half the men in the Yankees dugout that afternoon—signing an autograph was likely no longer so much a conscious act as it was a physical reflex.

"And this, too?" I said, holding out the lithograph so he could see the signatures of DiMaggio, Ford, and Rizzuto. "For me?"

"God," he said, finally smiling for a moment. "You're a persistent fucker, aren't you?"

I assumed his question was rhetorical.

"Gimme it," he said, adding another perfect signature to the three already on the back. "Now leave me alone," he said.

"Thanks, Mick," I said, and steered clear of him the rest of the day.

Old Timers' Day was followed immediately by the three-day all-star break. With the exception of center fielder Roberto Kelly, the one Yankee named to the all-star roster, the team's coaches and ballplayers scattered to homes and hometowns across the country for a brief midseason vacation. After the hiatus, the Yankees resumed play with one of their longest road trips of the season, an eleven-game West Coast swing.

I was grateful for the time off. I'd stumbled through the first two weeks of summer school, arriving late for class on two occasions, both after late nights at the Stadium. With presumably unintentional irony, I was warned the second time that I was down to my last strike.

We had been reminded of the ground rules when attendance was taken the first day. Class would meet five mornings a week for one month. Absent extraordinary circumstances, perfect attendance was required to pass the class. If you attended every class and passed the final exam, your grade would be raised from an F to a D and you'd be allowed to come back to school in September.

I caught my breath during the two weeks the team was away, but shortly after the Yankees returned to the Bronx, a marathon twelve-inning weeknight game did me in. The next morning in the clubhouse, I overslept by more than an hour. I ran from the Stadium to the subway in a panic, considering too late whether some sort of pseudo-official note from Nick might help my cause. I arrived at Regis just as class was ending. My teacher sent me directly to the office of the assistant headmaster, Mr. Walsh.

Mr. Walsh had worked at Regis for years, and he wore his dedication to the school and its students on his sleeve. He was the type of administrator who knew every incoming freshman's name, his family background, and which town or outer-borough neighborhood he hailed from. He not only knew the current rosters and records of Regis's basketball, debate, and chess teams, but was a regular spectator at the big matches of all three. In his capacity as assistant headmaster, he had the bearing of a demanding but fair college professor.

"Mr. Walsh," I panted. "I'm sorry I'm late."

"Sit," he said from behind his desk.

"I was working late at the Stadium," I said. "I'm sorry."

"Matt," he said, leaning forward in his chair. "We agreed at the beginning of the season that your job was an unacceptable excuse for any failings at school. You remember that agreement, right?"

I did remember the agreement, made just before Opening Day; it had been a warm and happy conversation. Mr. Walsh was a baseball fan, and he was in fact the Regis faculty member who'd interviewed me when I'd applied to the school as a thirteen-year-old eighth grader. He'd asked me in my interview to name three people, living or dead, I'd like to have as Regis classmates. I answered King Tut, having just read a book about the teenage pharaoh of ancient Egypt; Holden Caulfield; and then, after confirming that my potential classmates need not be of high school age, Mattingly. I knew Mr. Walsh liked me and had been pleased for me when I'd landed my job at the Stadium. But I could tell by his tone of voice that partiality would play no role in our conversation that afternoon.

"You know the terms of your scholarship," he told me. "And you know too that, by the book, you've failed summer school now."

I pictured myself starting my senior year at a new high school, friendless, unable to pronounce my own last name, my college hopes in shambles.

"Please," I said. "I don't want to leave Regis."

"That's not my call to make," he said. "That's up to Father Kuntz"—the Jesuit headmaster of the school—"and he's out of town this week. I can tell you one thing, though: if you miss another class between now and when Father Kuntz gets back, if you're even a minute late to another class between now and then, it's going to make his decision a whole lot easier."

"Okay," I said, my palms and shirt damp with sweat. "I understand."

"Go to class and see what Father Egan wants you to do to make up today's work," he said.

I didn't sleep very well at the Stadium the final two weeks of summer school. Waking up disoriented in the subterranean clubhouse in the middle of the night, trying to divine how many more hours I had left before morning, I might as well have been sleeping in a Las Vegas casino. I found an old windup alarm clock with Day-Glo numerals at home and took it to work, placing it each night beyond arm's reach of my makeshift bed in the players' lounge. Nick noticed and was supportive in his own way, promising to slap the sleep out of me if I wasn't awake each morning by seven.

Fear proved stronger than fatigue; I never reported less than an hour early to each of the last ten days of class. Father Kuntz never summoned me when he returned, and the first week in August, I passed the final exam.

Road Trip

With school finally out of the way and my summer days free again, the most beguiling clubhouse perk ballooned in my imagination: being invited by Nick to join the Yankees on a road trip. Jamie had traveled on the team's swing out to Seattle, Oakland, and Anaheim after the all-star break, and he returned home so elated with the experience that I didn't even need to hector him into telling me about it. For weeks afterward, Jamie freely volunteered details of the eleven-day luxury tour. The six-hour flight on the Yankees' chartered jet. The deluxe hotel suite he'd stayed in (albeit a deluxe hotel suite shared with Nick). The strangeness of wearing a road uniform instead of the home pinstripes. The long nights out on the town that the players had taken him on in each of the three cities they'd visited.

The problem for me was that joining the team on a road trip was a privilege generally accorded only to second-year bat boys, as a reward for more than a season's worth of hard work.

Asking Nick to make an exception in my case seemed out of the question; Robby and the Mule agreed that making a direct appeal to Nick would just about kill my chances. Still, as the only member of the clubhouse staff who hadn't yet traveled that season, they suggested a scenario in which Nick might feel obligated to take me on a trip, even a short one, before the season ended.

"Work hard," the Mule advised me. "Let the old man see you really busting your ass, and maybe he'll take you along."

I hustled to put in time outside of game days, working without pay. I showed up at the ballpark on off days, when the Yankees occasionally held extra batting practice for struggling hitters, and spent those afternoons shagging flies in the outfield and cleaning up the clubhouse after BP. I began helping out on unpacking nights, when the Yankees flew back to New York after the end of a road trip. The team usually arrived at an ungodly hour, in the middle of the night or very early in the morning, but now I started waiting with Rob and the Mule in the clubhouse for the ballplayers, their equipment, and Nick to appear. If the Yankees finished a series in, say, Chicago, with a night game ending there at ten o'clock, you could count on the team needing one hour after the game to shower and pack (eleven o'clock) and an hour to get to O'Hare Airport (twelve o'clock). Counting the time for the flight back to New York, plus the hour time differential, and then the bus ride from the airport to the Stadium, the team rarely arrived home earlier than three or three-thirty in the morning. And that's what time the night's work began. Unpacking nights left you the following day with jet lag–like symptoms as pronounced as if you'd crossed those time zones yourself.

Still, mindful of the dwindling number of road trips left on the Yankees' schedule before the end of the season, I met the team every time they came off the road in August. But by Labor

Day, with the beginning of the school year looming, no invitation from Nick seemed forthcoming.

It was clear by early September that the Yankees were not going to catch the Toronto Blue Jays in first place. After a stretch in which New York lost thirteen of sixteen games, even some of the most affable ballplayers on the roster couldn't hide their frustration with the turn the season had taken. I saw Mattingly lash out at a pair of front office interns who were indiscreetly laughing and joking in the clubhouse after a close loss. Nick escorted the interns, white as ghosts for having offended the Yankees captain, to the clubhouse door.

A week or so later, Steve Farr, the Yankees closer, capped a disastrous performance by the team's relief staff by destroying the big-screen television in the middle of the clubhouse. The bullpen had inherited a 6–1 lead against the Oakland A's in the top of the sixth inning and promptly gave up a grand slam to Jose Canseco. Farr, a rough-around-the-edges Harley-Davidson-riding guy with a Fu Manchu mustache, had come into the game in the top of the ninth, charged with preserving the now tenuous one-run lead. He allowed a single and a walk, and then, facing Oakland third baseman Carney Lansford, left a 3–2 pitch out over the middle of the plate. Lansford deposited the ball in the left-field seats for a three-run home run.

Upon entering the clubhouse after the game, Farr took a baseball bat to one of the concrete posts supporting the clubhouse roof. Thankfully, the concrete proved too durable to deliver the visual results Farr probably felt necessary for the catharsis he was seeking, and after a few *thwocks*, he went in search of something more satisfyingly fragile. The Mule was standing in front of his locker, close by the entertainment center, and I watched his eyes widen as Farr's intentions became apparent. The television was tuned to the Yankees postgame show, and the sportscaster was narrating video of the Yankees' meltdown. Farr's first swing went through the glass screen of the television, ruining the hopes of the one or two people in the room who may have been looking forward to watching more postgame analysis. Farr's second and third swings, two-handed and over the top, splintered the set's casing, scattering plastic and metal parts on the clubhouse floor across a ten-foot radius. Nick signaled the security guard at the door to hold the press outside the clubhouse until it was clear Farr was done, but it seemed like a moot gesture; I'd have guessed the ruckus was loud enough to be heard all the way to the Grand Concourse.

Such eruptions were common enough that we had a name for them in the clubhouse: "snapping." The targets were usually humble: the concrete pillars in the clubhouse; the oversized orange Gatorade tubs in the dugout. There is also a small bathroom located just off the dugout that ballplayers use during games to avoid walking all the way back to the urinals in the clubhouse. The bathroom is fronted by a heavy steel door, and visible on its face are dozens of dents, evidence of baseball bat beatings administered by frustrated Yankees hitters in the moments after bases-loaded strikeouts, popped-up sacrifice bunts, and inning-ending double plays.

Nobody acknowledges a snap while it's happening. A ballplayer might be splintering a bat against the bathroom door, cursing at the top of his lungs, and yet everyone would stare straight ahead, carrying themselves as nonchalantly as during pregame warm-ups. The mess left behind would be cleaned up either by the grounds crew or the bat boys, and the game would go on as if nothing had happened. A violent and ferociously noisy outburst, ten feet away? Where?

But I'd yet to see a snap as explosive and imaginative as Farr's. At the sound of shattering glass, every head in the clubhouse turned in the direction of Farr and the shattered television; I think even Nick was impressed, if that's the right word. Within a few moments, though, even before Farr tired himself out, dispassion (or at least the appearance of it) returned to the clubhouse. Farr dropped the bat and walked to the trainers' room to have his pitching arm wrapped in ice. The rookies and coaches continued to pick at their plates of mixed greens and baked ziti from the postgame spread. Rob and the Mule ineffectually ran a pair of vacuums over the shards of glass and plastic on the clubhouse carpet for a while, then finally just gave up and taped off the area. The media was ushered into the clubhouse.

There was no ignoring the gaping hole where the TV normally droned as players toweled off and got dressed in their street clothes. Ducking under the tape to retrieve dirty spikes from a pair of nearby lockers, I could hear the debris crunch under the soles of my sneakers.

"What happened?" one of the Yankees beat writers whispered to me as I passed by.

I shrugged.

"Don't know," I said.

The next afternoon, Farr walked into the clubhouse and laid five hundred-dollar bills on Nick's table.

"Let me know if it costs more than that," he said, loud enough for his voice to carry across the clubhouse. Nick was hanging uniforms in lockers only a few feet away, but he gave no indication that he'd heard the offer, and showed neither opprobrium for the damage caused nor gratitude for the restitution just made. The next day there was a new clubhouse television, slightly bigger than the one that had been there two games before.

The Yankees' mathematical elimination from the pennant race, inevitable for many weeks, actually seemed to lift the mood in the clubhouse. It was too late to make much difference in the standings, but between the pressure that had lifted and a few late-season additions to their lineup, the Yankees started to play better, or at least more spirited, baseball.

Major league rosters are normally capped at twenty-five men, but for the last month of the season, teams are allowed to carry as many as forty active players. When rosters expand, teams with only next year to look forward to promote their best minor league prospects, giving them a chance to face major league pitching or hitting, auditioning them in anticipation of the following year or off-season trade offers.

In mid-September the Yankees promoted the young stars of their top farm team, the Columbus Clippers, which had just ended its season on a high note. Down 4–2 in the deciding game of a best-of-five series for the AAA International League championship, the Clippers had rallied for three runs in the bottom of the ninth inning to win the game and their league's crown. The next day, half their starting lineup reported to the Bronx, and they carried with them the giddiness of their still-recent triumph.

The Yankees went to Baltimore and swept a three-game series, spoiling the playoff hopes of the second-place Orioles. At the Stadium a few days later, an exchange of brushback pitches sparked a bench-clearing brawl with the Chicago White Sox. I stood on the top step of the Yankees dugout and watched the two teams' relief pitchers stream in from the bullpens to join the scrum that had formed between home plate and the pitching mound. The forty-man-strong rosters of the Yankees and White Sox shoved each other around, letting off steam for a few minutes before retreating to their dugouts.

It was the second bench-clearing brawl at the Stadium that season, but the first in which I understood what my proper role was while the players resolved their differences on the field. The first time, mindful of the Yankees pinstripes I was wearing, I'd nearly gotten caught up in the excitement. Am I supposed to scrap with the bat boy in the other dugout? The idea seemed right, very briefly, before I remembered that the kid across the way was just Ray from the other clubhouse, dressed in a visiting uniform. Before I could take ill-advised action of any kind, the Mule came down the tunnel from the clubhouse and told me exactly where bat boys were to stay until a resolution was reached on the field: well within the dugout.

"You never went out there during a brawl when you were bat boying in Seattle?" I asked him, watching an umpire step between and separate two knots of players.

"Are you crazy?" he said. "I'll tell you what would happen if you left the dugout during a brawl. You'd go out there, and after one of the ballplayers finished kicking your ass, Nick'd kick your ass, and then somebody from the front office'd come down and kick your ass. You'd make *SportsCenter*, dangling from some six-foot-four ballplayer's neck, but it'd be the last you ever saw of your Yankees ID card."

With the end of the season on the horizon, the ballplayers began making preparations to leave New York for their off-season homes. The Yankees would end the season with six games on the road, three in Cleveland and three in Boston.

A few weeks before the Yankees' last homestand, Tim Burke, one of the team's relievers, called me over to his locker. Burke had been traded to the Yankees from the Mets in June and we'd spoken more than a handful of times. He was a devout Christian, and at one point in the season had given me a paperback book that profiled a few dozen born-again ballplayers, including himself; though it didn't inspire any epiphanies, I'd read the book and appreciated the gesture.

"So I was talking to Nick," Burke told me, "and I've got a proposition for you." Burke explained that he lived in New England during the off-season. After the last home game, he would fly with the Yankees from the Bronx to Cleveland and then Boston, but he needed to figure out a way to get his car up to Massachusetts so he could drive home directly from Fenway when the season ended.

"Do you have a driver's license?" he asked me.

"Sure," I answered.

"Well, I was thinking that you might be able to drive my car up to Boston in time to meet us there when we get in from Cleveland. We'll figure out a room for you in the team hotel, and you can catch a ride back to New York with the team when the series is over."

"Nick's cool with me coming to Boston?" I said. "I mean, you asked him?"

"I did," he said. "He said you're welcome to work the three games at Fenway."

"Jesus Christ!" I said, forgetting for a moment whom I was speaking with. "I mean: Wow."

I called home after the game to ask my parents' permission, fully anticipating that it might be a tough sell. I had graduated from learner's permit to driver's license only a few months before, and I'd never driven a longer distance than the twenty miles between my parents' house and Yankee Stadium. I breathlessly explained first to my mom and then my dad how unusual it was that I'd be allowed to travel with the team my first season as a bat boy. I couldn't hide my excitement at the opportunity, and with some give-and-take, we settled upon a solution: my dad would join me for the drive, drop both me and Burke's car off at the Yankees' hotel, and then take the shuttle back to New York the same night.

I would get my road trip after all.

My season-ending road trip was not the only reason to look forward to the last homestand of the season. For the club-house staff, the last home series of the year also meant end-of-season tips from the ballplayers, our just reward for six months of demands promptly met and errands well run.

Even for the bat boys, the tips were not insignificant: Jamie told me that in those three days you could match the salary that you'd made over the course of the whole season.

During the Yankees' final homestand, I was handed a dozen checks and nearly as many envelopes of cash, all of which Nick stored for me under lock and key in a safe-deposit box in the trainers' room. The players were generous: a check for a few hundred from Tartabull, the highest-paid player on the team, and lesser amounts from most of the other guys on the roster.

A handful of players ignored the conspicuous whirlwind of mutual thanks that dominated the clubhouse all weekend. Not giving an end-of-season tip, even a token one, was considered an inexcusable breach of clubhouse etiquette. Those baseball spikes didn't shine themselves.

As was his custom every season, Mattingly tipped last. After waiting to see what every other player had given, he would always beat the best tip by a hundred bucks. It was a characteristic move for the Yankees captain; a few years later, after a players' strike prematurely ended the 1994 season, Mattingly was one of only two players—Jim Abbott was the other—to seek out the three bat boys' home addresses and send each one an end-of-season tip.

The Yankees had an off day scheduled between their series against the Indians and Red Sox, and the team was to fly to Boston immediately after the last game in Cleveland. The afternoon of the team's flight, my dad and I took the train together into the City and the subway up to Yankee Stadium.

Burke had left the keys to his car with the security guard in the Yankees lobby. It was a Lexus sedan, a nicer car than I'd ever been in before, and my dad let me take the wheel for the stretch of highway between the New York and Boston city limits. As if by a sixth sense, my dad could tell without looking over at the speedometer the few times I inched over the speed limit; each time, he shot me a look that almost involuntarily separated my foot from the gas pedal.

We made the trip in about four hours, pulling up to the team hotel just before dinnertime. My dad handed the car keys over to the valet and walked me to the front desk of the hotel. I swung the small bag I'd packed up on the counter and gave my name to the hotel clerk.

"I'm here with the Yankees," I added, discreetly but proudly. "I'm staying with Scott Kamieniecki."

Kamieniecki, one of the Yankees' young starting pitchers, had offered to let me room with him after his wife decided to stay in New York to prepare for their own postseason trip to their home in Michigan. The clerk checked my name against the room list prepared by the Yankees traveling secretary and then slid a key across the counter to me.

"Any incidentals will be charged to Mr. Kamieniecki," she said before stepping away to help another guest.

"Incidental what?" I whispered to my dad.

"It means stay out of the minibar," he said. "And don't charge anything to the room."

I was saying good-bye to my dad when Bernie Williams and two of the Yankees recently promoted to the majors, Hensley Meulens and Gerald Williams, strolled past us through the hotel lobby. Three of the youngest players on the team, they had come up through the Yankees' minor league system together. I nodded to Bernie as he passed.

"I didn't know you were coming on the trip," he said.

I started filling him in on the task I'd just completed for Burke, then realized I'd failed to introduce my dad standing next to me.

"Oh, sorry," I said. "Guys, this is my dad. Dad, this is Bernie," and indicating Hensley and Gerald by their clubhouse nicknames, "and Bam-Bam. And Ice."

"Jim," my dad said, greeting all three but not tipping his hand as to whether he'd ever before met a Bam-Bam or an Ice.

"You sticking around for the weekend?" Bam-Bam asked me.

"Yeah," I said. "I'm staying with Kami."

"Your dad coming to the game tomorrow?" Gerald asked.

"Unfortunately not," my dad answered. "I'm flying back to New York tonight."

"We'll keep an eye on Matt for you," Bernie said.

"I'd appreciate that," my dad said.

"What are you guys up to tonight?" I asked the trio of ballplayers.

"Not sure," Bernie said. "We were just going out now to walk around for a while."

"Can I suggest Harvard Yard?" my dad said.

"Yeah?" Ice said.

"Oh, it's beautiful," my dad said. "Really a world-class campus. You should take a walk along the Charles—"

"C'mon, Dad," I cut him off, suddenly a little embarrassed. "I'm sure these guys don't care about seeing—"

Bernie cut me off in turn. "No, no," he said, chuckling. "Maybe we'll check it out."

"Have a good time," my dad told them before turning to me. "You too," he said, giving me a nudge with his elbow. "Stay out of trouble."

"Dad, c'mon, please," I said. "I'll see you guys later," I said to the ballplayers, and we exchanged good-byes. I walked with my dad to the front of the hotel.

"You all set?" he asked me.

"I'll be fine," I said.

"Okay," he said. "Thanks for driving."

"Thanks for letting me drive."

"Be good," he told me. He gave me a quick hug and then hailed a cab to take him to Logan Airport.

I spent most of the Yankees' off day with Robby and the Mule, walking around town and checking out two movies, back-to-back, at a theater down the block from the team hotel. When I got back to the room, Kamieniecki invited me to grab a bite with him and a few teammates, but I demurred; I explained that I wanted to be well rested and on the earlier of the two buses scheduled to take the team to the ballpark the next day. Kami seemed amused at my earnestness and insisted on ordering me a cheeseburger from room service before he left.

I woke the next morning to a beautiful late-summer Boston

day. Nick treated me to lunch at Charley's on Newbury Street. We sat outside at the sidewalk café, and I peppered him with questions about his many previous road trips to Boston.

"I'm very big in this town," he told me, his boasts punctuated by raggedy laughs. "Very big in Beantown, Matty. My town. Very big."

The early bus was empty save for myself and a handful of the support staff that chronically reports hours before first pitch: Nick, Rob, the Mule, the Yankees medical trainers, one or two coaches. A Red Sox attendant waved the driver down to the far end of Yawkey Way, and the bus dropped us off flush against the brick exterior wall of Fenway Park. We entered through one of the same gates that fans would use to enter the ballpark in a few hours. Unlike at Yankee Stadium, where both clubhouses are underground, the visiting clubhouse entrance at Fenway is off the same concourse that leads to the field-level box seats. Only a small wire cage and an elderly security guard with a thick Boston accent seemed to separate the visiting clubhouse from the throngs of Red Sox fans that would later pack the ballpark to root against the hated Yankees. If this is the security now, I wondered, what must it have been like before 1978, the year the Yankees famously took the American League East title from the Red Sox in a one-game playoff at Fenway Park?

I walked into the clubhouse and immediately recognized the Boston equipment manager who on Opening Day in the Bronx had given me twenty bucks and sent me up the block to buy a pair of bat stretchers. Nick reintroduced us, and he pointed out the locker labeled with a strip of white athletic tape: MCGOUGH. All the Yankees road uniforms, which had arrived two nights before from Cleveland, had been unpacked and hung neatly in the lockers, including my own. As Jamie had promised, it felt odd at first to dress in a gray uniform with NEW YORK printed across the front instead of the familiar pinstripes. But the road uni seemed to fit as well as the one at home.

One of the visiting clubhouse attendants came over and asked me if I wanted to see the inside of the old-fashioned scoreboard set into the Green Monster, Fenway's famous forty-foot-tall left-field wall. We walked down the tunnel to the dugout, then down the third-base line to the base of the Green Monster. There was a small door, just to the left of the window indicating the number of the player at bat, cut into the manually operated scoreboard at the bottom of the wall. Through the door was a small concrete room, furnished only with a three-legged wooden stool and a transistor radio. Trays of green metal plates painted with white numerals littered the floor; they were the same size as the vacant windows in the scoreboard through which I could see a Red Sox player taking BP across the field.

"Is he really three hundred ten feet from here?" I asked my tour guide. I thought it a trenchant question. For decades the Red Sox had insisted that that was the true distance between home plate and the Green Monster. For just as long, opposing teams had insisted that the distance was far shorter than that. It was part of the folklore of baseball in general and Fenway Park in particular. The *Boston Globe* once went so far as to use aerial photography to measure the distance at slightly less than 305 feet; the Red Sox ignored the exposé in their hometown paper.

"Three-ten," the clubbie told me.

"Sure it is," I joked.

I looked up and noticed that the raw concrete walls were adorned with hundreds of faint white scrawls, names of ballplayers who'd ducked inside the scoreboard over the years to add indisputable evidence that they'd once played in Fenway Park.

"There's a piece of chalk there if you want to put your name up on the wall," he told me.

"Really?" I asked.

"Sure," he said. "Go ahead."

I picked up a piece of chalk and marked my name and the date on the wall as high up as I could reach; I hope it's still there today.

We walked back to the visiting dugout, which remained empty pending the arrival of the late bus from the team hotel. The clubbie headed back inside and I took a seat on the bench by myself to watch the Red Sox take batting practice. I couldn't get over the fact that I was actually sitting in the same visiting dugout that Joe DiMaggio and Allie Reynolds and Tommy Henrich had in 1949; that Reggie Jackson and Thurman Munson and Bucky Dent had in 1978; that Darryl Strawberry and Lenny Dykstra and Dwight Gooden (Mets, but still, a great New York team) had in 1986, the first World Series of which I watched every single inning of every single game.

The Yankees gradually filed down to the field and filled in spaces on the bench around me. The moment the Red Sox ballplayers cleared the diamond and the head groundskeeper signaled that it was New York's turn to hit, I grabbed my glove and sprinted out into the sunswept Fenway Park outfield. I positioned myself in deep left–center field, the Green Monster looming large over my shoulder. The Yankees hitters took turns banging balls off the great wall; I stood at its base and tried to cleanly field the caroms.

A little more than a year before, I'd been sitting in the Yankee Stadium bleachers, watching the same two teams play a late-season game, when the idea of applying to be a bat boy first crossed my mind. Now I stood at the heart of one of baseball's foremost cathedrals, my name both on a locker in the visiting clubhouse and left as an artifact inside the cathedral's innermost sanctum. I was dressed in my own Yankees road uniform, catching balls hit off major league bats with a glove I'd broken in over a full major league season. I was in Fenway Park with the Yankees. I'd say I was living out a childhood dream, but I'm not sure that even as a baseball-crazed eight-year-old I ever dreamed just *this* audaciously. I couldn't remember ever feeling so happy.

Just after Fenway security opened the ballpark to fans, the Yankee pitching staff emerged en masse from the dugout. The dozen pitchers loped out to left field for their daily stretching exercises. I shifted farther over toward center, utterly absorbed by my surroundings and the fly balls being launched from home plate. Within a few minutes a few hundred fans had made their way down to the wall along the third-base line, drawn to where the Yankees pitchers were stretching on the warning track. I could hear the fans shouting down to the players below them, I presumed seeking autographs. The ballplayers seemed to be having fun bantering back.

As it was, though, I was more than a hundred feet away, in my own little world, and I didn't notice at first a few of the pitchers waving their gloves to get my attention, calling me over. They were grinning when I jogged up to the group of them.

My roommate Kamieniecki put his hand on my shoulder and pointed up to the stands, about twenty feet over our heads. The fans grew quiet and craned their necks to see what was going on. Kamieniecki pointed out a very pretty girl in a high school swimming jacket who stood right up against the wall at the front of the crowd.

"Matt," he announced to me and everyone else in the vicinity, "this is Teresa."

I gave Teresa a shy wave.

"Teresa, this is Matt," he said, draping his arm over my shoulder. "Matt's from New York."

He paused for effect, then continued, his voice projecting

even farther across the rows of seats slowly filling with fans: "Matt, you and Teresa are both seventeen years old, and Teresa doesn't have any plans tonight after the game."

The mob of fans, three hundred or more people, gawked at Teresa in the front row, and then at me down below on the outfield grass. Both of us blushed deeply.

"Uh, Teresa," I shouted up at her as quietly as possible, trying to create some privacy where there was none at all to be had, "do you wanna go out after the game tonight?" The crowd leaned forward, rapt, waiting for her answer.

"Sure," she said, sending the whole section of fans into a fit of hooting and applause. I told Teresa I'd meet her by the door to the visiting clubhouse as soon as the game was over. The Yankees bullpen extracted a series of embarrassed high fives before allowing me to retreat to the dugout.

The players made full use of the three-hour ballgame to tease me about my date, asking me what we were going to do, suggesting restaurants that I could take Teresa to, joking that Kamieniecki should move out and get a separate room for himself for the night. Fifteen minutes after the last out of the game, Teresa was waiting with her little brother where we'd agreed. She explained that she just had to walk her brother to where her dad was waiting to pick them up, and that we could then go out together.

"Great," I said, getting my bearings, feeling good about being back in street clothes. Small talk seemed easier now that we didn't have an audience of three hundred baseball fans listening in on our conversation.

Teresa's dad was waiting at his car in a parking lot a few blocks from Fenway. Teresa introduced us, explaining that I was up from New York for the weekend with the Yankees and that we were going to go out to dinner.

"I'm sure you're a nice kid, Matt," her dad said very matter-of-factly, "but my daughter's not going out with you tonight."

Teresa looked exasperated, as if this might have happened before.

"Maybe I can leave you tickets to the afternoon game tomorrow?" I said, trying to think fast. "It'll end a lot earlier, four or five o'clock, and we can go out for a while afterwards."

"That sounds fun," she said, smiling again. She wrote down her name and number on a scrap of paper while her dad waited in the car. I told Teresa to meet me after the game tomorrow in the same place outside the clubhouse and ran back toward Fenway to try to catch the Yankees bus before it left for the hotel. I boarded to a chorus of groans and heckling.

"Jesus Christ," someone shouted from the back of the bus. "What the hell happened?"

Making my way down the aisle, I explained that Teresa's dad hadn't let her come out; the ballplayers seemed to think that was the funniest thing they'd ever heard. They gave me a little credit, at least, for getting her to come back to the ballpark the next day. A couple of players offered to sponsor her attendance.

After the game the next afternoon, I gave myself what must have been the most unnecessary shave in the hundred-year history of Fenway Park's visiting clubhouse. I had just finished burning my cheeks with aftershave when I was approached by Steve Farr, the Yankees closer. I couldn't remember him ever having said two words to me before, and his snap in the Yankees clubhouse a month before was still fresh in my memory.

"Big date tonight, Matty?" Farr asked me gravely.

I nodded.

"Have fun, brother," he said, extending a handshake and very smoothly placing a C-note against my palm.

Notwithstanding the end-of-season tips that I'd collected

from the team, I felt as if I'd just won the lottery. This hundred dollars was earmarked for just one date, and at that point in my life, a hundred dollars seemed an impossible amount of money to spend on a single night out on the town. The credit card slots in my wallet held my newly minted driver's license and high school ID; I couldn't even have guessed how much a bottle of wine cost in a restaurant.

Teresa and I took a taxi from Fenway to a surf-and-turf restaurant—the wine was excellent—and a taxi from the restaurant to a jazz club that she had heard was nice, then walked back along Newbury Street to the Yankees' hotel. A half dozen ballplayers, including Kamieniecki, were at the hotel bar and immediately waved us over to buy us a round of drinks.

I was happy to see them. I had never taken a girl out in a town other than New York, and to be honest, I wasn't sure what was supposed to happen next. Each of the players introduced themselves to Teresa very politely, asking her where she went to school and joking about whether, after tonight, she was still a Red Sox fan.

After a while, I asked Teresa if she wanted to go upstairs to my room.

"Sure," she said.

While another player ran interference, Kamieniecki quietly told me he'd be down in the bar until last call, and that if I wanted him to stay scarce longer than that, I should leave the do-not-disturb sign on the door.

Teresa and I rode the elevator upstairs together to my five-star hotel room. We'd had an incredible night for a pair of seventeen-year-olds: a fancy dinner and drinks and jazz and brushes with celebrity. If we had been on the couch at one of our parents' houses, or parked in a car, or in a dark movie theater, or on a bench in Central Park, I'm sure we would have gotten along all right. Instead, overwhelmed by a world alien to both of us, we were too shy and awkward to even manage a kiss. We sat on the king-size bed, separated by a good three feet, and watched TV together.

"My dad'll be mad if I get home too late," she finally said after an hour or so.

"Okay," I said. I walked Teresa downstairs and put her in a taxi so she wouldn't miss her curfew.

The players saw me coming back through the lobby by myself and summoned me back into the bar.

"A beer for my man right here," Kamieniecki told the bartender.

"Good date?" he asked.

"Good date," I said.

"Good," he said, raising his bottle of Budweiser to mine. "Cheers."

Should We Tell the Kid?

By the time I returned from the Boston road trip, summer seemed a distant memory on the streets of New York. On the back pages of the tabloids, the Giants and Jets had eclipsed the Yankees and Mets. For me, it was back to school.

I shouldn't have been so disheartened by the changing of the seasons. But it wasn't just the games I missed. Baseball was no longer merely a diversion, as it had been when I was younger. Now this childhood passion had taken on grown-up meaning as well. All summer long it had filled my days and padded my wallet. I was already familiar with the exhilaration that accompanies the end of the school year, and I would learn later to recognize the relief felt in leaving a job, and all its burdens, in my wake. But not yet. Not this job.

There were, of course, baseball chores that I was happy to leave behind. No more lugging overfull garbage bags every night, tobacco juice and Gatorade leaking down my leg, to the dumpster outside the clubhouse. No more swabbing filthy sinks, shining baseball spikes, or collecting and carrying armfuls of strangers' damp, dirty laundry. Saturday mornings began, once again, later than 7:00 A.M., and no longer with Nick flicking on the fluorescent lights of the players' lounge over my head, which signaled that the coaching staff had arrived at the Stadium and that it was time for me to peel my skin off the vinyl couch I'd slept facedown on the night before.

None of these ugly memories consoled me much in math class that fall, though. I did not feel emancipated by all the free time I now enjoyed after school, at night, and on weekends. Days before, I had returned from Boston flush with excitement, cash, and stories, and the source of all these was no closer now than next Opening Day. It's hard enough ordinarily to return to school after summer vacation. But the loss of baseball made the transition feel even sharper than usual.

A full month of the school year had already passed by the time the Yankees played their last game of the season, packed up, and went home. Most of my classmates seemed to have used the head start to become fully immersed in college application decision-making. Regis did its part in fanning the flames. Throughout the fall, each of us met one-on-one with the school's guidance counselor, who cataloged and then winnowed our undeveloped ideas of where we might be headed. Preprinted postcards for requesting applications were handed out at Wednesday morning senior class assemblies. Ceaseless reminders pushed the topic toward the center of every conversation at school. All fall, thick brochures and course catalogs piled up at home. The growing stack of application materials on the table next to the TV kept the subject distressingly topical with Mom and Dad.

Toward Thanksgiving, the Stadium began to recede a little bit from my memory. Classes advanced toward midterms. I joined the CYO basketball team at my local parish and went to practice two nights a week. I met a girl who lived and went to school in Hastings, a few towns south of Tarrytown; she became my first steady girlfriend. I reunited with what felt like my long-lost crew at school. Most of my Regis friends hadn't seen each other more than once or twice the whole summer, and we converged daily on East Eighty-fourth Street between Park and Madison Avenues with the sense that we needed to make up for lost time.

We were seniors in high school, seventeen years old. We might have been aware on some level of how much we still had to learn, but we didn't dwell on it. We'd learned by trial and error how to make our way through the City and the school; on our best days we were convinced we ran both. We knew all the teachers, exactly what each teacher expected from us, and just how far each one could be pushed before dispatching you to the dean of discipline. Our senior year course work encompassed— at a Catholic high school, no less—free and heated discussions of abortion and euthanasia; a survey of world religions; contemporary American fiction and film; public speaking; the history of the Cold War; and a semester-long yoga class taught by a Jesuit priest. We no longer hung back, terrified and mute, at school dances that drew three times as many Catholic schoolgirls as there were Regis students. At lunch and after school, we roamed the Upper East Side, verbally jousting and egging each other on. We were defending state champs in basketball, nationally ranked in debate, and had the best chess team in the City. We'd earned our access to the senior section of the cafeteria and its enormous stereo, which was a machine of great power: though outnumbered three to one, we pitilessly imposed our choice of music on lunchrooms full of underclassmen. We found a bar on Eighty-eighth Street and First Avenue, full of old men, that never carded and served us frothy pitchers of Budweiser, though this step forward was halted the evening our English teacher, stopping in for a cold one after work, walked in on a bar full of his students.

We'd watched the three classes of seniors before us assume the mantle that we now wore; we'd seen how, by sheer presence and energy, they could dominate the classrooms and hallways, the cafeteria and gym, and the streets around Regis. Since day one, Regis and its teachers had pushed hard to expand our minds and impart the confidence we needed to engage the world outside of school; by addressing us, always, as "Men," they inflated our egos and boosted our self-regard. In a feat of alchemy, by the time we returned to school that fall, our latent talents and swelling self-regard made our great expectations seem reasonable. We had it all figured out. We could talk our way out of anything. We were too smart for our own good.

Between catching up with friends and on schoolwork, it was early December before I made my way back to the Stadium again. I'd yet to fully clean out my locker, and I was sure I'd left at least a few autographed balls inside, hidden but unguarded. I also wanted to see Nick and Rob, to check in and see if they needed help with any of their off-season work. I knew that Jamie wasn't likely to be back for 1993, and though Nick never said as much, I had a pretty good idea after he'd invited me to Boston that the top job would fall to me. I didn't know what off-season responsibilities the rising head bat boy might be expected to shoulder. But I was eager to cement the prospective promotion, and I thought it'd be a good idea to pay Nick and Rob a visit.

One day the week after Thanksgiving, I left school at three o'clock and took the subway up to the Bronx. I walked into a clubhouse that looked that afternoon closer to its state on the day of my interview, almost exactly a year before, than I'd seen it any day since. Boxes stuffed with Yankees gear and equipment once again covered tables, couches, and large expanses of the clubhouse floor. Most of the players' lockers had been cleared of their pinstriped uniforms, jackets, and spikes. All photos of families and girlfriends were gone as well, along with the teetering stacks of fan mail. In their place, Yankees road uniforms hung neatly from plastic hangers. Nick and one of the visiting clubhouse attendants stood alone at Nick's picnic table in the middle of the room.

Nick had a foot up on the bench and was stroking his chin with his fingertips. The door swung shut behind me and they both turned toward the front of the clubhouse. Their eyes tracked my progress across the room. I walked to my locker, past them, and through the doorway leading to the showers and trainers' room. Even with my back to them I could feel them staring at me. Not normal.

I threw my backpack at the foot of my locker and walked back out into the clubhouse. "What's up?" I asked.

The visiting clubhouse guy turned to Nick. He spoke out of the side of his mouth: "Should we tell the kid?"

Nick grunted with disgust and dismissed the idea out of hand: "Don't tell the kid." His reaction, in and of itself, was unremarkable. Nick grunted with disgust dozens of times a day, in response to any number of different provocations. Under most circumstances, Nick was far more likely to tell the kid off than tell the kid something constructive.

"Tell me what?" I asked. Robby stood off to the side of the clubhouse, stacking uniforms inside a locker. I wasn't sure if he'd been listening, but I tried to meet his eyes. If it truly was something special, I knew, Robby wouldn't leave me on the outside looking in.

"Don't tell the kid," Nick warned the guy from the visiting side.

I took a seat at the table. Nick probably realized that it was already too late to forestall the inevitable. "Tell me *what?*" I asked again.

"Matty, you don't have the money for *what,*" Nick barked.

"What's *what?*" I half barked back. The exchange was a *Who* and an *I Don't Know* short of an Abbott and Costello routine.

Robby left his locker of uniforms and walked across the clubhouse toward the trainers' room. Without stopping or making eye contact, he cautioned me as he passed by. "Don't worry about it, Matt," he told me.

I turned back to Nick. "I've got money," I protested. I had received nearly sixteen hundred dollars in tips from the ballplayers at the end of the season. But I'd spent the major share of that in one afternoon, the week after we got back from Boston, exchanging a half year's worth of errands and late nights for a stereo receiver, a five-CD changer, and a pair of speakers. What was left over had seemed to disappear by osmosis into the cash registers of the restaurants, record shops, and bookstores that lined my route to and from school. It was my first experience with the natural tendency of ready money in New York City. That afternoon at the Stadium, I had two twenties in my pocket. At home, I had four of the six hundred-dollar bills Mattingly had given me with a handshake two months before. That's all that was left.

I held my seat at the table. Nick probably realized that I'd hound him to exasperation if he didn't let me in on their conversation. "Should we tell the kid?" I mean, come on! What else could I do? I was prepared to wait him out.

A few minutes passed while Nick folded towels on the table in front of me. When he finally looked up and opened his mouth, he spoke unequivocally. There was some anger in his voice. "You don't have this kind of money," he told me.

"How much?"

"Fifteen hundred dollars."

Fifteen hundred dollars. Not two months before, I'd held just about that much cash in my hands, but only for as long as it took me to get to Crazy Eddie's to buy a sound system. Fifteen hundred dollars. About as much as I'd managed to dissipate in eight weeks' time. Was that stupid? Was I stupid? I rolled the number over in my head. For all my recent experience with the end-of-season tips, it still seemed a pretty abstract figure. Nick must have mistaken my blank look for unflappability; he was waiting for me to speak.

"For *what?*" I asked again.

The visiting clubhouse guy rejoined the conversation. "It's an investment. A piece of a business opportunity."

Whether or not I actually had fifteen hundred dollars seemed to me to be beside the point. I certainly wasn't going to turn the conversation in that direction right now. I'd never been approached with a business proposition before. I wanted in on the action. "What are we buying?" I asked.

The guy from the visiting side smirked. Nick cleared a corner of the table with his arm and flipped an invoice over to its blank side, then drew a marker from the waistband of his Yankees shorts. "You do it," he ordered the visiting clubhouse attendant, handing him the pen. On the paper he drew a stack of fifteen squares: eight on the bottom, four on top of those eight, two on top of the four, and one at the summit.

"This is the Network, Matty," Nick explained. "Fifteen hundred buys you a box." Each level had its own name. The box at the top belonged to the CEO. The CEO's level was supported by two presidents, who were in turn held up by four executive vice presidents. Eight vice presidents sat at the bottom.

The visiting clubhouse guy wrote my name in a box at the lowest level.

"This is you," Nick explained, jabbing at my name with his finger. "You're a vice president." He paused. I nodded. He continued. "When seven other people buy in, the CEO cashes out. Collects twelve thousand dollars. The Network splits. Then everyone moves up a level."

Cashes out.

The visiting side guy covered the top box with his hand and drew a line that vertically split the others. He picked up the explanation where Nick left off. "Eight more boxes come in underneath each new CEO. Every time eight more guys come in, it splits again."

Now, Nick: "The last couple of weeks, they've been moving eight or ten boxes a week. I put in three weeks ago. If three more boxes sell this week, I cash out."

"So you're here?" I asked, tapping the top box.

"Yeah," Nick answered. "From here," pointing at the bottom row, "to there," pointing to the top. "In three weeks. You want in?"

"Yeah," I told him. "Definitely."

"You have the money?" Nick asked.

"I don't know," I lied.

"Well, come to the meeting Thursday night. Check it out, meet some people. Listen. Then decide what you want to do."

Three nights later I told my parents I was going to meet my girlfriend at the movies and, following the directions I'd been given, drove my parents' car to a two-family house off the Saw Mill River Parkway in Yonkers. I checked the address against the scrap of paper in my pocket, parked the car at the curb, and walked up to the door. The house had a synthetic brick facade that gave way at eye level to a story and a half of gray aluminum siding. A blue awning overhung the short stoop fronting the twin entrances to the two sides of the house.

A big, blond, motherly woman answered the doorbell with a smile and invited me inside. From the door, I could see down a hallway into the crowded living room. Bottles of soda and a few six-packs of beer sat on a table against the wall. Every seat in the room was taken and a couple dozen more people stood in small groups, milling around, making conversation. Thirty or forty other people were already there when I arrived. I was the youngest person in the room by at least fifteen years. I spotted the guy from the visiting clubhouse talking with a secretary from the front office and a man I recognized as a Yankee Stadium electrician. Toward the back of the room a front office guy was talking with a couple of guys from the grounds crew. Nick sat by himself on a sofa in the corner. I'd never seen him wearing slacks before.

Nick caught my eye and motioned me over with one hand. With the other, he reached up and tugged the shirtsleeve of a man standing to the side of the sofa. I made my way through the crowd to Nick and his friend.

"Eric," Nick said as the man turned toward him, "I want you to meet Matty. Matty's one of the kids working in the clubhouse. He's a good kid." I extended my hand to Eric and he pumped my arm.

"Hey, whaddya say, Matty! Nice to meet ya, Matty." He spoke in one of the truest Noo Yawk accents I'd ever heard. "Is this your first Network meeting?"

I told him that I'd just heard about the Network a few days before. "Nick told me I should come check it out, see how this works."

"That's great, Matty," he grinned. "Listen: if you have any questions later on tonight, you just come to me, all right? You just let me know. You want a drink, Matty? A Coke, or a beer? Just help yourself, Matty." He slapped me on the back and left me and Nick alone.

I grabbed a handful of pretzels from a bowl on the coffee table and took a seat on the couch next to Nick. All around us, people chatted and laughed.

"How's school, Matty?" Nick asked.

"Fine," I told him.

"You're not gonna fail any classes this year, right, Matty?" he asked me, smiling.

"No way, Nick."

At seven-thirty sharp, Eric stood up to address the crowd. By then the whole house—living room, kitchen, front foyer, stairs leading to the second floor—was standing room only. There must have been over a hundred people there.

Eric began by introducing himself. "Welcome to the Network," he started. "How many of you are here with us tonight for your first Network meeting?" Fifteen or twenty hands went up. "Okay, great. Well, for you folks, I'm going to spend a couple of minutes explaining what the Network is, how it works. Then we'll take a look at where our Networks are now, and we'll give those of you who are here to invest an opportunity to get involved."

He took a breath and continued. "The Network is the opportunity of a lifetime. No other investment opportunity gives you the chance to turn fifteen hundred dollars into twelve thousand dollars in as short a time as you can here with the Network. No other investment opportunity offers you zero percent risk. You hear me, guys? Zero! And no other investment opportunity allows you to make the friends like you'll find among the people you'll meet through the Network. You probably came here tonight with a friend. After you join the Network you're gonna bring your own friends, and once you're in, you're gonna meet a whole gang of new friends. And become friends with their friends! You'll work together with all these friends to make the

Network grow, and you'll make big money together. And as I said a moment ago and will explain more in a minute, it's can't lose. You can't lose."

Eric pulled an oversized piece of poster board out from behind him and propped it up on the dining room table against the wall. The chart featured the same neat configuration of fifteen boxes that had been drawn out for me at the Stadium a few days before. And just as Nick had explained, alongside each row of boxes was written the name for that level of the organization, from CEO up top to vice president at the bottom.

"There's two more questions people sometimes ask that I want to answer for you right off the bat. Is the Network a pyramid scheme? And is it illegal? The answer to both questions: no and no. The only similarity between a pyramid and the Network is in their triangular structure. And as for whether it's illegal: I'm a cop. A New York City police officer. There is no law on the books that says that this Network, this investment opportunity for and between friends, and friends of friends, is illegal or improper in any way. And if there was, if it was illegal, there's no way I'd be standing up here, a New York City cop, putting my ass on the line, talking to you about it." People laughed.

Eric demonstrated for the novices how the vice presidents would ascend a level for every eight new Network members. "Now, let's say you put in tonight, and three weeks from now you've gone up two levels—you're a president—and for some reason, any reason, you want out. You want to take your money back and go home. No problem. Not for nothing, there's *always* people waiting to buy in at the lowest level, at the vice president level. Last week over twenty people joined the Network, and with this crowd it looks like we'll do even better this week. Now, if you want out, you just sell your box, at the president level, at the CEO level, wherever you are. That's why there's no risk involved. You'll find no shortage of buyers. Buyers who might even pay you *more* for your president slot than you paid to get in at the beginning. Because you're that much closer to cashing out. Why you'd want to quit at that point, I don't know, but the point is, you can get out whenever you want out. So," he said, grinning wide, "on that note, any of you presidents or CEOs out there want to put your box on the block tonight?"

People shouted "No way!" and shook their heads left to right, laughing and hooting as if they were at a religious revival.

With that, Eric retreated to the kitchen. From my seat I could see a folding table and two chairs pushed up against one wall. Eric took a seat in one chair. A woman I hadn't seen before sat in the other; she had brown hair and was about forty, more or less the same age as the woman who had met me at the front door. On the table sat a stack of photocopied blank Network charts. Three more, each partially completed, were taped to the wall behind Eric and the woman. Nick's name was scrawled in the box at the top of one of them.

More than a dozen men and women stood ready to join the Network that night. They formed a long line into the kitchen while I stayed off to the side with Nick and watched them come forward, cash in hand. One at a time, each handed over fifteen hundred dollars. The woman counted the cash out on the table and sealed it inside a plain number ten envelope. Then she looked up and asked, "Who invited you here tonight?" Eric located that person's name on one of the three charts behind him and pulled the appropriate duplicate from a folder on the table. After he nodded, the woman continued. "And what's your name, honey?" Eric wrote that name—first names only—in a box, working his way left to right across the row of vice presidents. The woman wrote the same name on the envelope. Then the next person stepped up. This procedure repeated itself for nearly half an hour.

Men craned their necks to see which boxes were being filled on which chart. Each new name brought high fives and cheers from another corner of the room.

Finally Eric hollered toward the living room. "Anybody else?" A few seconds passed in silence. Then Eric turned the charts around on the table so people could see them. Two of the three Networks, including Nick's, were completely subscribed; the third was one vice president short of splitting. Eric announced that it was "time for some people to get paid!" Nick and another man were called forward and handed eight fat envelopes each. People slapped each other on the back and crowed with anticipation and excitement. Nick told me to hold the envelopes while he tore them open one at a time. Twelve thousand dollars in cash came into view and then disappeared into his pockets. Nick smiled and showed his tooth.

He'd invested fifteen hundred four weeks before. I couldn't believe what I was seeing. It seemed like the multiplication of fish and loaves. Awe and greed churned up from the bottom of my gut.

Eric elevated Nick's two presidents to CEO, one of whom was Will, the front office guy I'd seen talking with the grounds crew employees earlier in the evening. Two new charts went up on the wall. A quick poll of those who filled the ranks of Will's new network netted sixteen "definites" who were said to be ready to come in the following week.

I did the math driving home. At that rate, the Network would split twice a meeting. At that rate, twelve thousand dollars in two weeks. Even quicker than Nick. It was as simple as it was brilliant. There was no risk. No downside. I couldn't wait to step up to the table. All I had to do was come up with the money. I needed a partner.

It was close to ten o'clock by the time I got home. Mom

and Dad were already asleep. I took the phone into my bedroom, shut the door tight, and called my friend Chris at his house on Staten Island.

As embryonic and uncertain as the plan still was in my mind, I had only one friend I thought suited to helping me put it into action: Chris Wiedmann. There was no second option. Though his background seemed vanilla—he lived on Staten Island, the only child of a substance abuse counselor and a schoolteacher—Chris fit in across the social spectrum in a way I respected and admired. He seemed to glide effortlessly through every scene he encountered. He played varsity soccer and joked easily with the other athletes. He knew the source and meaning of graffiti tags scrawled on streetlights and subway advertisements. He perennially scored a place in the school's most advanced math and science classes. In his pocket, Chris carried a digital noisemaker the size of a box of matches that he'd bought at Radio Shack and reprogrammed. When held up to the receiver of a pay phone, it mimicked precisely the tone of the phone being fed a quarter; in this way, Chris granted himself free citywide long-distance pay phone privileges. He was also an Eagle Scout. He coined put-downs so cryptic and inscrutable— "Oh yeah? Well your mom chews cinder blocks!"—that they left whole cafeteria tables stunned and speechless. He was editor in chief of the *Regian*, the school's yearbook, and thus sole guardian of keys to the *Regian* office, the quasi-private warren of rooms in the basement of Regis universally recognized as the best place to cut class. At least one or two mornings a week he came to school with bleary eyes and spoke of nightclubs he'd been at the whole night before; he had amazing stories of twenty-four-hour electronic music parties at abandoned outer-borough factories.

If he had set it as a goal for himself, Chris could have been the most popular kid in school. Instead, he allowed his personality to pull him in so many incongruous directions that I think classmates gave up trying to figure him out. Most thought of Chris as a "cool kid," if sometimes aloof; I considered him my most independent-minded and street-savvy confidant. Since freshman year, we'd been fast friends.

I saw in Chris the same virtues that, flattering myself, I imagined Nick and the visiting clubhouse guy had prudently recognized in me before telling me about the Network. He could keep a secret. He was open-minded and naturally predisposed toward adventure. He had a sharp and searching eye. He was levelheaded and trusted his instincts to lead him through any kind of trouble. No less than myself and more than any other friend, Chris had tasted something of the adult world and found himself up to it. Six months before graduation, we considered ourselves no more suited to high school than to grade school; we were just waiting for people older than us to begin to see us this way as well. That I'd been singled out to join the Network validated this impression of myself and further stoked the fire.

"What's up?" Chris said when he answered the phone.

"Where are you?" I asked.

"In my house."

"Yeah, I know that, Sherlock. I meant *where* in your house. Go somewhere we can talk, somewhere your parents can't hear you. I need to talk to you."

Chris put the phone down and thirty seconds later came back on the line.

"What is it?" he asked.

"You remember last week, when I went up to the Stadium?" I began. "So Nick put me onto this new business he's in, this investment thing. It's called the Network."

"Okay. And?"

"Listen," I continued. "They have meetings every week

where they explain how it works, and new people can buy in. So I went to a meeting tonight, at this house in Yonkers. Nick put fifteen hundred in like three weeks ago. Every time eight more people put money in, someone cashes out. Last night, Nick." With added emphasis: "Twelve thousand dollars."

"Yeah?" Chris asked. He didn't seem to be following me.

"Chris: Nick turned fifteen hundred dollars into twelve thousand dollars in three weeks." I took a breath. "And so can we. We put the money up. We get other people to come in. We get paid. That's it. And we can't lose. Anytime we want to get out, we can get out. You just sell your box to someone else. It's bananas."

"Wait, wait, wait. Boxes?" he asked. "What are you talking about?"

"Get a pen," I told him. "Draw a box at the top of the page, then two boxes below it. Like a three-block pyramid. Then draw four more below those two, and eight at the bottom."

"How?" he asked. "Start over."

"Are you drawing this out?" I complained. "You need to draw it out."

Five minutes' worth of scrapped sketches later, we were finally on the same page. Having conveyed its structure, I described how the Network worked, splitting again and again, minting two new CEOs for each one who graduates to a comfortable retirement. How it had happened just that way—twice—at the meeting earlier that night. How we'd ascend level by level, week by week, and ultimately be spit back out in a month's time with twelve thousand dollars in cash. I explained that it was legal—"It's run by cops!"—and that you could pull your money out whenever you wanted. I recounted everything I'd seen, with my own eyes, a few hours before. I told Chris: we have a week to come up with $750 each, and then we can go in together, as partners, at the next meeting.

"We've got to do it," I told him.

"Let's talk tomorrow. I'm not even sure I have the money," he confessed.

"Yeah, I know," I said. "Me either. But we've got to find a way to come up with it."

I walked into school the next morning an hour before classes started and went looking for Chris. I found him studying in the *Regian* office.

"Yo, put the math homework away," I started in, seating myself in the beat-up folding chair opposite his desk. I glanced over my shoulder to ensure we were alone. "So what do you think?" I asked him. The excitement of the previous night's meeting rushed back and flushed my face.

Chris pushed his spiral notebook and pencil across the desk to me. "Break it down for me again," he told me.

I sketched out the fifteen magic boxes. He asked me to explain again how you could pull your money out if you changed your mind. He wanted to know how many people were at the last meeting. How many people had joined. If I thought there was a catch. He asked me whether I had $750 in cash. I explained that I thought I had maybe half, and that I would try to borrow the other half from my girlfriend.

"We're going to have it all back, and eight times more, in a month," I reassured him. I spoke faithfully, as a friend. "There's no risk, no way to lose."

"Jesus," he said.

Chris went home that night and took a seat next to his dad on the living room sofa.

"Dad," Chris said, "I need to talk to you. I'm seventeen

years old. I think I'm old enough now to be responsible for handling my own money."

He was referring to the bank account into which his parents had deposited every five-, ten-, or twenty-dollar bill that a relative had ever tucked inside one of his birthday, Christmas, or graduation cards. The lessons his parents hoped to pass on to him—the value of carefully saving your money, the satisfaction of buying something for yourself—had been unspoken but imparted artfully. His whole childhood, Chris never touched the account himself. Upon deciding that he needed that new skateboard, or CD, or computer game, he would let his parents know what he wanted and how much it cost, and they would withdraw the money for him. Since he'd been very young, Chris and his parents had taken trips to the bank together to make these small deposits and withdrawals. Chris thought he'd accumulated about eight hundred dollars, more or less, over a lifetime of saving. It'd put him just over the bar we'd set for each other to split a box between us. But telling his parents what he intended to do with the money—withdraw it, then "octuple" it in four weeks—was obviously out of the question. This presented a problem: Chris was still a minor, and though the bank records were in his name, he lacked even joint access to the account.

"You're talking about your savings?" Mr. Wiedmann put down the newspaper he was reading. "What made you think of this now?"

"I've been thinking about it for a while, Dad," Chris answered.

"What's wrong with the way we've always handled things?"

"Well, it's kind of a hassle to need to wait for you or Mom to take me to the bank every time I want to buy something. And there's all kinds of stuff going on at school that I'm going to need money for soon. We have to put our deposit down for the prom in a couple of weeks. Plus, when I go away to college next year, I'm going to be in charge of my own money, and I just think that I'll be better prepared for that if I have some experience dealing with it now."

Chris kept his poker face while his dad thought it over.

"Well, if you feel so strongly about it," he said. "And if you're sure you can handle it. I suppose it'd happen automatically on your next birthday anyway."

"That's right," Chris replied. "Thanks, Dad."

Saturday morning, Chris and his dad went to the bank and signed the papers giving Chris full banking privileges on the account. It held $825. The bank was located all the way on the far side of Staten Island, a long car ride from where the Wiedmanns lived.

Monday afternoon, Chris took the Staten Island Ferry home from school but boarded a different city bus than usual at the ferry terminal. An hour later he transferred to an even farther-flung bus, which he rode to within a block of the bank. Fifteen minutes later he was back at the bus stop. His balance, by then, was down to two digits.

For my part, I sat in a parked car talking for an hour with my girlfriend of two months outside her high school. I explained the Network to her the same way that Nick, and then Eric, had explained it to me. The same way I'd explained it to Chris. I had come to believe the pitch so deeply that relating it was becoming second nature. I told her that this was too big to pass up, that Chris had already gone ahead and come up with the money on his end. That I'd have her three hundred back to her in a month. Six weeks tops. I really need you to help me out. Baby, please. There's no one else I can go to about this. And no matter what happens, I'm good for it. Trust me. I saw it all go down for Nick with my own eyes. Baby, I swear. With my own eyes!

· · ·

The next meeting was Thursday night, at a restaurant and wedding hall in the Throgs Neck section of the Bronx. Chris told his parents that he was coming up to Tarrytown to spend the night and work on a group homework assignment. We ate dinner at the kitchen table with my parents, brother, and sister. I helped clear the table and announced that Chris and I were going to the movies.

Ten minutes later I eased my parents' car onto I-87, the Major Deegan Thruway, heading south toward the Bronx. Chris traced our route on an old map and we navigated our way through the Bronx toward the address I'd scrawled down earlier that day on the phone with Nick.

"I think you can get on the Cross Bronx from the Major Deegan," Chris mused, tilting the map to catch the dim headlights of the car behind us. "And it looks like the Cross Bronx leads right into the Whitestone Bridge." The names of these outer-borough roads were vaguely familiar from a childhood's worth of overheard talk radio traffic reports—"Three-car pileup on the Pulaski Skyway. Jackknifed tractor-trailer causing big delays on the Belt Parkway, backed up all the way to the BQE"—but neither of us had ever driven them before or could even remember ever having been in this corner of the City. We took the last exit before the Whitestone Bridge and pulled off the highway onto the local, residential streets that run alongside the East River.

We parked on a side street near the water. You could see the underside of the bridge and hear the traffic passing over it. The first real cold snap of the winter had descended on New York just a few days before, and we were still dressed for fall. As we walked toward the restaurant, a bitterly frigid gust came off the water and assaulted our faces at what felt like forty miles an hour. I leaned into the wind and dug my hands deeper into my pants pockets. In one, I had my wallet, which held my high school ID and driver's license; in the other, the keys to my parents' car and an envelope with $750 in cash. Mine was cobbled together from the fifteen twenties my girlfriend had lent me, Mattingly's four leftover hundreds, and an assortment of fives and tens. Chris, who'd pulled his straight from the bank, held his $750 in eight bills.

We checked our coats at the cloakroom and were pointed straight to the back, to the restaurant's ballroom. We walked through the dining room, past tables of elderly couples and families of five quietly eating dinner, and out onto the ballroom's parquet dance floor. The room was ringed with tables for eight and seemed set for a wedding reception or bar mitzvah. Easily three times as many people as had been at the house in Yonkers crowded the room. I saw Nick when we walked in; he was there with his son Paul. The Yankees grounds crew and front office were once again well represented. I introduced my friend Chris to the guys from the Stadium.

Eric the Cop began his seamless presentation. It was identical to the one he'd delivered the week before, right down to the same jokes told on the same beats, but the size of the audience and the setting boosted the energy level even higher than it had been in Yonkers. Unlike in Yonkers, there was no longer a TV running off to the side of where Eric had the Network diagrammed on a piece of poster board propped up against the living room wall. Now Eric spoke with a microphone; his chart rested on an easel. His tone was half business pitch, half wedding toast. He stood in front of a floor-to-ceiling wall of glass that framed the bridge and its reflection, which twinkled on the surface of the East River. Eric smiled beneficently down on the few hundred in attendance and spoke of future riches and happiness; everyone beamed back at him and at each other.

At the end of the presentation, Chris and I joined the long line of investors in waiting. Five separate Network charts were being filled that night, and after we reached the table and laid our money down, we selected one of the two pyramids borne of Nick's having cashed out the week before.

Five of the eight vice president slots had already been bought. Our money was counted out and both our names squeezed into the sixth box in the bottom row of the chart. Right after us, Nick's son Paul took the seventh spot. The line was still a dozen people deep when the final box went as well. A cheer went up from the crowd that stood off to the side, watching which name Eric placed where. Chris and I had been in the Network less than ten minutes, and we'd already advanced a full level closer to the top. Eric printed our names onto a fresh chart and posted it on his easel. More people laid their money down on the table, filling five of the eight new vice president slots in our Network. By the end of the night, Chris and I were co–executive vice presidents, along with Paul Priore and two guys who owned a pizzeria in the Bronx. I recognized neither of the two presidents above us, and they never introduced themselves to me, or to Chris. Our CEO was Will, who worked in the Yankees front office. We huddled over our chart as busboys stacked chairs around us. Will broke off to speak with Eric, then came back and announced that we'd meet the next week at a different restaurant, a sports bar in the North Bronx. We took down the address and exchanged phone numbers.

"Everybody bring people," pizzeria owner one exhorted the group. "Everybody bring two people next week."

One of the two presidents in the circle spoke up: "Two people each and this thing'll split every week."

Chris and I looked at each other and read mutual panic: we didn't have even one person to recruit. We, as seniors in high school, were supposed to know people who had fifteen hundred dollars in cash? Definitely none of our classmates had it. My list of adult acquaintances was pitifully short. All the people I knew at the Stadium were either already in the room that night or had decided not to get involved. Was I supposed to ask my teachers at school if they wanted to make some money on the side? Relatives? Neighbors? My parents' friends?

We left the restaurant with Will and walked together to our cars. I'd always liked Will. He was one of the few guys in the front office who took the time to learn the names of the kids working in the clubhouse. During the season he'd often come downstairs after games and had a beer while we picked over the leftovers from the players' postgame buffet.

I confided to Will our fears about whether or not Chris and I would be able to find anyone to invite to the meeting the next week.

"Don't worry about it, Matt. I've got a couple friends—three, at least—who I'm gonna bring and who are gonna come in for a full box each. You and Chris can have two of them," he promised. "You guys can tell people you brought them in, and you'll have done your part. You'll be square with everybody."

"Oh, man. Will, that'd be great."

We arrived at Will's car. Chris and I both shook his hand; I felt so grateful I wanted to give him a hug. We stood by while Will started his car.

"I'll see you next week," our CEO said. He saluted us with two fingers and drove away.

Chris and I drove back to my house delirious with anticipation.

We had it made.

It was late enough that the highways were almost empty, and as we crossed the Bronx, Chris put a hip-hop mix-tape on and turned the volume up as loud as it could go. Banging the steering wheel with both fists, I sounded the car horn in time with the music. Chris opened the windows and sunroof and shouted lyrics into the winter night.

We were three people away from being elevated to president. Will had told us that *at least* three people were coming in the next week, and two of them would be *ours*. There was no doubt that, within the month, we'd be rolling in cash. The only question was whether it would take two weeks, or three. Two weeks or three weeks? How much longer until we'll never be broke again? I was sure, having seen the size of the meeting the week before and the rate at which the Network kept growing, that we'd cash out in two weeks' time. Chris was certain that everyone had agreed upon the "bring two people" mantra at the end of the meeting; that meant we'd cash out in three meetings.

Chris asked me what I was going to do with the money. I had no answer to this question; I hadn't really thought about it. I told him that maybe I'd just save it, put it away.

"Save it?" he laughed. "Man, you don't even have a bank account!"

"Yeah, neither do you," I said. "I mean, not anymore. Not since you cleaned it out. Sucker."

"I'm gonna put every dollar back," Chris said. "Plus some."

We passed the last few miles in near silence, our faces set in giddy grins. Hurtling down the highway, we did not fantasize about winning the jackpot; that was already a foregone conclusion, and our thoughts had moved beyond it. We made mental lists of what we'd do with all that money once it was placed in our hands.

We parked the car in my parents' driveway and bounded up the front steps. As was usual by ten o'clock at night, the whole house was already asleep. I took a seat on the sofa and turned on the TV.

"So, seriously," I asked Chris. "What are you gonna do with your half?"

"I don't know," he shrugged. "There's this snowboard I've had my eyes on for like two years. But I think it's only maybe five hundred bucks. Maybe I'll buy a car."

"I'm gonna buy a closetful of clothes," I announced. "And some silk suits, like the ballplayers wear."

"When are you going to ever wear a suit?" he laughed.

"Yo, we can get some nice Italian suits and wear 'em to school," I joked. "Picture it: all splurged out in the back row of math class."

We were laughing so hard I was worried we'd wake my parents up.

"No, no, no," Chris said as we got hold of ourselves. "I'll tell you what we should do. We should take a trip."

"Yeah? Where?"

"I don't know," Chris said. "Somewhere warm."

"Somewhere *hot*," I corrected him. "Let's go to Puerto Rico. No, no—Hawaii! Let's go to Hawaii." I was so full of excitement I had to stand up.

"Anywhere eighty and sunny."

"Eighty and sunny," I dreamed aloud.

Chris stood up as well. We were elated, literally bouncing around the living room again. "Eighty *and* sunny *and* where the girls are at."

"Let's do it," I said. I clapped my palms together like a quarterback coming out of a football huddle.

"Let's do it," Chris replied. We clinched hands, then tiptoed up the stairs to my room to get ready for bed. It was late, and we had school in the morning.

. . .

Surrounded by rush hour commuters on the train to Manhattan the next morning, Chris and I spoke in low voices. I often saw neighbors and friends of my parents on the train on my way to school, and I didn't want to risk being overheard.

We picked up the conversation where we'd left off the night before. We revisited the two-weeks-or-three-weeks discussion. We reaffirmed our travel plans. We debated whether or not we could tell anyone else at school about the Network. On this last point, we agreed: it just wasn't a good idea. None of our friends, we thought, were likely to have both the cash at hand *and* the temperament to take the plunge. One or two might have had the former, and one or two the latter, but we couldn't think of one who had both. Besides, the last thing we wanted anyone to think was that we were showing off. *Kids* bragged and couldn't keep their mouths shut. We, on the other hand, were now involved in an adventure clearly on the grown-up side of the adult-adolescent divide. For us, it was a top priority to live up to this new station in life, to act like we belonged on the far side of the line. To serve notice: when this is all said and done, we're not crossing back over to the other side. No way. We agreed: no running around school, lips flapping. No acting like a couple of dumbass kids.

So all week, conversations in the cafeteria and between classes carried on as normal: who was going to the dance coming up at the Academy of the Sacred Heart, the girls' high school on Ninety-first Street; whether or not the Knicks should have traded Mark Jackson to the Clippers; which plays were going to be on the Shakespeare exam; who'd asked which teachers for recommendations to which colleges. Chris and I sat and listened and chimed in only every now and then. Our minds were elsewhere. With the possible exception of the college applications—"Wait, we have to ask teachers for recommendations? By when? No! Shit!"—the topics all seemed less compelling than they'd been just the week before. I thought about the Network while standing in the subway on my way to school; during class; eating a sandwich at lunch; watching the evening news with my parents; lying in bed trying to fall asleep. I was hooked on the clandestine nature of our involvement. Along with the amount of money we'd put in, and the amount we stood to collect, the cloak-and-dagger business further boosted the allure of the enterprise. I couldn't not think about the Network, and Chris and I couldn't not talk about it. Many times that week the two of us retreated by ourselves to the back room of the *Regian* office, where we sat with our feet up on the desks and counted off the days until the next meeting.

When we arrived at that Thursday night's Network venue, in the back room of the sports bar in the North Bronx, some differences from the week before were readily apparent.

Sitting around a half dozen tables were fewer people than had been at the meeting in the house in Yonkers, and maybe only a quarter as many as had filled the wedding hall in the Bronx. But it was not only the numbers; the character of the group felt changed as well. Looking around the room trying to find someone familiar to sit down with, I recognized most of the faces I saw. But I knew them only from seeing them at previous Network meetings; there was almost no one I actually knew. With the exception of Will, who with his college buddies filled a table toward the back of the room, and Paul Priore, Nick's son, there was no one from the Stadium left. No front office secretaries. No guys from the mailroom. No grounds crew. No visiting clubhouse guy. No Nick.

Chris and I sat down at a table with Paul Priore and the two pizzeria owners.

At seven-thirty, a man I'd never seen before—not Eric—stood up and began speaking.

"Eric's sorry he couldn't be here tonight," he began. "Given how many people have been joining the Network over the past couple weeks, and how many times it's split recently, the meetings were getting a little big. We were having a hell of a time finding someplace large enough for us to get together every week. So the Network's been split off into a couple of smaller meetings, and Eric's with one of the other Networks tonight. He'll probably be back with you guys next week."

He paused to make sure the room was still with him.

"So," he continued, brightening up. "How many people here have never been to a Network meeting before?"

Four hands at Will's table went up. One of the pizzeria owners nodded to two guys sitting to his right. They raised their hands as well.

Six people total? That was it? I looked over at Chris and shrugged my shoulders. At least we had an answer to our question. "Three weeks," I mouthed across the table.

Eric's stand-in gave a decent presentation, but nowhere near as polished as the ones I'd heard the two weeks before. Unlike Eric, this guy was apparently not a New York City police officer; if he was, he didn't volunteer it. He spoke little of meeting new friends and of new friends making money together. The strong point of his speech was a very succinct and direct description of the Network's mechanics, which in its entirety went something like this: "For every eight new people who come in at the bottom, the guy on top cashes out." When he finished, there were no questions from the audience. Three of Will's four friends lined up and put their money down, taking the last three empty boxes at the base of our Network. Will cashed out. The stand-in gave him his eight envelopes, three of which were filled with money his friends had handed over moments before.

Two more new Network charts came out. Each of the names left below Will's on the old chart was copied over, one level higher than before. Chris and I watched them pencil us in. Chris and I had advanced again, to president, and were now just two splits short—sixteen people—from cashing out ourselves. I tried to check my excitement and keep it cooler than the previous week. Chris and I nodded at each other with quiet confidence.

All administrative business concluded, the group huddled again. We agreed that we'd meet back here, at the sports bar, the following week. Someone verbalized what everybody had noticed but nobody had said out loud: the Network slowed down tonight. The same battle cries as the previous week were sounded. Everybody brings two people next week. No coasting. Everyone's got to pick up the slack.

Will and his friends adjourned to the bar. I thought of reminding Will of what he'd told us the week before—that in terms of bringing in recruits, two of his buddies counted for Chris and me. But it didn't seem like the right moment. Will was busy celebrating his windfall. Surrounded by his friends, I realized that maybe I didn't know him so well after all. One of his buddies who'd just bought into the Network raised his beer and demanded that Will buy a round for everyone in the place. Will had his envelopes jammed into the back pockets of his jeans; I don't think he could have sat down if he'd tried. He pulled three hundreds from his twelve thousand and waved the bartender over. Chris and I left a moment later.

"Kind of weird tonight, huh?" Chris asked me on the way home. "You think it's gonna be okay?"

"Yeah," I answered. "I'm sure it'll pick up again next week."
But it didn't.

From the first moment we walked into the bar the following Thursday, the same unease I'd felt the week before surfaced again. There was no one left in the room whom Chris and I knew. Eric again was nowhere to be seen. Will was probably home counting his money. The Network was stale news at the Stadium; aside from Paul Priore, who was now in a separate Network than us, anybody Yankee who might once have been in had already come out the other side. For the first time since Yonkers, I noticed that everyone there had a good ten years on me.

When the time came for newcomers to identify themselves, one hand in the room went up. Sighs and groans were audible wall to wall. Will's friends seemed confused; everything had gone so smoothly for Will the week before. The new guy didn't even end up putting his money down. I'm not sure I would have either; I saw nothing that night that might inspire the excitement I'd felt at my first Network meeting.

After the meeting, the ritual plea for recruiting newcomers was tinged for the first time with some finger-pointing. Accusatory looks shot back and forth across the table. Congratulatory comments and camaraderie gave way to bitter sarcasm. I was sick of hearing the pizza guy give orders about how many people everyone else needed to bring each week. How many guys had he brought in, I asked Chris a bit too loud. The pizza guy turned on me in a rage.

"How many people have I brought in?" he repeated. "Me? Three. Who the fuck have *you* brought in?"

The whole circle spun in my direction. I opened my mouth to explain that two of Will's friends should be considered part of Chris's and my count. Then, just in time, I realized the absurdity of what I was about to say. Will's two friends, neither of whom

I'd even been introduced to, were sitting across the table listening to the exchange, and I was about to claim that Chris and I, and not Will, had recruited them. I stammered weakly. The pizza guy shook his head in disgust. I felt my face flush. My eyes went to my shoes.

Chris jumped to my defense.

"Who did *we* bring in?" Chris said, addressing the pizzeria owner but speaking before all that was left of the Network. "Man, don't blame us! We're seniors in high school. Who do you expect us to know who has fifteen hundred dollars in cash? You guys are *adults*. Don't look at me and Matt to start producing businessmen when it turns out you guys can't." His voice trailed off. It was a truthful speech, and I thought courageous as well, but it failed to assuage or hearten the crowd.

"Fuck me," said the pizza guy, picking up his jacket. "Fuck this."

As we had the previous four weeks, the next Thursday afternoon Chris and I took the train up to my house after school. By this time, both his and my parents were getting pretty used to his weekly visits to the McGough house.

"That's some big assignment you guys are working on, huh?" Chris told me his mom had asked him the night before.

After dinner, I shouted up to my parents' bedroom that Chris and I were going out to the movies. My sister, brushing past us, asked Chris what we were going to see. "We don't know," I blurted, trying to take my friend off the spot. "Whatever's playing."

Any movie we might have seen would have been better than the Network meeting that night. In terms of turnout, it was the worst one yet. If even one newcomer had shown up, he would have been set upon by CEOs and presidents eager to trade their eminent positions for even money, or less. Because there were no new faces, there was no presentation. Will's friends were apoplectic, arguing among themselves about whether they'd be able to get their money back from Will. I think everyone realized even then that we weren't likely to see each other again. A proposal was made to meet every two weeks rather than one; we'd be more likely to find recruits, someone suggested, if we had more time to talk it up. People were too sullen and surly to even respond.

Late into that night Chris and I sat at my kitchen table while he diagrammed pyramids and punched numbers into a calculator.

"Hey, check this out," he said. "You know how many people you'd need to fill all the open boxes after it split ten times?" He turned the calculator toward me. "Sixteen thousand three hundred eighty-four."

"What?" I asked. "How?"

"Trust me," he said. "I did the math."

He went back to his scratch pad and calculator.

"And after a hundred times?" he offered.

I wasn't sure I needed to know. "How many?"

"Over sixteen million," he said.

I could only state the obvious.

"That's nuts," I said. "That's twice as many people as live in New York."

There was no next Network meeting.

I knew it was over, definitively, two nights later, while watching the ten o'clock local news on the couch in the living room. My dad was dozing in the easy chair to my left. "And now, a special consumer report," the anchor said. "Pyramid schemes sweep the tristate area." A trio of dollar signs gleamed from the graphic box over his left shoulder as I watched in stunned silence. "It's called the Network," the television droned. "And it's pitched as the deal of a lifetime. But tonight officials are sounding the alarm. Across New York and New Jersey, hundreds of people are learning that it really is too good to be true . . ."

Chris knew it was over, definitively, the next morning when the starting forward on our high school basketball team approached him in the *Regian* office before class. "Chris, you've got to get in on this. Listen: you want to turn fifteen bucks into one-twenty?" Chris almost hit him.

The whole thing, it turned out, had been a con game in the truest sense of the old expression. As long as everyone had full confidence that the Network would deliver a 700 percent return on their investment, it usually did. Week after week you watched people line up and clamor to put their money down. You saw friends, and strangers, walk away with thousands of dollars in cash. You believed, until it was too late, that it would end that way for you, too.

But after the Network first faltered, people's confidence eroded and a fear of complete stagnation was introduced to the delicate equation. Even Chris and I weren't so naive as to think that the Network had ever been about making new friends. But as long as things were going well, the impulse to get your friends involved was fully altruistic. You were making money yourself and putting your friends—or relatives, or coworkers—on the same path as well. This is why I don't blame Nick for what was at the time a staggering loss. I don't think he was trying to take advantage of me; as far as I know, his own son lost fifteen hundred dollars as well.

. . .

Neither Regis High School nor Yankee Stadium held a moment of silence to mark the dissolution of the Network and the death of our big-money dreams.

There were final exams to take just before Christmas vacation, and college applications had to be postmarked before the first of the year. By the holidays I'd narrowed my list to fourteen colleges; I realized only later that no friend had applied to half that many. I spent New Year's Eve shuffling papers in the backseat of my parents' car while my father did seventy down the West Side Highway, bearing down on the only twenty-four-hour post office in greater New York City. Dad was furious that I'd procrastinated to the last possible moment, and even more furious that I'd managed to time our mad dash to the main post office—ten blocks south of Times Square—for midnight on New Year's Eve. A precinct's worth of cops blocked every other intersection and any hope of curbside parking. With ten minutes to spare, we walked into the vaulted lobby. I was exhausted and eager to leave for college, and my dad probably shared those sentiments.

We reached the front of the line at five to twelve. A neon light came on and directed us to our left. I cradled my applications and took a hurried step forward before I felt my father's hand on my shoulder.

"You sure you don't want to apply anywhere else?" he asked.

"What?" I said.

He shrugged his free arm so that his wristwatch came clear of his sleeve. He pointed to the face of his watch. "I mean, I think you still have a little time," he poker-faced me. "If you want."

"Yeah, real funny, Dad," I said.

A forgiving grin broke over his face. "Come on," he told

me, clapping me on the back. I slid my fourteen fat envelopes across the counter and on to college admissions offices across the country.

In late January I visited the Stadium. Nick and Rob had already begun packing for spring training in Fort Lauderdale, and they put me to work moving boxes and sorting uniforms. Some guys from the grounds crew were working in the clubhouse that afternoon as well, including a couple I recognized from those months of backroom Network meetings. But nobody mentioned the Network. In fact, as quickly as the Network had come to dominate all of my conversations at the Stadium that winter, the fruitless scheme was never really raised or discussed at work ever again.

Not so with Chris. It took us a while to let any of our other friends know the truth. We never, of course, told our parents. It took me three months to save up enough money to pay back my girlfriend; I'm not sure if Chris's bank account was ever made whole again. Even in the immediate aftermath, though, our friendship never wavered. We'd both been true believers, after all, and we'd each witnessed the other's financial self-immolation. It took only a couple of weeks before the Network became just more material for us to draw on as a source of black humor. The jokes were tentative at first, but then came on faster and without shame. And to this day, I still can't buy Chris a beer without him subtracting it—"$750 minus five" again and again—from a perpetually open tab.

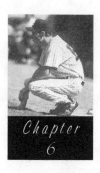

Chapter
6

Spring Training

The next time I heard from the Yankees was on a rainy Saturday in March. Robby and Nick had been in Florida for spring training since the beginning of February. The start of the baseball season was just two weeks away. Even weekend days seemed to drag on forever.

I was lying on the couch when the telephone rang. "It's Rob," my dad told me, his hand over the mouthpiece of the receiver. "From the Yankees," he added unnecessarily. I took the phone into the next room.

"Robby, what's up?"

"Not much. Sick of Florida. Can't wait to get back to New York. How's school?"

"Fine. Almost done. Still waiting to hear where I got into college."

"Good, good," he said absentmindedly. "Listen, I've got a proposition for you."

I cringed, thinking of the Network, but Robby carried on. Would I be interested, he wanted to know, in taking a trip south to spring training for a few days?

"To do what?" I asked. "Work? Or hang out?"

"Both. Hang out for a day or two, and then drive one of the ballplayers' cars back up to New York. We play our last game here on Thursday, April 1. Right afterward we fly to D.C. for an exhibition game there Friday against the Mets. Then back to New York for the Mayor's Cup games Saturday and Sunday." The Mayor's Cup was a two-game exhibition series between the Mets and Yankees, one game each at Yankee Stadium and Shea, traditionally held the weekend before the season opener. "A lot of these guys drove their own cars down here in February, but when we pack up and go, we're flying home."

"Yeah?"

"Yeah," he said. "Somebody rented a tractor-trailer to take a dozen cars north, but it filled up in a day, and guys got frozen out. Matt Nokes asked me yesterday if I knew anybody who'd want to drive his car back to the Bronx. I thought you might be interested."

Matt Nokes was the Yankees starting catcher. Like most catchers, he was stocky and slow—I'd have bet a week's pay that Nick Priore could outrun him in a footrace—and his batting stance, left-handed, matched his build. Nokes stood in at the plate as if he were actually seated on an invisible hard-backed chair placed in the first base half of the batter's box. But twenty or twenty-five times a season, he'd connect with one of his rigid uppercuts and power a ball into the right-field seats.

Off the field, Nokes was a family man. I don't remember him hanging out too much with the other players, but he got along with the bat boys as well as anybody on the roster. It wasn't so much because he'd pal around with us like some of the other guys, shagging fly balls during batting practice or talking in the dugout during games. We liked Nokes because there was an element to his personality that set him apart from almost everyone else on the ballclub: within his six-one frame was the uncorrupted personality of a thirteen-year-old boy. Nokes liked gadgets and muscle cars. He'd stare transfixed at action-adventure movies playing on the clubhouse TV. He listened to classic rock and roll. Back issues of *Road & Track* magazine littered the floor of his locker. He walked around the clubhouse looking hyper and lost in thought. Nick called him a space cadet.

I knew Nokes best from one exchange we'd had the summer before. It was a night game late in the season—I was already back in school—and I sat down next to him toward the end of the dugout. He must have been given the day off by Showalter. We sat and watched the game in silence until the fourth or fifth inning, when, making conversation during a pitching change, Nokes asked me what was new at school. I told him about an assignment I was working on in physics class, something about volume and pressure and equal but opposite reactions. Nokes nodded and started in on a story about a homemade cannon he'd built when he was a kid.

"You could launch a potato three hundred fifty feet," he bragged. We sat in the dugout and looked straight out to the outfield, past the baseball game being played in front of us, toward the left-field wall. Painted on the fence, just inside the foul pole, was printed in six-foot-high type: 318 FT.

"No way," I said.

"Oh yeah," he laughed, nodding his head. "Easy."

Nokes got up and went into the clubhouse, and came back to the dugout holding a cup of coffee. He sat back down and sipped his beverage, silent, thinking hard. A few innings passed.

We watched the Yankees take the lead, then fall behind by a run. He said nothing until the seventh-inning stretch.

"I bet we could make one," he mused aloud.

"Make what?"

"A cannon," he whispered.

"A potato cannon? Come on. You're joking."

"Three hundred and fifty feet," he said quietly, almost to himself, gazing out toward the left-field seats. He squinted his eyes like a professional golfer mentally calculating the distance to the green. "You think you can get some duct tape and tennis ball cans?" he asked me. "Or like three feet of PVC pipe, this wide," he said, holding out his thumb and index finger a few inches apart. He spoke, not unreasonably, in a low and conspiratorial voice. "And lighter fluid," he instructed. With each word, his eyes became more animated. "We'll need lighter fluid. Can you get some lighter fluid?"

The first day of the next homestand, a couple of hours before batting practice began, we sat in the dugout with the raw materials for a cannon. Except for Nick, who was folding towels in the clubhouse, the Stadium was empty. Nokes used a can opener to take the tops and bottoms off two metal tennis ball cans. We duct-taped them end to end on top of a third can, whose bottom we left intact. Using a hammer and nail I'd borrowed from the grounds crew, Nokes punched a hole near the base of the cylinder, now about three feet long. Following his directions, I squirted half a can of lighter fluid into the hole. Down the cannon's hatch I dropped a medium-size Idaho baking potato; I pushed it down the full length of the cylinder, using a fungo bat as a ramrod. We propped the cannon up against the top step of the dugout and angled its mouth toward the left-field seats. I took a full step back while Nokes flicked a Bic lighter at the small nail hole. The fluid ignited, hissed, and sucked the lighter's flame down into the tube. A half second later there was a weak pop, and the potato burst lamely from the hole, coming to rest a few feet away.

"Darnit," Nokes said. It was about as strong as his language got; I'd never heard him curse.

Nokes scratched his head and we set to work diagnosing the problem. "We must not have gotten a tight enough seal between the cans," he speculated, fingering the seams we'd taped over. "There's some air that's getting in there." We added additional layers of duct tape and then tried it again, and again, until we ran out of lighter fluid. Nokes's disappointment was palpable. "Next time we'll use PVC piping," he promised, slapping me on the back as we walked together up the dugout tunnel to the clubhouse.

At no point did either of us ever acknowledge the lunacy inherent in our little science experiment. The absurdity, that is, of Nokes—a man paid a million dollars a year for the use of his hands—training me in the lost art of potato mortar construction, then flicking a flame at a metal tube full of lighter fluid. All in the service of—if everything went as planned—painting the left-field seats with mashed potatoes.

It was senselessness bordering on madness. Still, it was hard not to like how Nokes's happy-go-lucky personality hid an equally good-natured wild streak. Nick may have been right. Nokes was something of a space cadet. But I thought he was one of the coolest guys in the clubhouse.

Nokes was also renowned among the bat boys as a first-rate connoisseur of fast and flashy cars. I remembered him arriving at the Stadium before one game in a brand-new Dodge Viper, a car that bore a closer resemblance to a stealth fighter than to an ordinary automobile. I was upstairs at the entrance to the players' parking lot when Nokes pulled up.

"Holy shit," the parking attendant in the players' lot blurted to no one in particular as he waved the car through the gate. "You see that shit?" he asked aloud, his voice crescendoing. "Do you see that shit? Damn!"

I walked Nokes downstairs to the clubhouse and watched him toss the keys to Robby. "Can you ask one of the kids to fill me up?" he asked. Robby looked to me. It turned my stomach to admit that I couldn't; I didn't have my driver's license yet. The privilege fell to Jamie instead. I rode shotgun while Jamie drove Nokes's race car the few blocks south to the service station on 149th Street. A trio of high school girls passing by while we pumped gas stopped dead in their tracks in front us. I took a seat on the hood of the car and stared back, trying to hold my poker face. Jamie threw a nod in their direction. The message was clear: Yeah, ladies, this is our car.

Robby still held the line.

"What kind of car is it?" I asked him.

"I don't know. But Nokes is willing to pay you five hundred plus expenses. Hotel for the night, gas, food, whatever. You've just got to get yourself down here."

"Five hundred?"

"Yeah. You need to be down here for next Thursday. Can you do it?"

"Hell yeah!" I said. "Definitely."

I hung up the phone and went back to the couch. "What did Robby want?" my mom asked me.

"One of the ballplayers needs his car driven back up to New York at the end of spring training. I'm gonna fly down next week and drive it back before Opening . . ."

My dad cut me off. "No you're not, no way. You've had

your driver's license less than a year. You're not ready for a drive like that."

I threw my head back in frustration. "Dad, c'mon," I said. "I drove Tim Burke's car all the way to Boston last season."

"And I was with you for that trip," he said. "This is a twenty-four-hour haul you're talking about. I don't think you have enough cockpit hours for a drive like that, all by yourself." My dad had pioneered the concept of "cockpit hours" when he taught my older sister to drive. Each one represented an hour spent behind the wheel, with my dad as instructor and copilot. Driving privileges increased in step with the number of cockpit hours you accumulated. Driving alone. Driving alone on the highway. Driving alone on the highway at night. Driving alone on the highway at night into the Bronx or Manhattan. You never knew exactly how many more cockpit hours you needed to graduate to that next level. Until he had decided you were ready, Dad just told you that you were short of the minimum.

"What if I do it with somebody?" I countered. "What if I get Chris to come with me? We can split the driving."

"I don't know," my dad said. "I'll have to think about it. Both of you guys are young for a drive like that."

I needed a different approach. I eyed the stack of college application materials on the table to the side of the television. It'd been three and a half months since I'd cast my lot with fourteen different admissions offices. Half a dozen parent-son weekends had been spent that winter driving up and down the East Coast, visiting schools and ticking their names off my long list of potential choices. Dad and I had made it as far west as the Pennsylvania-Ohio border; Mom and I cut a sweeping path north, across Vermont and New Hampshire to Maine and then back south through Massachusetts and Connecticut. By March my parents' reserves of vacation days were pretty much exhausted, as was their patience for long-haul drives. Of the fourteen schools on my list, only a few were left that we hadn't visited. To their credit, my parents wanted me to see every college firsthand, to be able to meet with students and attend a class or two. Some of these schools were just too far-flung from New York for us to visit, though, and for these it was understood that I'd have to make do with secondhand reports from classmates and the application packets' glossy photos.

"Dad," I said, "this is the only way Chris and I will get to visit Duke." I saw Mom perk up on the sofa.

"Chris applied to Duke, too?" my dad asked me.

"Yeah. I think it's one of his top choices, too."

Dad considered this new justification for the trip. He looked to Mom, who shrugged her shoulders, signaling neutrality, or at least lack of opposition to the proposition. I could feel the momentum shifting in my favor.

Finally he spoke. "I don't want you guys driving through the night," he said sternly. "I don't care if you have to spend money on a hotel, you're going to take two days to do this trip."

I was on the phone with Chris a moment later. I broke down the details as Robby had explained them to me: we'd have to buy our own airfare down to Florida; Nokes would cover our hotel room our first night in Fort Lauderdale, along with gas on the drive up. Mindful of the tipping point in McGough family negotiations minutes before, I counseled Chris on how to proceed: "Tell them Duke's my first choice, too. Tell them I can't go if you can't go. Tell them we won't drive through the night." Chris wanted to know how much it'd cost to fly to Florida. Neither of us had ever bought an airline ticket before; I guessed about a hundred bucks apiece. We knew that Duke was in Durham, North Carolina, and that North Carolina was about halfway between Florida and New York. Chris consulted a world atlas and reported that, as if by destiny, Durham looked to be almost exactly halfway between Fort Lauderdale and New York. As prospective students, we knew it wouldn't be hard to find somebody on campus to crash with. If we were adding up the numbers right—mindful of our past miscalculations, we double-checked our math—we'd have about two hundred dollars to split at the end of the trip. Maybe even two-fifty. Not Network numbers, but not an insignificant sum, either.

Chris called me back a few minutes later: he'd convinced his parents as well.

We would have our vacation—the vacation we'd planned on putting all our Network profits toward, back when that investment seemed so promising—after all.

I called Robby the day before Chris and I left New York.

"We're flying in on the SkyBus," I told him proudly.

"What the hell is a SkyBus?" Robby evidently hadn't heard of SkyBus Airlines.

"It's this new airline I found out about: thirty-nine bucks one-way, LaGuardia to Fort Lauderdale."

"Jesus! Thirty-nine bucks? Do they have seats on the plane? Or are you flying in with farm animals?"

I was slightly stung that Rob didn't share my pride at my own thriftiness. "No assigned seats. No luggage allowed. No peanuts. But it's a good deal, right? The cheapest way to go."

"Yeah, sure sounds like it," he laughed. "Well, give me a call when you guys land. The plane does have landing gear, doesn't it? I'll send somebody to pick you up at the airport."

The Yankees' last spring training game was scheduled for that Thursday morning. The way Chris and I planned it, we'd take Wednesday, Thursday, and Friday off from school—visiting colleges out of state, we explained in advance to Regis's dean of discipline—and fly to Fort Lauderdale as early as possible Wednesday morning. We'd have all day to hang out at the beach or the ballpark, and Wednesday night at the Yankees' hotel. Thursday at dawn we'd go back to the ballpark to pick up Nokes's car and get on the road bright and early. Durham, North Carolina, by 8:00 P.M. Parties at Duke—college parties!—Thursday night, and a leisurely drive Friday the rest of the way back to New York. I wanted to be in uniform for the game at Shea Saturday afternoon.

Chris and I disembarked the SkyBus—there had been landing gear, but few frills—and were met at the airport gate by Shawn, a kid a year or two older than us. Shawn wore a Yankees T-shirt and cap, and introduced himself as one of the team's spring training bat boys.

"I work in the clubhouse for the Fort Lauderdale Yankees, too," he explained as we walked to his car. "They're single-A," the lowest level of the minor leagues, "and their season starts right after spring training ends."

"Yeah?" I asked. "What's that like?"

"Oh, it's cool," Shawn said as he slid behind the wheel. "Rookie ball. Most of these guys come here straight from high school. Me, I'm taking classes at the community college. I'm older than most of the players. Even last year, I was already older than most of 'em. But they're cool guys. We hang out." He eased the car out of the parking lot. Chris and I had our heads nearly out the windows, checking out the palm trees and trying to catch sight of the ocean.

"So," Shawn asked earnestly, "you guys really work in The Show?"

I didn't understand at first; I hadn't imagined that people in the minors actually referred to the major leagues that way. I'd thought it was just a line from *Bull Durham*.

"Matt does," Chris answered from the backseat.

"Wow," Shawn marveled. "That's awesome."

"Yeah," I said. "It's fun."

"I went up to New York a couple years ago. Right at the end of spring training, with my brother. Nick let us bat boy a couple games at the Stadium. Not Opening Day, but still. It was awesome. Stayed in a hotel right near Times Square. I'd love to move up there, but I don't know; New York's a crazy town."

I nodded.

Shawn steered the car through a gate in the chain-link fence surrounding Fort Lauderdale Stadium. A security guard waved him into the players' lot. The lot was full of luxury cars, which I scanned, without luck, for Nokes's Dodge Viper.

I pulled my knapsack from the trunk of the car. I didn't own a suitcase yet, and I'd packed what I needed for the trip in the same beat-up book bag I used for school.

The grounds of Fort Lauderdale Stadium were as impressively sprawling as Yankee Stadium is vertically imposing. The Stadium was only a story or two high and, unlike its counterpart in the Bronx, it was not hemmed in on all sides by buildings, parking garages, elevated subway tracks, and the Major Deegan. The Bronx County Courthouse did not loom large beyond this right-field wall. In fact, nothing at all loomed beyond the right-field wall. Dozens of lush baseball diamonds radiated out from the Stadium. A few ballfields over, I saw a few guys in Yankees uniforms running sprints in the outfield. A dozen others performed fielding drills in the infield, bounding off the mound and circling behind first base to back up a coach's throw from second base. Sprinklers threw mist into the air over countless other diamonds. The whole scene was bathed in bright sunlight. I could smell salty air coming off the ocean some distance away.

"This way," Shawn directed us to the clubhouse, leading the way not through a network of underground tunnels but around the back of a freestanding cinder-block building. "So who's your favorite ballplayer?" he asked me as we reached the door.

"Mattingly," I answered without hesitation.

"Definitely," he agreed. "Best with the buck."

"That's right," I said. "No doubt."

"Best with the buck," Chris repeated, laughing at our clubhouse lingo.

Shawn swung the clubhouse door open and held it for us as Chris and I walked through, reporting for spring training.

The spring training clubhouse was comparable to the one at the Stadium in size only. The room was cool and damp and seemed purely functional, with none of the amenities the players (and clubhouse staff) enjoyed in the Bronx. No big-screen television in sight. No leather couches. No blown-up photos of pin-striped Hall of Famers, immortalized in moments of glory, staring down from the walls. No wall-long wire rack sagging with the weight of a convenience store's selection of snacks. Through the open door of the manager's office I could see unadorned concrete walls painted battleship gray and Yankees blue, and a desk bare except for a beat-up rotary telephone. The trainers' room was even plainer than the manager's office: two rub tables against the wall and a half dozen steamer trunks that doubled as a counter for various salves, bandages, and medications. It was a clubhouse fit for minor leaguers, and appropriately so: with the exception of February and March, that's exactly what it was. The clubhouse was no more than a way station, hopefully to AA or AAA—the higher levels of minor league ball—and eventually, with any luck, on to the majors. And if not up to those higher levels, then out of baseball. Going down from the Class A Fort Lauderdale Yankees meant going home and finding a new profession; there's no such thing as Class B professional baseball. The clubhouse was not much more than a place for getting in and out of uniform. Nobody made himself at home there.

The relatively spare appearance of the spring training clubhouse belied the sheer number of players that the room accommodated. The amount of space given over to one locker in the Bronx was split between two in Fort Lauderdale, and even as late as this last day of spring training, a Yankees uniform hung in every one of them. Though the official roster had been scaled down by then to thirty-one names—close to the twenty-five-man Opening Day limit—this seemed hard to believe given the number of crowded lockers in front of us. Easily sixty pin-striped jerseys were arrayed around the room; many of them carried preposterous numbers, numbers better suited to a wide receiver or nose tackle than a baseball player. Few players had ever taken the field at Yankee Stadium wearing numbers like 77 or 81. The name of each locker's occupant was written by Nick—I recognized his big block-lettered penmanship—on a strip of white athletic tape affixed to the locker's crossbeam. I knew most but not all the names. Alongside those of players who were guaranteed a place on the Opening Day roster, I recognized names of veterans who, rehabbing injuries, had been designated for extended spring training. Other lockers were inhabited by nonroster invitees, more than a dozen of whom were still fighting on that last day of spring training for the final spot on the Yankees bench. The balance of the lockers held the uniforms and equipment of a handful of rookie minor leaguers, nominal participants in spring training who remained around only because the team had decided they would begin the season with the Fort Lauderdale Yankees. These were the players assigned the high numbers.

At a glance, I understood what Rob had once mentioned in passing the summer before: for him and Nick, February and March were the most demanding months of the year, full of work and nothing else. Exhausting days, fifteen or sixteen hours long, seven days a week, for two full months. For the guys working in the clubhouse, spring training was even busier than Old Timers' Day. Spring training meant twice as many ballplayers to outfit. Twice as many pairs of shoes to shine, uniforms to wash, equipment bags to pack. Twice as many guys asking favors and hassling you for gear.

Of all the players reporting for spring training, the rookies, I'd understood, were the toughest to deal with. Few had ever been treated as major leaguers before, and only one in a hundred acted as if he were there to stay. Before reporting to the big league camp, they'd known nothing but the hand-me-down uniforms and equipment major league teams supplied to their minor league affiliates. There was no limit, in quantity or quality, to what they demanded of Nick and Rob. They wanted—no, needed—everything they saw emerge from Nick's storeroom: sneakers, windbreakers, wristbands. One of every T-shirt stocked by the team, two pairs of Yankees athletic shorts, three or more baseball caps. Even heavyweight sweatshirts, despite the fact that they were playing in Florida. They helped themselves nightly to six-packs of Budweiser from the fridge in the players' lounge, which they squirreled out of the clubhouse in brown paper bags.

Listening to Nick complain, I felt embarrassed not only for them but also for myself, remembering with some mortification my own rookie behavior on Commemorative Pin Day the May before. It was the first giveaway day held at the Stadium since I'd been hired, and as was the case every promotional day, a few cartons of the giveaway item had been delivered to the clubhouse during the game. As soon as I saw them, I rushed to grab a handful of boxes. Each box held a hundred or so tin pins. I stowed them under the bench in my locker. Greedy, grabby, anxious, I wanted dozens, mostly because every other fan in attendance only got one each. I wanted them because they were there, and scarce, and free. One worthless pin wasn't nearly enough for me as a rookie.

I'd been looking forward to bringing Chris around to meet Nick and Rob for a long time. It hadn't happened in the Bronx. Chris, of course, had heard a great deal about them over the previous year, not to mention while we ran the Network gauntlet together. I knew with near certainty that, to Nick and Rob, the introduction would carry little meaning. And maybe to Chris as well. To me, though, these were the people who best represented the two worlds by which I'd come to define myself, and the pending introduction held great import: my best friend and my Yankees mentors. I was eager but apprehensive. What if it didn't go well? What if Chris couldn't play it cool? What if he did or said something that embarrassed me in front of the guys? What if Nick failed to live up to the implausible but true stories I'd been telling Chris about him since my first day on the job? What if Nick and Rob ignored me in front of my best friend? I wasn't half as concerned about introducing Chris to the ballplayers as I was about him meeting the clubhouse guys. I did my best to keep my fears concealed.

I needn't have worried; Nick's greeting was nothing less than fully characteristic. He saw Chris and me follow Shawn through the door and greeted the three of us from across the room with a gesture that was half wave, half karate chop. He took the wet cigar stub from his mouth and loudly harrumphed to get Robby's attention.

"Hey!" Rob called out from the other side of the clubhouse. "Look who's here!"

I walked up to Nick and spread my arms wide like I was about to give him a hug. As I leaned in, Nick cocked his arm across his chest, as if to strike me with the back of his hand. I don't doubt he would have if I'd actually tried to embrace him. I flinched and twisted out of the way, grinning.

"That's right," Nick spat at me, his rough voice filling every corner of the clubhouse. "I'll break you in half. When are you going back to New York, you lazy fuck?"

"Tomorrow, I think," I told him.

"Not soon enough," Nick immediately deadpanned. He raised his pointer finger and pressed it into the center of my chest. "Let's get one thing straight: you are here to work. There will be no time on the beach. There will be no piña coladas, no seafood dinner. You are not here on spring break."

"Nick," I interrupted. "This is my friend Chris."

Chris warily extended his arm for a handshake. Nick stuck his cigar back in the corner of his mouth and grasped Chris's hand. He looked him up and down, then gestured in my direction. "Are you as dumb and lazy as your friend here?" Nick asked him.

A long second passed while Chris considered whether he was being asked a trick question. Chris turned toward me and shrugged his shoulders apologetically. "No?" he finally ventured. I tried to signal him that it was cool, that I thought he'd answered acceptably. I made a mental note to explain later that Nick's invective was not only normal but might actually suggest a growing endearment. With Nick, the more he showered you with verbal abuse, the less you doubted his genuine feelings. If he didn't like me, he'd have ignored me; to those he was partial to, Nick could be ruthless with his affection. With few exceptions, even great stature within the Yankees organization was insufficient to protect you from Nick's ad hominem attacks. The only people I never saw him lay into were Steinbrenner, Showalter, and Mattingly; these three he addressed always and only as Sir. Everyone else was fair game. I saw him level both barrels and unload on ballplayers and front office executives in front of a full clubhouse audience, just the same as he would on me or Robby or the Mule. Nick would disregard you for days at a time and then erupt in your direction, knocking you over with a pitch-perfect torrent of insults. In the Yankees clubhouse or during his stint in the navy, he had collected an apparently bottomless reserve of off-color insults to fit most any fault or transgression. As long as you understood that Nick's very personal slurs weren't meant to be taken personally, his routine was fall-over funny. It was somewhat less hilarious when he laid into you rather than somebody else, but even then it was hard sometimes not to laugh. He could have enjoyed a second career emceeing Friars Club roasts.

That day, in front of Chris, I felt lucky that Nick had insulted only my intelligence and work ethic, and not any alleged physical or moral shortcomings, as he'd done before. As in: "And bring back my change, you gangly son-of-a-bitch thief."

"Good," Nick responded to Chris's tentative answer. "Then you should know enough to get the fuck out of here before I put you to work, too." He turned and walked across the room. "And take your no-good friend with you," he shouted to Chris over his shoulder, then disappeared into a stockroom.

Chris exhaled deeply and let out a nervous laugh. "Jesus Christ! Is he always like that?"

I answered truthfully. "Just when he's in a good mood."

"He seems real happy to see you," Robby teased me. "That is, for a dumb, lazy fuck." Chris laughed again.

"Yeah, I really missed him too over the winter," I postured, masking my feelings with the sarcasm his vitriol demanded that I show in turn. I'd never been so proud of myself for having been publicly derided as a slothful half-wit.

"Listen," Robby said. "He wasn't kidding you just then. Unless you guys want to get stuck here at the stadium working until midnight, you should jet right now. There's two split-squad road games that the whole team just left for, and this place is going to go to hell when the buses get back this afternoon. I've got to stick around the ballpark to help pack up for New York, but you guys should get out of here. There'll be enough work for you to do once we get back to the Bronx."

I nodded.

Rob dug into his pocket and pulled out a set of keys. "Take my rental car," he said.

I shouldn't have been so surprised by Robby's largesse. I had already learned that there were two ways of doing things: the normal every-man-for-himself way, and the Rob Cucuzza way. Robby was the first guy I'd ever met who not only always handled his own affairs in first-class fashion but also went out of his way to make sure any friend close by was taken care of just as well. He never expected—nor, probably, would have tolerated— expressions of gratitude or promises of I'll-get-you-back. Rob left no man behind. Or, rather: he left no broke, car-less seventeen-year-olds behind. Not on their first trip to Florida.

"Where should we go?" I asked him.

"I'd drive down to the Strip," he told me. "There's tons of action over there. Half the people in Lauderdale right now are college kids in town for spring break. Take the car and go to the beach. We can meet up at the hotel later tonight." He held out the car keys. "It's the red convertible out in the players' lot," he said, almost as an afterthought.

Classic Cucuzza. Chris and I both grinned stupidly. "Nice," we said in unison.

We stepped out of the clubhouse into bright Florida sunshine. The handful of clouds that our SkyBus had descended through had burned off completely. We walked up and down two long rows of gleaming cars and found our red convertible at the far side of the lot. Robby had left the top down for us.

Matt Nokes himself would have been impressed with the affection and attention Chris and I showed our new ride: circling it; admiring its paint job, its tires, its black leather interior; running our hands across its hood, trunk, and down the length of its flawless frame. Chris took a three-step running start and swung both his feet parallel to the ground, vaulting over the car's door into the driver's seat *Dukes of Hazzard*–style.

"Yo, check it out!" he said, both arms aloft, as if soliciting applause from passersby. "Yo, take a picture!"

We finished the roll of film, then shot it out odds and evens. Chris took two out of three and won the right to drive first. Radio privileges fell to me, riding shotgun.

Chris eased the convertible out of the lot onto a long boulevard lined on both sides by shopping centers and fast-food franchises. I switched on a Beastie Boys mix-tape as loud as the radio could go. Robby had left a hotel-issue map of Fort Lauderdale in the glove compartment. I held the map on my lap, below the sight line of passing pedestrians, and called out directions over the music. "I think we want A1A," I shouted as we pulled into traffic.

"What?"

"A1A," I repeated louder, pointing to the thin line on the map that ran north and south the full length of Fort Lauderdale. "The road parallel to the beach. A-1-A!"

"Chill!" he said. "I heard you the first time." Chris grinned.

"If you're gonna flip out every time I need directions between here and New York, you might not even make it to Duke."

"Left, left!" I shouted. We were quickly closing on an over-sized highway sign—⇐ROUTE A1A⇐—that was now almost directly over our heads. "Make this next left! You've got to get in the left lane!"

Chris calmly checked the rearview mirror for room to merge left into traffic. Cars flew by us on the driver's side at forty miles per hour. Over and over, Chris inched the car forward and left before being forced to slam on the brakes. The guy stuck behind us leaned on his horn a few times, then started throwing aggravated hand gestures in our direction.

"Go, go, go," I hollered, calling out each seam that momentarily opened in the flow of traffic. The turnoff to A1A was almost even with our front bumper and still one lane over. The chorus of car horns swelled behind us and threatened to drown out "No Sleep Till Brooklyn." I was about to demand that Chris surrender the driver's seat when he swung the wheel hard left and gunned the engine. The force of our acceleration and the sudden burst of wind coming over the windshield lifted the sunglasses off my face and deposited them on the backseat. Tires screeching, wisps of smoke rising from the pavement in our wake, we crossed two lanes in a half second and shot out onto the coastal road.

We hadn't even traveled a few hundred feet of the Strip before it became clear that Robby had actually understated the degree to which, that last week of March, Fort Lauderdale was given over to Spring Break '92. I'd attended sold-out Division I football games and seen fewer college kids than Chris and I could see from our vantage point at the base of A1A. Our vantage point, that is, from the front seat of Robby's late-model red convertible sports car.

Just ahead of us in the Strip's median was a street sign that declared NO CRUISING in oversized letters. Below that admonition, in slightly smaller type: CARS PASSING ANY SINGLE POINT ON A-1-A THREE TIMES IN ONE HOUR SUBJECT TO $250 FINE. Identical signs were positioned prominently every few hundred feet up the road as far as we could see.

Over the next four or five hours, we took the convertible on forty or fifty victory laps the full length of the Strip; I have no idea how we avoided police detection. Nor do I have any memory of what Chris and I could possibly have discussed over the course of such an extended tour; I can say with some certainty that there was a great deal of self-satisfied grinning. The car radio was not once lowered below its maximum volume; there was not one beachside bar that we didn't idle outside of at least twice.

Close to sundown the beaches began to empty. We hit a red light mid-Strip and found ourselves watching through our windshield a parade as stirring as any I'd ever seen before. Hordes of spring breakers flush with sun and booze stumbled past us, presumably headed back to their hotel rooms to prepare for the big night ahead.

I sat behind the wheel and, when the feeling struck me, revved the engine; Chris rode shotgun, sunglasses lowered to the tip of his nose, mouthing lyrics off the radio. The light had just turned green above us when I felt Chris's arm across my chest.

"Hold up, hold up," he said, pointing at two girls in swimsuits who had stepped out into the crosswalk a few feet in front of the convertible. The car in the lane next to us accelerated, and the girls pivoted back toward the curb. For a split second, as they turned, I made eye contact with one of them, a strawberry blonde.

Everything turned slo-mo.

It had just dawned on me that a beautiful college girl was looking right at me. Or maybe just at my nice car. Not that it mattered much: either way, it was enough to set my heart racing. For a long moment, I'm sure my eyes broadcast nothing but panic. She was beautiful.

I thought her face reflected similar anxieties. In hindsight, it seems more likely that it had just dawned on her that she'd stepped out into moving traffic. She was probably concerned that I was about run her over.

We shared a deer-in-the-headlights moment together.

"Whoa," I exhaled.

"Damn," Chris said. "We should offer them a ride."

The girls scampered back onto the sidewalk.

Back in the world of our all-boys Manhattan high school, cruising around in a car trying to pick up college girls was about as familiar a pastime as badminton or bull riding. Not that we didn't have an idea how it was all supposed to go down. But between the everyday lack of wheels and New York's subway culture, it wasn't something we'd ever had an opportunity to practice. Nor did I know anyone at Regis who hung out with girls much older than themselves; New York's high school girls, not its boys, were extended invitations to parties at NYU or Fordham or Columbia. Give us some Dominican Academy or Sacred Heart girls at the Central Park Sheep Meadow or at a table adjacent to ours at Cosmo's Pizzeria, and we'd have made introductions just fine. But this was altogether new territory.

I pulled the car up a few feet and stopped in the crosswalk.

"Hey, ladies, where you headed?" Chris hollered from the seat next to me. The car stuck behind us honked its horn. Without turning around, I threw my hand up above my head, index finger extended, signaling that we'd just be a few seconds. Miraculously, the honking stopped. The girls looked at us, and then at each other.

Chris turned down the radio and repeated his question.

"Our hotel, I guess," the blonde's friend—taller, and with long brown hair—answered.

"You want a lift?"

The girls exchanged shrugs and smiles. "Sure, why not?" the blonde said.

"Hop in, hop in," I offered, so smoothly I surprised myself. The girls took a step toward the car. "In the back," I blurted, undoing the confidence boost I'd just given myself. The convertible held only four, and Chris and I were already sitting up front; the sole alternative seating arrangement would have had our new friends sitting on our laps. I gripped the steering wheel harder, to keep myself from slapping my own forehead.

The girls let it pass and clambered over the side of the car into the backseat.

"Which way?" I asked.

"Straight ahead," the blonde answered. "We're at the Holiday Inn. All the way at the end of the beach."

I put the car in gear and turned the radio back up.

Chris turned around in his seat to face the girls. "You guys from Fort Lauderdale?" he asked.

"No, we're just here on spring break," the brunette answered. "We go to school in Iowa."

"Wow," Chris said. "What school?"

"Iowa State."

"Cool," he replied. Chris and I exchanged a look. Iowa State? What the hell were we supposed to say to that? Then a quick, almost imperceptible nod between us: don't worry, I've got your back. I'll follow your lead.

The strawberry blonde leaned forward in her seat. "What about you guys?"

"Yeah," Chris answered casually. "We're down here on spring break, too."

"Where are you in school?"

Chris paused a beat and glanced over at me.

"Michigan State," I said.

"Cool," the brunette approved. "What year are you?"

"Sophomores," I said.

"We're seniors."

Wow. Seniors. They were probably only twenty-one years old, but still: the word seemed to carry enough weight to negate whatever street smarts edge we might have hoped New York, New York, would give us over Ames, Iowa. I pictured David Lee Roth's music video for "California Girls," burned into my memory since early adolescence. The video still served as a crude shaper of my expectations regarding regional differences among American women. I almost started humming the song aloud, trying to remember the relevant lyrics. *Midwest farmers' daughters . . . Make you feel all right?*

We rode a few blocks in silence. Silence, that is, conversationally: the Beastie Boys tape still blared at full volume. The sun had begun to set but continued to bathe the convertible in warm light.

Chris broke the lull in the conversation. "I love spring break," he announced.

"Totally," the blonde said.

"So what are you guys up to tonight?" I asked.

"I don't know," she answered. "Probably get some dinner now, maybe check out a bar later on."

"Oh yeah?" Chris said. "You know some good bars?"

"Yeah, one or two," she said.

"Why don't we get some dinner together, and then check one out after?"

The girls conferred for a second behind us. "Yeah, sure," the brunette said. "Can we just drop our stuff off at the hotel and change real quick?"

"Oh, yeah, definitely," I said.

"No problem," Chris confirmed.

A traffic light a good distance in front of us turned green to yellow. I gunned the engine and accelerated through it. The blonde threw her head back and smiled, face to the sun. Her friend raised her arms into the breeze coming over the wind- shield.

The brunette smiled and shouted into the wind. "This is a nice car," she said.

"Isn't it?" I said. Then, completely inexplicably: "It's my uncle's."

"It's your uncle's car?" she said.

"Yeah."

A long pause.

"But it's a rental car," she said. In unison, both Chris's jaw and mine dropped nearly to the dashboard.

"What?" I said. My face flushed. "What do you mean?"

"I mean it's a rental car," she said. "It's got rental car plates."

I remembered something I'd seen on the news a few months before: a German tourist had been robbed and shot in Miami, and the police suspected he'd been targeted because he was driving a car whose license plate started with the letter Z— as did all Florida rental cars. After the crime, there'd been some talk of changing that convention, to make tourists less easily iden- tifiable. The talk evidently hadn't amounted to much legislatively.

Chris did his best to cover: "It's his uncle's rental car."

I nodded agreement.

"Oh," the brunette said, clearly unconvinced. We neared the end of the beach.

"There's the Holiday Inn," the blonde said, pointing across the street. I swung the convertible into the driveway and pulled up under the canopy in front of the lobby.

The girls hopped out and grabbed their towels. "We'll be down in like two minutes," the blonde told us.

"Cool," we answered together.

The girls disappeared into the hotel lobby.

"Aw, man," Chris moaned, "we're totally busted."

I lowered my head to the steering wheel. "I know."

"What do we do now?" Chris asked.

"I don't know."

"We better think fast. The girls'll be down in a minute."

I looked right, over my shoulder, into the empty lobby. I had a premonition of the four of us sitting in silence around a restaurant table. This was followed by an even more distressing vision of Chris and I getting carded at a bar and then being unceremoniously thrown out of the place in front of our new girlfriends. At least Christ had a crappy fake ID; I was defenseless against even a nominally inquisitive bouncer or bartender.

I threw the car into gear. "We're out of here," I announced.

"We're just gonna jet?"

"You want to stick around and talk about what classes you're taking at Michigan State?" I asked him. We peeled out of the hotel parking lot and back onto the Strip. Not until the Holiday Inn fully receded in the rearview mirror did either of us open our mouths.

"Jesus," Chris said, doubled over laughing. "That was horrible."

"Yeah, really bad," I said, grinning sheepishly. "Sorry about that. My bad."

"What the hell were you talking about?"

"I don't know. I thought it'd sound good at the time."

"Your uncle?" he asked incredulously. Chris was laughing so hard he had to take his sunglasses off to wipe the tears away from his eyes.

"I know," I said, now laughing harder myself. "My bad, man."

"Why didn't you tell them we got it from the Yankees?"

I shrugged, knowing that what I was about to say would just inspire more hysterics. "I don't know," I said. "I didn't think they'd believe me."

We took one more lap down the Strip to savor the day's last sunrays.

"It's almost seven-thirty," I said, checking my watch. "You hungry?"

"Starving."

"Let's eat," I said. "We should go somewhere real nice."

We turned off A1A, heading away from the beach, and soon saw a T.G.I. Friday's looming up ahead of us.

Perfect; just what we had in mind.

We feasted, and after settling the tab, Chris waved our waitress over.

"Can you recommend someplace cool around here," he asked her, "where we could go for some drinks?"

"Where *you guys* could go for drinks?" she said.

"Yeah," Chris said. "Maybe somewhere with good music? Like a bar?"

"You mean somewhere they won't ask you for ID?" she asked us, smiling coyly.

Chris smirked back at her. "Exactly," he said.

She scrawled a crude map and the name of a place on a napkin and wished us luck.

We followed her directions to a small roadside strip mall not far from the restaurant. Neon beer logos glowed from a storefront at the corner of the L-shaped shopping center. To the bar's left side was a former laundromat, its abandonment announced by its soaped-up windows. To its right was a tanning salon. A behemoth in cutoff jeans and sleeveless T-shirt sat on a stool outside the bar's front door.

"Shit," I said. "Looks like there's a bouncer."

"I'll handle it," Chris said. "I talk my way into parties in New York all the time."

"Yeah, but we're not in New York anymore. And I don't have any ID."

"Man, just park the car," Chris said, hopping out of the convertible. "Watch me work."

By the time I'd parked and walked to the door, the bouncer had Chris's ID out and was giving it the once-over, tilting it back and forth in the poor light cast by the neon signs in the window.

"Go ahead," the bouncer told Chris. "ID," he said to me.

Chris spoke up on my behalf: "He forgot his wallet back at the hotel."

I nodded. The bouncer looked me up and down and pronounced judgment: no ID, no entry.

"He's twenty-one," Chris insisted. "He just doesn't have ID."

"Can't come in."

"Aw, come on, man," Chris said. "We're down here from New York for one night."

"Can't help you."

"We heard about this place in New York. We drove all the way out here to check it out."

"I can't let you guys in without ID."

I watched the conversation like a tennis fan sitting at center court, my head pivoting side to side, following the exchange of volleys. Left as Chris lofted another argument at the bouncer, right as the bouncer artlessly smacked it down. Left again as Chris improbably returned the ball to his court, trying to sneak one past him.

The dialogue reached another impasse, this one apparently final.

"Can't you just help us out?" Chris said, his voice by this time tinged with a bit of desperation.

"Nope," the bouncer said.

I started back toward the car.

I heard Chris say something from over my shoulder about the Yankees.

"*He* works for the Yankees?" the bouncer asked him, pointing at me.

"Yeah," Chris said.

"You work for the Yankees?" the bouncer now asked me.

"Yeah," I said.

He turned back to Chris. My best friend and the bar bouncer were discussing me, in front of me, as if I were a deaf-mute.

"What does he do for the Yankees?" he asked Chris.

The truthful answer posed something of a problem given what we were ultimately trying to convince him of.

"He's an assistant general manager," Chris told him after a moment's hesitation.

"Does he have Yankees ID?"

Chris gave me a look that said I'd better. I pulled out the wallet I'd ostensibly left at the hotel and presented my Yankees identification, which thankfully listed neither job title nor birth date.

"You should have told me that before," the bouncer said, holding the door open for us.

The bar was nearly empty and the deejay wasn't on par with what Chris had become accustomed to in his escapades at the Limelight or Palladium back in New York.

"This place is lame," Chris said as we polished off our first and only beers. "Let's get out of here."

We woke the next morning at six, well rested after an otherwise uneventful night of cable TV, room-service pizza, and minibar soft drinks; we never gave a thought to touching any of the hard stuff.

It was still dark outside when we met Rob to carpool over to the stadium. None of the players had arrived when we got there—we beat everybody to the ballpark but Nick and Showalter—so Chris and I sipped coffee and kept vigil in the folding chairs in front of Nokes's locker.

The players started filing in, sleepily, around 7:30. Chris and I were on our second cups of coffee by the time Nokes stuck his head through the doorway. "Come on," he shouted to us, beckoning us out to the parking lot. "I'll show you guys the car."

Between the caffeine, the clear blue sky lit by the sun rising over the horizon, and our high expectations for the car—bring on the Viper!—we were primed to get on the road. Nokes walked us down a long row of cars, past Robby's convertible and a half dozen other sports cars, and depressed a button on the key chain he'd pulled from his pocket. A car alarm chirped from somewhere behind an enormous sport-utility vehicle, parked directly in front of us, that blocked everything in our view.

I peered around the side of the truck. Chain-link fence.

Nokes called me over to where he was standing. "Okay, fellas, first things first. You control the alarm system from here," he said, holding the key chain out to us in the palm of his oversized hand. "It's a brand-new model—1993 Chevy Suburban—so it's got the latest everything: alarm, CD changer, the whole nine."

So, no Dodge Viper. That's cool, I told myself. I had no idea what a Chevy Suburban looks like, but odds are it's still a nice ride. Maybe even another convertible, I figured. "So wait, where's the car?" I asked.

"Right here," Nokes said.

"Where?"

Nokes rapped his knuckles against the hood of the mammoth SUV. My eyes went to the chrome Chevrolet nameplate on the rear of the truck, which definitively dashed our expectations of racing up the East Coast in a high-speed, flashy ride.

"This is it?" I asked, trying to hide my disappointment.

"Yup," Nokes answered. He was much too focused on completing our two-minute crash course in Chevy Suburban operation and getting back inside the clubhouse to even take note of our crestfallen eyes and forced smiles. "This button turns on and off the car alarm," he said, "and you use this one to open the trunk. Which you guys shouldn't do, or it'll take you all day to fit whatever falls out back into the car."

The Suburban's back and side windows had appeared at first to be fully opaque. I now realized that this was an optical illusion; the truck's windows were in fact only slightly tinted. What I had initially seen as empty space I now could see was actually the opposite: every inch of the truck's enormous cargo hold was so completely packed with crap that all light was blocked out. The back of the Suburban probably ran near ten feet deep, seven feet across, and four feet high, and it was clear that Nokes hadn't been kidding about not opening the trunk. Solely on the side of the car on which I was standing, I could make out a pair of suitcases, half a dozen stacked cardboard boxes, a set of golf clubs, and a television. Even more prominently positioned, pressed flush against the windows, was an array of children's toys—most still in their original packaging—sufficient to have contented an elementary school full of eight-year-olds. Opening a channel from the tightly packed payload would have loosed a torrent of Nokes family possessions.

I remembered the story of a bat boy a few years earlier who, on a similar drive up from spring training, hadn't even made it out of Florida before flipping the player's car. The car, which had been packed as tightly as Nokes's, was totaled in the accident; both the bat boy and the cargo had escaped injury, somewhat miraculously. The bat boy, stranded with the lion's share of the ballplayer's personal possessions, ultimately found his way to a ticket counter in Jacksonville International Airport and bought a ticket back to New York. "How many bags are you checking?" the ticket agent asked him. "Thirty-three," he answered. The player grudgingly reimbursed him nearly two thousand dollars in overweight baggage fees.

Nokes counted off last-minute instructions on the fingers of his left hand. "Registration and insurance card are in the glove," he said, his eyes searching the sky for the details he wanted to remember. "Here's my wife's phone number, if you need to get in touch with her, just in case. I'm gonna give you a couple gas station charge cards that you guys should use to fill up along the way. When you get to the Stadium, just park the car in the players' lot and leave the keys with security." Nokes then pulled five hundred-dollar bills out of his wallet, handed them to me along with the charge cards, and shook both our hands.

"Drive safely," he told us.

"We will," I promised.

Chris and I clambered up into the cockpit—you had to step up to get into it, as the seats were easily four feet off the ground—and jammed our few possessions back behind the front seat. I succeeded in adjusting the driver's seat to account for the fact that I was half Nokes's size, but the rearview mirror was hopeless.

"Jesus Christ," I said. "You can't see anything back there. There's so much crap."

Chris stuck his head out the window on the passenger side to see if there was anything or anyone behind us.

"You're clear," he said. "Let's go."

The route we'd planned from Fort Lauderdale to Durham was direct and uncomplicated: I-95 north for nearly a thousand miles—through Florida, Georgia, and the Carolinas—and then, once we reached Duke's latitude, due west.

We made a surprisingly quick peace with the fact that we were driving not Nokes's Viper or another sports car but instead—not counting those trucks with eighteen wheels—far and away the largest passenger vehicle on the road. The commanding view of the highway afforded by the height of our perch and the bloated size of our vessel lent a sense of being at the helm of an ocean liner. Even the car's thunderous horn sounded vaguely nautical.

Maybe it wouldn't have been so fun, after all, to sit contorted in low-slung bucket seats, six inches off the ground, for a dozen hours straight. Maybe we were better off behind the wheel of the Suburban. Everything about Nokes's truck was oversized; we might as well have been barreling down the highway in a pair of jet-powered La-Z-Boy recliners. It was comfy, at least up front, and well suited for eating up road at a steady if not head-turning clip of seventy or so miles per hour.

Chris and I had settled on trading off driving time in two-hour shifts, and I was about halfway through my second turn behind the wheel when we saw the first road sign for Daytona Beach.

Daytona Beach was familiar to me and Chris as the location of MTV's spring break beach house. The name of the town alone was enough to provoke a Pavlovian reaction, at least among guys our age. An average seventeen-year-old boy's description of how The World's Most Kick-Ass Party might look and sound would correspond pretty closely to the images being broadcast from there. Waiting out a sleet storm on my parents' sofa earlier that month, watching MTV, the scene strained credulity.

Which of those televised images wouldn't we have dreamed of seeing in person? "Daytona Beach" signified sun and sand and marathon pool parties. Vast seas of beautiful bikini-clad girls, girls who so loved partying and dancing that they took no pause at the multiple TV cameras getting all up in their business. Surprise appearances by every band of the moment and every action movie star you'd ever dream of meeting. Nonstop and socially sanctioned immature behavior, each joke more sophomoric than the one before. All broadcast on national television back to your friends watching at home.

Daytona Beach? Spring Break '92? The words were nearly a rallying cry. We deliberated for about two seconds before deciding that this was a mandatory pit stop.

"It's not that far out of the way," Chris said, squinting at a small corner of our map of the entire eastern seaboard.

"It can't be that far," I said. "Anyway, it's just a detour. We'll just check it out for a minute. We've been making real good time this morning already."

"Yeah," Chris said. "We don't need to get to Duke that early anyway, right?"

"Nah," I shrugged. "But even if we hang out for a while, we'll probably still make it there for dinner."

"Or we can just eat somewhere on the road."

We passed a sign indicating that we'd entered the Daytona Beach city limits.

"Hey, turn up the radio," I said.

Chris turned the dial the opposite way.

"Louder, man," I said.

"Wait," he said, a look of gravity suddenly on his face. "If you tell some girl here this is your uncle's car, you're walking home."

As we entered downtown and approached the shore, we could sense the ocean in front of us. But not by the normal signals. The breeze off the water carried not the expected scent of salty ocean air but instead a surprisingly identifiable fragrance of Hawaiian Tropic tanning oil, pizza, and fries. In cars or on foot, all traffic was headed in the same direction, and we merged into a long line of vehicles—convertibles and jeeps, mostly—surging toward a swing-arm gate and guardhouse.

"Where do you think we should park?" I asked Chris.

"What's this line for?"

"Parking, right? Look at all these cars."

"Yeah, I guess."

We inched our way up to the gate. The guard manning it wasn't more than a couple years older than we were. He wore a brown rent-a-cop uniform shirt over shorts, a Smokey the Bear–style hat, and mirrored wraparound sunglasses.

"Afternoon, dudes," he addressed us through the open passenger window. "Your pass, please."

"A parking pass?" Chris asked.

"Parking's that way," he said, pointing back toward the end of the line.

"So what's in front of us?"

"Daytona Beach, dude."

"So where are all these cars headed?"

"To the beach."

"Yeah," Chris replied. "That's where we're trying to go, too."

The gatekeeper posed what was almost certainly a rhetorical question: "You guys from out of town?"

We nodded.

"Daytona Beach's for drivin'," he explained. "You heard of all the speed records set on this beach? The sand's packed down. It's like a one-lane highway."

We nodded again.

"You want to buy a pass to drive on the beach or what?"

We exchanged ten dollars for a piece of date-stamped cardboard. The gatekeeper lifted the guard-arm and waved us under. I steered the Suburban along the faint tracks left by the jeep that had entered ahead of us. We drove straight toward and almost to the water, then made a right to pull parallel with the shoreline.

I could see now that we were at the rear of a long caravan of show cars. But not exactly a caravan; what we'd joined was a *parade* of show cars. An audience of many thousand vacationing college students lay out on the beach, drinking, tanning, partying, watching tricked-out cars pass by.

From the cockpit of the Suburban, eight feet in the air, we had a pretty good view over the beach, but even with my sunglasses on, I had to lower the visor and squint into the high-noon light to see where the column of cars ended. On our left hand, a few dozen feet of sand separated us from the ocean. The shoreline ran ahead of us, perpendicular to the horizon, to a bungee jumpers' crane that effectively split our view out the windshield straight down the middle. Everything to the left of the crane was water; everything to its right was either beach towel or body. The thin spit of sand directly in front of us over which the jeep had passed was clear of beach towels, but not people. Thanks to our extended exchange at the guardhouse, a few hundred feet had opened between the Suburban and the jeep leading us. As if following a law of physics, a mass of well-tanned college kids had poured into the void and now stood milling about in the middle of the "road."

To absolutely no effect, I sounded the horn. Nothing happened. No one even turned around.

Since we'd passed the guardhouse, Chris had been flipping through the handful of CDs we'd brought down from New York and hadn't even noticed the impasse I'd reached behind the wheel. He selected an album—*The Chronic*—and slipped it into the Suburban's CD changer.

The Chronic was Dr. Dre's first solo album. It had been released just a few months before and had quickly gone platinum, introducing West Coast rap to the rest of the country. The whole album was run through with an aggressively heavy, slowed-down bass line, and its lyrics were boastful and dirty, just like the beat.

The CD took a few moments to load, and Chris turned up the radio just as the stereo registered the first track. Between Fort Lauderdale and Daytona Beach, we had yet to test the Suburban's system very intently. But from the second the bass kicked in, it was apparent that Nokes hadn't skimped on speakers.

There's a famous photo, by the street photographer Weegee, of a summer afternoon in Coney Island's prewar heyday. The shot takes in an astoundingly large crowd. Maybe a million people are packed together on the beach and boardwalk, with no space between them; even deep into the background, the crowd shows no sign of thinning. The only thing more remarkable than the sheer number of people in the frame is that *everyone* on the beach appears to be looking directly into the camera. It's unfathomable how Weegee might have pulled it off.

And yet when the first beats of "Nuthin' But a 'G' Thang" came over the car stereo, my first thought was of that photo. The very improbable juxtaposition of Matt Nokes's Chevy Suburban sound system and Dr. Dre's *The Chronic* turned so many heads so instantly that it made our tour in Robby's convertible seem like a spring training exercise for this, the World Series. Spring breakers whirled around en masse to see the source of the tremendous sound. From our height above the crowd we saw the effect ripple out along the beach; even people out of earshot turned, just to see what everyone else was looking at.

The cargo in the back didn't so much block the awe-inspiring bass emerging from the speakers as redirect it, first around the car and then out the sunroof and open windows. The sound waves rattled the truck's frame; I felt the steering wheel vibrate against my fingers in 4:4 time.

The crowd in the road before us parted like the Red Sea.

Sorority girls grabbed their sisters and pulled them to the side by their elbows. A knot of people surrounding a boom box stopped moving to their own music and started dancing to the beats emanating from the Suburban. Entire fraternities stood and started throwing drunken and aggressively primal gestures at each other, honing pecking orders in time with the music. A few people blanched, whether at the sheer force of the bass or the coarseness of the lyrics, I'm not sure. Others animatedly rapped along with each song.

We pushed forward at a few miles per hour along the suddenly empty thoroughfare.

As we moved down the beach, we noticed another phenomenon take shape: our rapport was stronger with the spring breakers twenty or more feet from the truck than with those inside that radius. Until we got real close, people hooted and raised cans of Budweiser in our general direction, dancing like a camera crew might be nearby. As we got closer, though, we could see facial expressions shift from rapture to curiosity. Like something didn't add up.

I remember one girl standing up ahead of the truck—pretty, animated, deeply tanned. The very image of Daytona Beach Spring Break, this girl belonged on MTV. I saw her when we were still some distance away and, driving so slowly, she was in my sight line for a full two or three minutes. Her face was so expressive, as we approached and then passed her, I felt I could follow her thoughts.

She was clearly feeling the Dre CD, utterly unfazed by some of the dirtiest lyrics ever set to music. She danced in place, by herself, her eyes closed, her face toward the sun, her arms raised to the song's chorus. Guys on the beach turned away from the truck to watch her.

As we pulled even with her, she opened her eyes and looked right into the car. She was unable to disguise her surprise at seeing not some all–Big Ten defensive tackle half the size of the truck or some guy with designer sunglasses and fat gold chains, but me and Chris instead. She didn't seem so much disappointed as confused. There was no hiding the fact that we were only seventeen, still closer in time to eighth grade than to college graduation. Or, given the West Coast gangsta rap we were broadcasting from the truck, she may have been surprised that we were white. Or maybe just that we were *so white*. Not meaning state of mind. Meaning literally. The morning before, we'd woken up in forty-degree New York weather. We were the least-tan people on the beach. We may have had the worst tans in metropolitan Daytona.

And then, as we kept moving forward at just a few miles per

hour, she watched the Suburban's ten feet of back windows pass her at eye level. Beats and lyrics still rattling the frame of the truck, she noticed the Suburban's cargo hold, packed full of children's toys. From just behind our heads, all the way to the hatchback door, the truck's windows framed Nokes's kids' toys as well as any Christmas shop's display. Bright yellow Tonka trucks. "Age 6 & Up" Milton Bradley board games. A pink girl's bicycle with training wheels. Two pairs of Fisher-Price My First Roller Skates, still in their boxes, particularly prominent, pressed flush against the glass.

In the sideview mirror, I watched her facial expression descend from mild confusion to complete incomprehension.

Our one concession to responsibility on the way out of town was forgoing the two-for-the-price-of-one bungee jump offer at the far end of the beach. Fueled by beef jerky, Cheez Whiz, and two 2-liter bottles of Mountain Dew charged to Nokes's gas card, we made it to the Duke campus shortly after midnight.

The weather in Durham the next morning was as beautiful as it had been in Florida, and almost as beautiful as the Duke campus itself. Duke seemed to have everything I could wish for in a college. The school had been among my top choices from the very beginning, probably for arbitrary reasons having to do with watching Christian Laettner and Grant Hill perennially lead Duke deep into the NCAA basketball tournament. Now it rocketed to the top of my list, probably for arbitrary reasons having to do with it being my first-ever glimpse of a college campus in the throes of spring fever. Chris and I walked through quadrangles framed by rough-hewn stone buildings, across lush lawns where athletic guys and pretty girls played Frisbee and read books on the grass. College life to the fullest. Everyone looked happy to be there.

We visited the library and Cameron Indoor Stadium. I bought a Duke basketball T-shirt in the school bookstore. After roaming the campus, we lay out on the college's central lawn soaking up the sun, plucking blades of grass and watching students walk to and from class.

"It'd be nice to go to school here," I said.

"So nice," Chris agreed.

Our drive up the East Coast from Durham was uneventful through Delaware, where we developed a technique behind the wheel to ensure our swift passage the rest of the way back to New York. In short, the technique involved keeping the Suburban's cruise control locked at eighty-five miles per hour and flashing our headlights the moment another vehicle appeared in our lane. For a hundred miles we bore down on cars traveling a mere twenty miles per hour over the speed limit, signaling them to move over as soon as they appeared on the horizon.

A few miles short of the exit for the Goethals Bridge to Staten Island, another car came into view up ahead of us. Chris gave it the high-beam strobe light treatment, but even as we came up on its back bumper, the car refused to budge.

"Out of the way!" Chris shouted, flashing the lights ever more furiously.

The driver eventually took the hint, sliding over a lane to let us by. After we passed him, he calmly moved back in behind us and flipped on the police lights concealed in his car's grill. Pulling over onto the shoulder of the turnpike, Chris pointed to the City's lights reflected in the foggy night sky up ahead of us; we were that close to home. We watched out of our sideview mirrors as the trooper, hand on his sidearm, approached Chris's window.

"Son," the trooper said to Chris when he reached the Suburban, "you were coming up on my ass like a heat-seeking missile."

"I'm sorry?" Chris said. I couldn't tell if he was expressing regret or seeking clarification, but the trooper took it as an apology.

"You should be, driving like that, ninety-one miles per hour. License and registration, please."

Chris dug his wallet out of his pocket while I rifled through the glove compartment for Nokes's registration and insurance card. The trooper took the paperwork back to his undercover cruiser. When he came back, he had a stern look on his face.

"This is not your car," he said.

I leaned across Chris and addressed the trooper directly. "We're driving it north from Florida for Matt Nokes," I said.

"Matt Nokes, the Yankees catcher?" he asked me.

"Yeah," I said. "I work for the team. We're driving it up from spring training for him."

"Really?" the trooper asked, then returned again to his car.

"You think he's gonna let us off the hook?" Chris asked me. "He seemed like a Yankees fan, right?"

"Yeah," I said. "No way he tickets us. It's just like that bar we got into in Florida."

But what worked in Fort Lauderdale didn't work a half mile from the New York City limits. The trooper presented Chris with a ticket not for speeding but for "improper use of headlamps." I suppose we got off easy.

"Damn," Chris said as we crossed the Goethals Bridge. "Does it say how much it's for?"

"I think it says a hundred twenty," I said, scrutinizing the numerals scrawled on the ticket. "Don't worry about it. We'll split it, take it off the top."

Just as Chris and I had done en route to and from our Network meetings, we discussed the balance sheet and profit potential of this latest joint venture. Five hundred bucks less the eighty we paid for our SkyBus flight, less our meal at T.G.I. Friday's and the beers afterward, less our room service at the Yankees' hotel, less the ticket, left about two hundred to split between us.

"That's not bad at all," Chris said as we pulled into the driveway of his house.

"Yeah," I said. "Thank God we never took those Iowa State girls out for dinner. We'd be broke right now."

Nick, Rob, and the Mule were already at work when I walked into the clubhouse with Nokes's car keys at 8:45 the next morning.

"Ohhh," Robby mewed. "The kid's back in town!"

I smiled broadly.

"Make good time on the road, Matty?" Nick asked me.

"Yep," I said.

"Good." Nick tossed me a pair of travel bags and pointed to a trunk of gray Yankees road uniforms. "Now get to it," he said.

He hovered over me as I stuffed the bags full.

"You will set a good example for the new kids, Matty," Nick told me. "You will work very hard this summer."

I looked up at Nick and nodded.

"New season, Matty," he said. "New season."

The Veteran

Much had changed at Yankee Stadium since the previous October.

Though Nick, Rob, and the Mule returned to the clubhouse in their prior capacities, Jamie was gone, a victim of Nick's strict two-season term limit for Yankees bat boys. I was promoted to fill Jamie's position, head bat boy, and two rookies filled the spots that Hector and I had occupied a year before. My new charges were Bill, a classmate at Regis whom I'd convinced Nick to hire, and Silverio, nephew of the owner of the red-sauce Italian restaurant in the Bronx from which Nick regularly ordered the team's postgame spread.

Upstairs from the clubhouse, a vastly more famous face, if a familiar one at the Stadium, had returned to the front office. George Steinbrenner's two-and-a-half-year suspension from baseball had ended in March, and at the beginning of the season he retook his place at the helm of the Yankees. No one expected

The Boss to remain a detached spectator for very long. He had in fact appeared on the cover of *Sports Illustrated* astride a white horse and dressed as Napoleon Bonaparte the day his suspension was lifted. The front office had made two major trades and spent $35 million of Steinbrenner's money on free agents during the off-season, and both he and the fans had steep expectations for the team.

The Yankees won their season opener in Cleveland behind eight innings of three-hit pitching from one of their heralded off-season pickups, the left-hander Jimmy Key, and the team returned to the Bronx a week later to open their home schedule against the Kansas City Royals.

Opening Day at the Stadium drew its usual sellout crowd of fifty-six thousand plus. Reggie Jackson, recently elected to the Hall of Fame, roamed the clubhouse before the game. I watched Steinbrenner and Mayor Dinkins applaud politely in the owner's box above home plate as the Yankees took the field to wild cheers, and winter in New York officially ended.

After the first inning, a dozen Broadway showgirls in short pin-striped skirts came out and danced on the roof of the Yankees and Royals dugouts. To the disgust of the baseball traditionalists in attendance but to the great amusement of the ballplayers, the dancers returned to perform a new routine every few innings. The marketing initiative was short-lived—to be precise, it lasted just one day—but sitting on the top step of the dugout, doing bats, I had a great view of both the showgirls and the new-look Yankees. Both lineups were startlingly impressive.

Starting across the infield from Don Mattingly was Wade Boggs, the longtime Red Sox third baseman whom the Yankees had lured away from Boston as a free agent. Boggs was a legendary hitter, a sure bet Hall of Famer. Every year of my childhood I'd watched him and Mattingly, rivals and icons of their respective teams, battle for the American League batting title; this summer I'd watch them play together as teammates. Boggs drove in the first run of the Yankee Stadium season with a two-out single in the bottom of the third inning.

I knew little about the Yankees' new outfielder, Paul O'Neill, who had been obtained from the Cincinnati Reds for Roberto Kelly, New York's lone all-star the season before. In his Stadium debut, O'Neill filled Kelly's shoes more than adequately: he went four-for-four with two RBIs. To fully appreciate what O'Neill brought to the lineup, though, Yankees fans would need to wait for a night when he was less than perfect at the plate. O'Neill played baseball with a grim determination, and when he failed to deliver in crucial situations, his frustration with himself was visible from the top rows of the upper deck. If anybody was keeping track at the Elias Sports Bureau, O'Neill almost certainly led the league in public displays of disgust and self-loathing. Striking out with the bases loaded, he would leave the batter's box and, seething, bat in hand, head straight to the Gatorade bucket sitting in the corner of the Yankees dugout. After beating the liquid out of it, O'Neill would grab his glove and retake the field muttering to himself like someone you might avoid sitting too close to on the subway. It was clearly not an act, and the fans loved it, and him, and the fire he brought to the Yankees.

I would become more personally acquainted with O'Neill's trademark intensity later in the season, during games when I was stationed down the first-base line and O'Neill was playing right field. Warming up O'Neill between innings was nothing like the easygoing game of catch it was with any other Yankees right fielder. This was especially true after O'Neill had just made the third out in the previous frame; God forbid he had stranded runners in scoring position. After he stalked out to his position, I would loft the ball to him in a soft arc. He would fire it back at me so fast, and with such palpable frustration, that I was afraid to move my glove an inch from where I held it up to him as a target. O'Neill had an incredible arm, and my saving grace was that he had good control. He was in fact at the top of the pitching depth chart if the Yankees needed a position player to fill in on the mound in an emergency. When he threw the ball in a bad state of mind, it actually made an audible sizzling sound before exploding with an angry *pop* in the pocket of my glove. It was not much better when I worked bats; after making an inning-ending pop-up or groundout, he would hurl his batting helmet in my direction, sending it skipping at shin-shattering speed across the grass in front of the dugout.

Even more than Boggs and O'Neill, though, I was most taken with Jim Abbott, the Yankees starting pitcher that Opening Day.

The Yankees had traded for Abbott to address the team's perennial Achilles' heel, poor starting pitching. And Abbott was a talented left-handed pitcher, so gifted that, after being drafted out of college, he skipped the minors and was sent directly to the major leagues. I don't need to check the baseball history books to confirm that, of the few players to have gone that route, Abbott is the only one to have also won both a Sullivan Award as America's premier amateur athlete (in 1987) and an Olympic gold medal (in 1988). In the first few years of his career, playing for the California Angels, Abbott had earned a reputation as one of the American League's best pitchers. He'd gone 18–11 with a 2.89 ERA in 1991, finishing third in Cy Young Award voting, and his 2.77 ERA in 1992 was among the five best in the league.

What I didn't fully appreciate until that day was that Abbott had accomplished all of this, along with his eighty-three-pitch complete-game masterpiece on Opening Day, with his left arm alone. Abbott had been born without a right hand, a fact that seemed to lift his long list of achievements nearly into the realm of implausibility.

Until I saw him pitch, I'd never considered how the simple mechanics of it might work. After releasing the ball, he would smoothly shift his glove over to his pitching hand, ready to field a ball hit back to him as fast or faster than he'd just thrown it. After catching the ball, he'd shift the glove back to his right arm, palm the baseball with his left hand, and throw the runner out. He seemed to make defensive plays beyond the ability of the many pitchers unburdened by what Abbott had overcome. Opening Day, I sat mesmerized on the top step of the dugout, my mouth half open, impressed beyond words, watching him outduel David Cone, the Royals starter that day.

For obvious reasons, not least of all his performance on the mound, Abbott was adored by Yankees fans. I shared their affection. I'd grown up with posters of sports icons on my bedroom wall, Mattingly among them, but it wasn't until Abbott came to the Yankees that I understood what it truly meant to have a hero.

He quickly became my favorite player off the field as well. Abbott was well-spoken, gracious and perpetually accessible, and universally respected by reporters, his teammates, and the clubhouse staff. Abbott was the type of person who, after I told him one night during batting practice that my sister Sarina was coming to the game, spent fifteen minutes chatting with her beside the dugout, teasing her about how she had put up with her little brother for so long. After the players' strike ended the 1994 season and robbed the clubhouse staff of the sizable end-of-year tips customarily received from the ballplayers, Abbott and Mattingly were the only Yankees to seek out the bat boys' home addresses and mail each one a few hundred dollars.

Abbott was also responsible for my clubhouse nickname, "Spider," by which I'm still known among the friends I made working at the Stadium. Abbott tagged me with it in the dugout one game after a few of the ballplayers had watched Martin Scorsese's film *Goodfellas* on the big-screen TV in the players' lounge. The movie was the main topic of conversation on the bench that night. Abbott asked me at one point to get him a cup of Gatorade and, feeling comfortable and very much the dugout veteran, I shot back a joke, telling him that fetching drinks wasn't part of my job description. If he wanted one, I told him, he could walk down to the end of the dugout himself.

"Watch yourself," Abbott warned. "You don't want to end up like Spider."

He was referencing the defiant barkeep in the film, a teenage kid first shot in the foot by Joe Pesci's Tommy for running drinks too slowly, then later done in for talking back to the mobsters.

The nickname caught on quickly. By the end of the month, even Nick had stopped addressing me by my given name.

Though Steinbrenner spent most of his time in Tampa, where he lived and had situated the Yankees brain trust's back office, his presence was felt on a daily basis in the Bronx. The Boss had instituted a number of new policies when he returned from his suspension, among them one edict that had sparked grumbling in the clubhouse from ballplayers and bat boys alike: no more food runs.

In addition to performing his Yankees ownership duties, Steinbrenner had long served in various capacities on the United States Olympic Committee. Effective immediately, his ballplayers would follow the same nutritional regimen as the U.S. Olympic team; no food deemed unsuitable by the Olympians' nutritionists in Colorado Springs would cross the threshold of the Yankees clubhouse. He charged the Yankees' medical trainers with enforcing the ban.

For the ballplayers, it meant no more pregame Extra Value Meals, no jelly doughnuts, no pepperoni pizzas, no tins of baked ziti from Silverio's uncle's restaurant. Plates of skinless chicken breasts and trays of raw vegetables replaced the fast food that had been a staple of the clubhouse diet. For the bat boys, it meant the loss of our most reliable source of tips; Nick even banned us from eating fast food in the clubhouse, lest we provoke cravings or offend a hungry ballplayer.

As with any other unpopular edict from above, though, the proscribed conduct was merely driven underground. Bags of McDonald's or Popeye's Fried Chicken were smuggled to the Yankees weight room instead of being delivered directly to the player's locker as before. Tips rose in recognition of explicit warnings from the front office that bacon-cheeseburger running was an offense that could cost a bat boy his job. In any case, you couldn't say no to a Mattingly or an Abbott if he requested a pregame fast-food fix. For a ballplayer who hadn't tipped the October before, though, the same request would yield just an apology: "We're not allowed to make food runs anymore."

We developed a code, effective if transparent, to pass the word on a given day that food runs should be made with an elevated level of stealth and caution: "Elvis is in the house." Steinbrenner occasionally traveled to the Bronx on short notice, and you could sense that the Stadium operated at a different pace when he was in the building.

You could never tell which minor fault in clubhouse conditions might trigger The Boss's temper: a wet spot on the linoleum floor outside the showers; a stray baseball on the floor that a ballplayer might trip over; a gallon of milk left out on the counter and not promptly returned to the refrigerator by a clubhouse attendant. So when Elvis was in the house, everyone snapped to it, wiping down tables that were already clean, straightening already tidy lockers, refolding folded towels.

Only the rookie bat boy Silverio seemed oblivious to Steinbrenner's expectations. I recall a morning when Steinbrenner made a surprise visit to the clubhouse a few hours before first pitch. Silverio and I were alone in the players' lounge when The Boss strolled into the room. I was eating a bowl of cereal at one of the tables near the lounge entrance, reading the sports page; Silverio was sprawled out on the leather couch in front of the television. As soon as I saw Steinbrenner, I jumped up and started alphabetizing the stack of morning papers, but Silverio didn't budge. The Boss walked up to the couch he was laid out on and, arms crossed against his chest, glared down on his teenage employee.

"Oh," Silverio said, finally looking up but not shifting from his languorous position. "Hiya, George," he said.

I wasn't sure whether to stick around for the imminent outburst or find cover in another room of the clubhouse.

Steinbrenner held his hands up, palms out, in Silverio's direction.

"Are you comfortable?" he said sarcastically. "Can I get you anything? Anything at all?"

"Nah," Silverio said, changing the channel with the television remote. "I'm fine."

"You sure?" Steinbrenner said. Silverio reflected on the offer for a moment.

"Yeah," Silverio said. "Thanks, George."

The Boss shook his head side to side with disgust and walked back out of the lounge.

I waited a few days for the other shoe to drop on Silverio; Steinbrenner had certainly fired people for less. But it never did.

. . .

The Yankees were playing at the Stadium the day in mid-April that college acceptance and rejection letters arrived in the mailboxes of high school seniors across the country. After batting practice, when I knew my mom would be home from work, I walked to the press room, where there was a bank of pay phones.

"Are you sure you want me to tell you?" my mom asked me. "You don't want to wait until you get home tonight and open them yourself?"

"No," I said. "Tell me. Open them."

My top choice of schools, thanks to Chris's and my idyllic visit on the way home from Fort Lauderdale, was Duke. But the Duke admissions office had sent me a thin envelope; the letter inside that my Mom read to me over the phone expressed regret that there was not room for me in the freshman class. Thick envelopes had arrived from a handful of other schools, though, among them Williams College, which wasn't far behind Duke on my wish list, and Holy Cross, which was both my father's alma mater and the college at which my sister Sarina was then a sophomore.

The difficult decision was complicated by the financial aid packages that I received from the schools over the next few weeks. Holy Cross offered me a good deal of scholarship money; Williams offered a less generous package. My parents were frank with me that paying the tuition at Williams—upward of twenty-five thousand dollars a year—would require significant sacrifices on the part of the family.

"If Williams is where you decide you want to go," my dad told me, "we'll figure out a way to make it work. But Holy Cross is a good school—Sarina's doing well there, and I think you'd do well there—and you need to think carefully about whether you can be happy at Holy Cross."

I had a month to notify the schools of my decision. I was in the clubhouse one afternoon when one of the executives in the Yankees front office overheard me talking about the dilemma with Bill, my bat boy classmate at Regis.

"You know Steinbrenner went to Williams," the executive said.

I hadn't known it.

"Maybe you should drop him a note and explain the situation," he counseled me. "Maybe the Yankee Foundation can help you. Write a letter, ask for help with lab fees, or books, or whatever else you think you might need."

I knew the Yankee Foundation, knew that it had rebuilt a number of Little League baseball diamonds in New York's inner-city neighborhoods, among other charitable projects around the City. I did not know that it might also grant college scholarships.

"Give it a shot," the executive advised. "You never know with The Boss."

I sat down that night and wrote a letter directly to Steinbrenner. I explained that I had worked in the Yankees clubhouse since the beginning of the 1992 season. I related the news that I'd been admitted to Williams, and having visited the school the previous fall, wanted nothing more than an opportunity to join the freshman class in September. I informed him how much a year of classes and room and board cost, and the fact that my parents had told me, given the modest amount of financial aid Williams had offered, that it would be a stretch for them to meet the cost of tuition. The only piece of advice that I didn't follow was asking for help with specific needs, like fees or books or room and board; I left my request open-ended.

"I don't know whether the Yankee Foundation offers college scholarships," I wrote in conclusion. "But I would greatly appreciate being considered for any assistance it might be able to offer me."

I hand-delivered a copy of the letter to Steinbrenner's personal secretary.

"Is he coming up from Tampa anytime soon?" I asked her.

"You never know with The Boss," she said.

A week later, shortly after batting practice, the phone rang in the clubhouse. Nick answered it.

"Spider!" he shouted across the room. "You're wanted upstairs. David Sussman's office."

Sussman was the Yankees general counsel. He welcomed me into his office and told me to take a seat. Three or four other men whom I didn't recognize stood around him behind his desk. I was the only person in the room wearing sneakers, shorts, and a sweaty Yankees T-shirt.

"Did Nick tell you why I called you up here?" he asked.

"No," I said.

"Well," he said. "Mr. Steinbrenner received your letter, and the Yankee Foundation has decided to give you a ten-thousand-dollar scholarship for your first year at Williams."

"What?" I said.

"Congratulations," he said. I didn't recover my breath until a long round of handshakes had been concluded. I traveled directly from Sussman's office to the pay phones in the press room. My mom answered the phone at home.

"I got a scholarship from the Yankees for college," I told her breathlessly.

"Yes?" she said.

"Mom," I said, "you don't understand. I got a ten-thousand-dollar scholarship from the Yankees for Williams. I'm gonna go to Williams."

"Oh, Matthew," she said, and started to cry.

No one but me and Regis's assistant headmaster knew just how close I'd come to flunking out of high school because of my job with the Yankees; now, a year later, the same job had become the basis for a college scholarship.

It was not the only irony. In his letter to me the day I first reported to work at the clubhouse, my dad had encouraged me to resist kicking Steinbrenner in the shins if I saw him. Suddenly the man had made it possible for me to attend one of the best liberal arts colleges in the country. I could appreciate why he was a lightning rod for criticism; but I knew at that moment I'd never feel anything but gratitude to Steinbrenner.

At the end of May, a few weeks after my high school graduation and the day after my eighteenth birthday, Abbott had his best start in pinstripes to date. The Yankees were hosting the Chicago White Sox at the Stadium, and it wasn't until the fifth inning that I took note of all the zeros Abbott had thrown up on the scoreboard. As is the superstition and custom in baseball, no one in the dugout spoke of the fact that Abbott had yet to give up a base hit. But there was little doubt that Abbott was aware of the line score; from the sixth inning on, the crowd stood for every pitch. Abbott retired the first hitter in the top of the eighth inning, which brought up Bo Jackson, one of Chicago's best hitters. With Abbott ahead in the count, Jackson fought off an inside fastball and managed a bloop single to shallow center field, breaking up the no-hit bid with five outs to go. The fans gave Abbott the longest ovation I'd heard in my fourteen months at the Stadium.

After the game, Nick called me over to his picnic table.

"You get one road trip this season," he told me gruffly. "Where do you want to go?"

The traditional choice for Yankees bat boys was the West Coast, which was generally the longest road trip of the year and offered a chance to see the relatively exotic cities of Seattle, Oakland, and Anaheim. But I had studied the Yankees' road schedule in anticipation of Nick's question; with little hesitation, I gave a different answer than the one he was likely expecting.

"I want to see the SkyDome and Camden Yards," I told him.

Both Toronto and Baltimore had recently built new ballparks for their respective teams, and both had been hailed as masterpieces of baseball architecture.

The SkyDome, in Toronto, was the first stadium in the world built with a fully retractable roof. Under its crown, the SkyDome housed not only a baseball diamond and seats for sixty thousand, but also a hotel and multiple restaurants. Toronto Blue Jays fans are not renowned for their love of baseball, but in three of their first four seasons playing at the SkyDome, the Jays managed to draw over 4 million fans a year; few other teams drew over 3 million.

Camden Yards, in Baltimore, couldn't have been more different from the SkyDome. The Orioles' ballpark was a self-consciously nostalgic throwback to the baseball stadiums of the first half of the twentieth century. Situated on land once occupied by Babe Ruth's father's saloon, Camden Yards was built new with many of the old-fashioned architectural flourishes associated with much older ballparks like Tiger Stadium in Detroit and Fenway Park in Boston. The Orioles' architects even incorporated into the ballpark's design the brick facade of a turn-of-the-century warehouse beyond the right-field wall. Camden Yards—intimate, quaint, and quirky—would become the model for half a dozen other major league stadiums built over the next decade.

An oversized Yankees schedule hung on the wall of the clubhouse, and I pointed out to Nick the dates I had in mind: a six-game road trip in late June, three games in Toronto followed by three in Baltimore.

The three days I'd spent in Boston the year before had been the longest I'd ever traveled outside New York without my parents. This road trip would have a very different feel than the one to Fenway. For starters, it was twice as long. And unlike the trip to Boston, I wouldn't be driving up with my dad for the start of the series and traveling home by bus afterward. This was a full-fledged major league road trip: the Yankees would fly from New York to Toronto, Toronto to Baltimore, then back home to New York.

The fact that the Yankees would travel by plane also meant that I'd have to make additional preparations than those that had been necessary for Boston. Suits were mandatory attire on the team plane, and unless I wanted to wear the now-too-small suit I'd worn to my eighth-grade confirmation, I'd have to buy a new one. I was also mindful of the problem Chris and I had run into in Fort Lauderdale, at the strip mall bar that had almost turned us away. If I were going to go out with the players wherever I liked in Toronto and Baltimore, I'd have to come up with a decent fake ID.

Both would require, in Yankee Stadium parlance, "cake." I'd been listening closely to the lingo Nick and Rob and the Mule threw around the clubhouse and had expanded my vocabulary significantly: "cake" was cash; your "lumberyard" was the sum of your cake holdings, usually held together by a money clip, or in Nick's case, a thick rubber band.

I decided to procure a new driver's license first. Armed with a hundred dollars and a passport photo, I met three friends from Regis, Ned, Ben, and Steve, who were also eager to artificially up their age. We met on a street corner a few blocks away from Times Square.

Times Square was still several years away from its transformation into a squeaky-clean theme park. On summer nights in the early nineties, the side streets of the neighborhood were still crowded with characters furtively hawking a wide range of illegal goods. We wandered up and down the block, avoiding eye contact with the weed dealers and men mumbling "Young girls, young girls." After a few minutes, a pusher came up and started walking alongside us.

"Fake ID?" he said out of the corner of his mouth.

Ben nodded discreetly.

"Follow me," the man told us.

We followed him into a McDonald's a block or so away from the heart of the neon glare. The five of us sat down at a table in the back of the restaurant.

"You guys looking for some fake IDs?" he asked us.

"Driver's licenses," I said assertively.

The fake ID hawker looked anxiously over both his shoulders to see if anyone was eavesdropping on our conversation. The restaurant was nearly empty.

"You already have a photo?" he asked us, his voice low.

"Yeah," I said. "We've got 'em."

"Good," he said. "Licenses are a hundred dollars each. You give me fifty dollars now, and I'll come back in half an hour with the licenses. You guys give me the other fifty then."

Steve reached for his wallet but I put my hand up, signaling him to hold on.

I chose my words carefully.

"You're not getting any cake off my lumberyard," I said, "without showing us a license first."

"What did you say?" he said.

"I said: no license, no cake."

"What the hell are you talking about?" he asked me.

"Cake, cake!" I repeated. "You know: money. Cake!"

"What the hell are you talking about?" Ned asked me.

"Oh, cake!" the guy said, harnessing the quizzical look on his face. "I, uh, thought you said something else." My friends were looking at me as if I'd sprouted an extra head. "You give me fifty bucks' worth of cake," he continued, "and I'll bring you back an ID in an hour."

"No way," I said. "Not without seeing what kind of IDs you've got."

"Wait here," the grifter told us. "I'll be back with a sample in five minutes."

We waited ten, then left the McDonald's. It was as close as we got that night to achieving our mission.

"Cake!" Ned laughed gleefully as the four of us crossed Forty-second Street. "What the hell were you talking about?"

"That guy might not have known what I was saying," I said. "But he sure knew what I was talking about."

My suit purchase, at Macy's Herald Square, went much more smoothly. I peeled three pieces of cake off my lumberyard, and the suit was mine.

As getaway day approached, it became clear that, at least from a baseball perspective, I couldn't have chosen a better road trip. The Yankees rattled off nine wins in the eleven games before the Toronto-Baltimore swing, the last victory an 8–0 shutout at the Stadium that gave them a four-game sweep over the Minnesota Twins. The win put them twelve games over .500 for the season. The Yankees would travel to Toronto in third place, but only one game behind the second-place Blue Jays and three games behind first-place Detroit. The Orioles trailed New York in fourth.

The Yankees would fly on the off day scheduled between the Twins series in the Bronx and the first game in Toronto. After the last win against the Twins, David Szen, the Yankees traveling secretary, handed me a copy of the team itinerary and informed me that my roommate on the road trip would be Nick Priore.

"Ugh," I joked.

"Sorry," he said. "A lot of the guys are bringing their wives along, especially to Baltimore. So there weren't many options."

The night before the trip, my mom gave me my passport in a pouch I could carry around my neck. Together, we packed my clothes into the Yankees suitcase that Nick had given me to take on the road.

It was hard to tell what my parents made of the adventure I was about to embark on. My mom, I think, imagined the Yankees on the road as something akin to a tour group on a luxury sightseeing vacation. She must have known I wouldn't be babysat, but I think she assumed that there would be tour guides, activities planned to entertain the group, and at least some formal supervision of her son. My dad, who by then had been down to the clubhouse and met Nick a couple times, probably had a more accurate sense of what it would be like to travel with the team. I think he just trusted me to keep my eyes open and myself out of trouble.

I dressed the next morning in my new suit, and before leaving for the Stadium, I gave my mom the official Yankees itinerary; she posted it on the fridge with a magnet.

I got to the clubhouse early enough to pack my own equipment bag—baseball spikes, my cap, T-shirts, socks, stirrups, glove. At the airport, the team bus drove onto the tarmac and pulled right up to the jet. The plane's interior was different from any I had ever seen before. All the seats were leather and spacious, no more than four per row. At the middle of the plane there were no rows at all, but a window-to-window lounge with easy chairs and coffee tables. If not for the lack of Secret Service agents, I might have guessed we'd just boarded Air Force One.

There were no boarding passes or assigned seats, so I followed the ballplayers past the coaches and picked a row for myself toward the back. David Szen came down the aisle handing out envelopes of cash, the meal allowance that, despite their huge salaries, all players receive as a matter of right for every day of every road trip. Nick had told me I wouldn't be paid for games I worked on the road, but Szen handed me an envelope, too, which held $150. Once the plane had taken off and dinner— lobster or steak—was finished, the ballplayers sitting in the rows ahead of me started playing blackjack with the cash they had just been given. I stood in the aisle and watched a few hands—twenty bucks' ante—before one of the guys looked up at me and asked if I wanted in the game. I wasn't sure if the offer was serious, but I said sure. I knew how to play blackjack; I'd learned addition by playing it with my dad on the floor of our living room.

The ballplayers cleared a space for me to sit down. Including the per diem, I had about $250 to last me the six days on the road. I figured that at twenty bucks a round, I could afford to lose three or four hands without running out of money before the end of the trip. I placed a twenty down on the table and was dealt in on the next hand.

Fifteen minutes and eight straight losing hands later, I went to see what was going on in the lounge. Nick snickered when I told him how much I had lost. When I returned to my row after the pilot announced we were landing, I found that someone had left a hundred-dollar bill on my seat. Melido Perez, a Dominican pitcher who spoke very little English but had been in the black-jack game, winked at me as I sat back down.

"Gracias," I told him discreetly as we filed off the plane. I wished I'd known enough Spanish to be able to tell him that I would be sitting out the card game on the flight to Baltimore.

We got into Toronto well after midnight but were received at the hotel lobby by more than a dozen fans fully decked out in Yankees gear. They swarmed around the weary team with photos and Sharpie markers as the players inched toward the elevators.

When I woke up the next morning, I wasn't sure exactly what to do with myself. Nick had already left the room, probably for the ballpark. Game time wasn't until 7:30 that night, and the team bus wasn't scheduled to leave the hotel until three or four in the afternoon. I decided to call Abbott to see what he was up to. I looked up his room number on the master list of aliases and dialed his room. It was 10:30 in the morning.

"Yeah," Abbott groaned into the phone.

"Jim, it's Matty," I said. "You want to have lunch?"

"Jesus, Spider," he said wearily. "What time is it? I have to pitch Friday."

I could sense I'd made a mistake calling him up; maybe we weren't as good friends as I'd thought. It hadn't crossed my mind that he might not also be kind of bored and hungry; that he wouldn't want to hang out.

I started to apologize profusely and told him I'd see him at the ballpark later.

"Listen, Spider," he said. "Meet me downstairs in an hour and we'll get some lunch, all right?"

"Okay, cool," I told him, and hung up the phone.

An hour later, feeling bashful, I met Abbott in the lobby. We hopped a cab to the SkyDome; Abbott suggested we try the Hard Rock Cafe that was actually part of the restaurant complex built into the ballpark. The waitress sat us at a table right up against the floor-to-ceiling plexiglass window overlooking the field. Having skipped breakfast, I was starving. The menu listed every type of pub food imaginable, a teenage kid's dream. I was still young enough that, when I went out for dinner with my family in New York, I wouldn't order an appetizer without asking my dad for permission ("As long as you finish your entrée."). Abbott smirked when I gingerly raised the topic. He told me I could order whatever I wanted. We split three plates of buffalo wings before moving on to burgers and dessert. I must have had three or four Cokes. When the check came, I made a motion for my wallet. Abbott laughed out loud. It's not that I thought he was going to take me up on it. It just seemed like the right thing to do.

After each of the games in Toronto, a couple of the players invited me to join them out on the town. My lack of positive ID never seemed to be a problem at any of the bars we visited. The ballplayers introduced me to the women who crowded around them everywhere we went.

"He's so cute! How old is he?" they asked the players right in front of me, as if I weren't there. Bartenders kept handing me fresh beers. I tried to appear nonchalant amid the glamour of the scene, tried to act like it was nothing special, as if I spent all my New York nights partying with the Yankees, surrounded by beautiful women.

The trip from Toronto to Baltimore was uneventful except for the slight speed bump I hit passing through U.S. Customs at Baltimore-Washington International Airport. The Yankees' usual fast track through customs was held up until the officers could locate one Matthew McGough, who had declared the toothpaste and deodorant he had purchased while on his business trip to Canada. The only people more amused than the customs agents were the ballplayers. Everyone on the team plane had been sleeping when the stewardess handed me the customs form. I'd never filled one out before and had carefully followed the directions, itemizing the toiletries I had purchased abroad and was bringing back into the United States.

I was still hearing customs jokes on the team bus to Camden Yards the next afternoon. The Yankees and Orioles would play three games in Baltimore: night games Friday and Saturday, then a day game Sunday.

As Szen had tipped me off, I'd seen a number of the players' wives in the hotel lobby the previous night, awaiting the team's arrival, and understood that it was unlikely I'd be invited to join any of the intimate postgame dinners being planned at Baltimore's better restaurants. Unlike in Toronto, where the ballplayers had taken me under their wings, I would be responsible here for my own nightly entertainment.

Working bats Friday night, I noticed a trio of teenage girls sitting together in the stands just above the Yankees dugout. I was mindful that my only plans for later that night involved watching television with Nick in our hotel room. I should have been more mindful of my girlfriend back in New York, but at age eighteen, I had not yet learned the value of romantic fidelity or mastered the art of self-restraint in the face of temptation. One of the three girls was especially cute. I stole glances at her through the first few innings, finally catching her eye just before the seventh-inning stretch. Encouraged by the giggling and laughing and elbowing that I seemed to have elicited from her and her friends, I decided to take my chances. I grabbed a baseball from the dugout and, between innings, ran back to the clubhouse for a pen.

"I'm down from New York for the weekend," I printed on the ball as small and legibly as possible. "If you know a good place to go out after the game, I'd like to treat you to dinner." Jim Leyritz, one of the Yankees bench players, happened to come down the tunnel to the dugout just as I was adding my name to the bottom of the proposal.

"Whaddya got, Spider?" he teased me.

"Don't worry about it," I muttered.

I entrusted the baseball to a grandfatherly usher stationed at the side of the visiting dugout.

"Could you please give this to the girl in the red shirt, five or six rows up?" I asked him. He smiled, as did the girl when he gave her the ball.

The game ended badly for the Yankees—a 7–6 loss, on a bases-loaded walk in the bottom of the tenth inning—but my disappointment was eclipsed when Cathy, the girl in the red shirt, came down to the top of the dugout and cheerfully accepted my invitation.

"I have to drive my friends home first," Cathy told me. She had the most amazingly sweet Southern accent I'd ever heard. "But I'll come back into town, and we'll go out."

"I'll wait for you at the hotel," I told her, and gave her the address and the number of the room I was sharing with Nick.

The phone rang in our room shortly before midnight. I jumped up and grabbed the phone before Nick, lying on his bed watching TV, might have been able to answer it.

"Matt?" Cathy said.

"Hey," I said. "You downstairs?"

"Actually," she said, "it was a little late by the time I dropped my friends off, and my parents don't want me to drive back into Baltimore tonight."

"Oh," I said, thinking back to the date that had been similarly short-circuited outside Fenway Park the fall before. "Are you busy tomorrow?"

"No, I'm free."

"Tomorrow's a night game," I said. "Why don't you come in during the day? We can have lunch, and then I can leave you a ticket to the game."

Nick looked askance at me when I hung up the phone.

"What?" I said.

"Nothing," he smirked.

Cathy was waiting for me at noon in the lobby of the Yankees' hotel. Wearing a floral print sundress, she looked the very image of a pretty Southern belle. We walked over to Baltimore's Inner Harbor and picked a restaurant with a nice view of the water. Our crab cakes had just arrived when two Yankees pitchers, Jimmy Key and Neal Heaton, walked over to our table; they'd apparently been eating across the room. Key and Heaton politely introduced themselves to Cathy and made small talk with us for a minute.

"You coming to the ballpark?" Key asked me.

"Yeah, but I might be late," I said. "Cathy's coming to the game tonight, so I might keep her company for a while more."

"So we'll see you around game time then," Key said. "Have fun."

I didn't feel bad about not reporting to the clubhouse at the time prescribed for the ballplayers. I was having a nice time with Cathy, and given the fact that I wasn't being paid to work the games on the road, I considered my attendance at batting practice strictly voluntary. Cathy and I finished lunch, then spent the next few hours walking the harbor hand in hand. I left her around six, a little more than an hour before the game was scheduled to start.

I hadn't taken two steps inside the clubhouse before I heard Abbott's voice from clear across the room.

"Jesus Christ," he shouted, his voice thick with mock outrage. "Finally! Who the hell do you think you are, walking into the clubhouse forty-five minutes before first pitch?"

"I had a date," I said, walking past him toward the locker I'd been assigned near the entrance to the shower room.

"A date?!?" he said, trailing right behind me and trying to get in my face.

"Yeah, a date," I said. "If you'd had a date like mine, you might have been late, too. Ask Jimmy Key—he saw her."

Abbott whirled around in the direction of Key's locker. "Jimmy," he said, "you know anything about this?"

"Yeah," Key said, smiling. "She was a real good-looking girl. A nice catch."

"See?" I said to Abbott. "I told you."

"I don't know what to say, Spider," Abbott sputtered. "You're way out of line. Again."

During the game, I kept the strident facade up, telling Abbott that I might skip batting practice tomorrow, too, depending on how things went with Cathy later on that night. The ballplayers couldn't have been more amused by the goo-goo eyes Cathy and I made at each other as I ran back and forth between the dugout and home plate. The pace of the game allowed more than enough time for teasing. Thanks to multiple pitching changes and seesaw scoring—the teams combined for thirteen runs in the first five innings—it seemed like one of the longest games of the season. I ruefully watched the hours pass on the clock on the Camden Yards scoreboard, wondering at what time Cathy's parents might put the kibosh on our plans to go out after the game.

When it finally ended—12–10 Orioles, another tough Yankees loss—Cathy came down to the roof of the visiting dugout.

"You think we can still go out?" I asked her.

"I think so," she said, motioning toward the outfield clock. "If you hurry."

The Orioles' visiting clubhouse bat boys were happy to take over my share of the dugout cleanup duties, and I sprinted up to the clubhouse to quickly shower and change. Given how the last two games had ended, the Yankees clubhouse was fairly morose; players stood at their lockers quietly fielding questions from the New York beat writers about blown leads and missed opportunities. I stripped off my uniform, jumped in the shower, then race-walked back to my locker.

I couldn't find my boxer shorts. I remembered having hung them on a hook, and I spent a few frantic seconds searching the floor for where they might have fallen. Nothing. A handful of T-shirts hung from hangers inside the locker, and I pushed them off to one side. At the back of the cubicle, lying flat on the bench built into the wall, were the missing shorts. I reached out and grabbed them, then recoiled my hand. My boxer shorts were not only wet, but cold. Someone—I had a decent idea who—had evidently taken them during the game, dipped them in water, and then frozen them. They were as stiff as a piece of corrugated cardboard.

"Oh no," I muttered to myself. "No, no, no."

At that moment, Abbott walked past my locker on his way to the shower room.

"What happened to your shorts, Spider?" he asked me.

Considering the mood in the clubhouse, there was little more for me to do than shrug mutely in disbelief. Key walked by as well, shaking his head in resignation.

"Oh, that's too bad," he said, before continuing on to the showers himself.

I hustled my underwear to the players' lounge, where I microwaved them back to pliability. They were still wet when I put my jeans on over them. Running upstairs to where I'd told Cathy to wait for me, I prayed that I hadn't lost too many precious minutes. I prayed too that my blue jeans were dark enough to mask the wetness I could already feel seeping through the denim.

"Sorry I'm late," I said when I ran up to her, trying to regain both my breath and my composure.

"I didn't mind waiting," Cathy said. "But it's almost midnight. I'm not sure we have time to go out."

My heart sank.

"But if you want, maybe you can come over to our place," she said. "My dad'll be here in a couple minutes to pick me up."

"How will I get back to the hotel?" I asked her.

"My dad can give you a ride," she said.

"Really?" I said. The idea that the father of a pretty seventeen-year-old girl might be willing to welcome an eighteen-year-old boy into his home, let alone one down from New York City with the Yankees, then drive him home in the middle of the night, seemed incredible to me.

But ten minutes later, I was sitting with Cathy in the back of her dad's car, driving out to their home in suburban Maryland. When we arrived, Cathy's dad told her to let him know when I was ready to go back to the hotel and then said goodnight, leaving us alone on the couch in the living room. We spent the next two hours watching TV and kissing, which seemed a step forward from my last road trip date. Around 2:30 in the morning, Cathy went upstairs and woke her dad, and the three of us drove back into Baltimore together. Cathy walked me back into the hotel lobby, where we shared a last kiss goodnight.

"Let me get this straight," Abbott said on the bench during the next afternoon's game. "The girl's father drove you all the way out to their house, then left you alone to make out with his daughter while he went to sleep upstairs?"

"Yeah."

"And what happened with the girl?" asked Troll, the Yankees strength and conditioning coach.

"We just made out for a while," I said.

"And then, at three o'clock in the morning, her father got up out of bed and drove you back to the hotel?" Abbott asked.

"Yeah."

"Wow," they said in unison, as astonished as I was.

"Wouldn't have happened that way," I told Abbott, "if you hadn't frozen my boxer shorts. So thanks."

"I don't know what you're talking about, Spider," he replied, poker-faced.

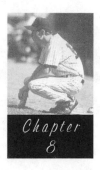

Chapter 8

Spider's Web

The day I first reported to work at the clubhouse, I never could have anticipated all the adventures that would follow. Fifteen months later, my childhood dreams—playing on the Stadium field, wearing a pin-striped uniform, meeting my baseball heroes—had not only been met but exceeded; what had been dreams became memories. Incredibly, there weren't many aspirations left to fulfill on my Yankees wish list.

I'd flown on the team plane to three separate cities and ridden the team bus between the Yankees' hotel and nearly a dozen road games. I knew what these bus rides were like after wins and after losses, and I'd learned to carry myself accordingly, just like the ballplayers. Waiting for the last man to board after a loss, I sat solemnly in my seat, listening to music on headphones and staring out the window. After wins, I stood at my row, one knee up on the seat where my ass belonged, my arms sprawled across my seat back and that of the seat in front of me, chattering and crowing at the jokes being cracked up and down the aisle of the bus. I'd been invited out by the ballplayers to restaurants and night-clubs, and now I found myself being pulled into the types of con-versations on the bench that I'd previously felt welcome only to eavesdrop on.

Just as my Regis friendships had been cemented through shared antics, I came off the road trip with material enough that dugout conversations seemed to propel themselves forward. I was now as sure of my place among the ballplayers as I'd felt among my classmates at Regis. This sense of acceptance overpowered what was left of my adolescent shyness. I spoke freely with the ballplayers, teased and joked easily. I was hanging out with Yan-kees.

It was not only in the dugout and clubhouse that I now felt so at home. Walking down the main hallway of the team's front office, I knew the faces, names, and something of the dispositions of most of the team's executives. I knew each of their secretaries and most of the interns who banged out the major share of the paper—press releases, marketing materials, statistical research—that issues daily from the Yankees offices. The grounds crew, the electricians and carpenters, the people in the ticket office, the guy who delivered boxes of fan mail to the clubhouse; all these peo-ple were no longer only familiar faces. I knew by name every one of the security guards who policed the Yankees lobby: the ones who wore tailored suits on game nights and dispensed VIP tick-ets to celebrities, and the one in the off-the-rack navy blue blazer who safeguarded the Stadium through the overnight shift.

Curiously, it wasn't until my camaraderie with the ballplay-ers became evident to people on the periphery of the clubhouse that everyone seemed to know me. Mattingly or Abbott would shout to me in a crowd of people in the Yankees lobby or in the players' parking lot after a game, and pretty soon people around the Stadium I'd never been introduced to were addressing me as Spider as well.

I'd always known that everything at the Stadium orbits the ballplayers. But by midsummer, I was close enough to that inner circle that I occasionally became susceptible to the notion that things actually revolved around me.

It's not that I became insubordinate; my corruption was imperfect, more subtle than that. On-field duties had never been so exciting, thanks to my cresting rapport with the guys on the roster, and I fulfilled those responsibilities as dutifully as ever. But off the field and in the clubhouse, where the day-to-day routine had become close to second nature, my focus shifted to doing what I needed to do to stay out of Nick's doghouse. Pre- and postgame chores promised none of the fun I was having hanging out with the players. Each day my priorities drifted a little further afield from where they'd been when I'd first walked through the clubhouse door.

I no longer feared that I'd never be accepted by the ballplayers the way I'd seen Jamie accepted the year before. I'd been accepted, and now I stood in the elevated position that Jamie had vacated the previous fall when his two years were up. This sense of myself as the favorite son swelled my self-regard and undermined my work ethic. The more I felt included by the ballplayers, the more assured I felt of those friendships, the less I exerted myself doing the things that had earned me that station to begin with.

My productivity as a Yankees employee began to decline nearly as steeply as the learning curve I'd ascended my first few weeks on the job. I led the junior bat boys Bill and Silverio less by example and more by something like decree. I pulled rank and delegated chores the same way that I'd so resented Jamie for doing almost exactly one year before; I even started parroting Jamie's old "Don't worry about it" tag. I spent nearly as much time trying to pass off my duties as I might have spent just doing them myself. Preparing cold-cut platters before games, wiping down sinks and emptying trash cans after: these were tasks I now thought most appropriately attended to by Bill and Silverio. I preferred and felt best suited to those jobs that kept me around the ballplayers. These personal errands not only promised more time with the guys but also, and not incidentally, more and better tips. I performed these errands as conscientiously as I had once shined blemishes off the players' game shoes or paused while vacuuming to hand-rub a persistent stain off the clubhouse carpet. Running their errands quickly and smoothly further deepened the players' trust in me, which produced more and more complicated jobs that were not part of my original job description.

Upon request, I would pick up a player's wife at the airport or go to Midtown to buy tickets to a Broadway show. Making reservations for players at popular restaurants in Manhattan, I became proficient at "dropping the Y-bomb," the clubhouse euphemism for mentioning your affiliation with the Yankees in expectation that it might get a player (or you) a better table or better service.

I spent more and more of my hours at work not working but hanging out, waiting for my services to be engaged, as if I were no longer a salaried employee of the ballclub, but a mercenary. I'd seen Jamie on the same track the summer before and knew that it was a somewhat standard trajectory for second-year Yankees bat boys. My knowledge that this was so went a long way toward smothering whatever my conscience may have had to say about my diminishing job performance.

Nick watched me and of course knew exactly what was

going on. Given the dozens of seasons he'd worked for the Yan-kees, supervising successive crews of teenage boys, there's no doubt he not only knew the pattern but could see me assuming the mantle of my no-good predecessors. It was surely the reason behind his two-years-and-out rule.

The saving grace, for Nick and maybe myself as well, was that I was nearing the end of my run at the Stadium. I'd be leaving for college in a little more than a month and a half, and after that, we both knew, I'd be gone for good.

The gradual degeneration of my principles was well under way by the morning of the weekend game in mid-July when I saw a man in the clubhouse handing out CDs from a duffel bag stuffed with music. He walked around the perimeter of the room, near the lockers, talking with the ballplayers. At the end of each conversation, he reached into his bag and doled out CDs by the half dozen. After he passed Kamieniecki, I approached Kami and asked what the story was.

"That's the CD Guy," he told me.

I understood from overheard clubhouse conversations that for every specie of consumer goods a ballplayer might have a taste for, there was a "Guy" who'd hand it over for free. The players got the goods; the Guys got the satisfaction of associating with big league baseball players. The relationships were fleeting, trans-actional, and—for the ballplayers, at least—lucrative.

A constellation of these Guys were scattered across the country, one or more in each and every major league city. Ana-heim, California, had the Wine Guy. Toronto had an Armani Guy. Boston had the Reebok Guy. I had learned too late for my own benefit that New York had a Suit Guy, but now knew that it had a CD Guy as well. There were Car Guys. Jewelry Guys who specialized in fat, gold rope chains and custom diamond settings. Hotel Guys, and Ticket Guys in the reservations departments of most major American airlines. Home Audio Guys and Television Guys. It seemed to me that a Yankee could go through an entire playing career without once needing to dip into his wallet.

In the clubhouse we called some of the more relentless Guys "greenflies," a pejorative earned for the way they buzzed around money and celebrity, relentlessly pestering, desperate to make a connection. We used the label derisively, dismissing them with that word. Unlike the rest of us in the clubhouse, who considered our relationships with the ballplayers to have been earned over time, we saw the greenflies trying to buy both their friendship and the self-esteem that came with it.

I suppose it's possible we were selling the Guys' business sense short. Whatever the value of what they gave away, they might have considered it a write-off, or an endorsement. Maybe the Suit Guy sold a dozen more suits a month simply on the basis of having, all over his store, photographs of himself shaking hands with the all-stars he outfitted every time they came through town to play the Yankees or the Mets. The Guys could probably get tickets to any game they wanted, good seats, and some of them had likely accumulated sizable memorabilia collections from what they had solicited from the ballplayers.

Still, we regarded them as charlatans, which goes some distance toward explaining another lesson I learned in two years with the Yankees: never purchase an autograph without some foolproof evidence of its authenticity. A significant percentage of the autographs that emerged from the Yankees clubhouse during my time there were signed not by the players themselves but by other hands in the clubhouse, including my own. This was not done with any particular ill will toward whoever the ultimate recipient of the autograph might have been. Nor was it necessarily done behind the backs of those players whose signatures we'd spent hours imitating, practicing, and perfecting.

It was done to save time, both our own and the ballplayers'. The demand for autographs never slackened, and there weren't enough hours in the day for the team's stars to fulfill all the autograph requests that came down to the clubhouse daily. As Steinbrenner, the man who signed the checks, often reminded us: the Yankees were paid to play ball, not sign autographs.

We learned quickly never to ask a player to sign anything in The Boss's presence. "Who's that for?" he'd furiously demand, shooing us away from whatever player we'd just approached, ball and pen in hand. Added to this official disapproval, most pitchers found it distracting and disruptive to sign on days they were scheduled to start; balls that for whatever reason had to be signed that day would be signed by someone else. Other guys just hated signing, period. It was no fun to need to gauge a guy's mood and risk getting chewed out just to get a ball signed for someone you didn't even know. We discovered the hard way that rather than courting trouble from The Boss or a grouchy player, it was often easier and quicker to go to the bat boy you knew had down cold the autograph you needed.

We perfected our autographs—or rather, their autographs—through countless hours of practice. We trained our hands for the challenge of it but also just to kill time, waiting for the game to start or for the whites to come out of the dryer at the end of the night. The bat boys sat around the players' lounge and filled up the back side of ticket envelopes, then put our efforts side by side to compare and critique them.

"Jesus, that's horrible," we'd mock each other. "I could do a better Tartabull left-handed."

"With my foot," someone else might chime in.

"With the pen between my teeth." And so on.

In truth, though, the vast majority of the signatures were

not only passable but spot-on. Seeing one against the genuine article, I'd have had a hard time myself picking out the fake. Unsurprisingly, the most practiced autographs were those of the most popular players, the ones most frequently sought and the most sought after. These players' signatures were thus also the first ones learned by the most junior bat boys. I wasn't working at the Stadium more than a month by the time I could do a respectable Mattingly. Everyone had a Mattingly. I practiced mine so assiduously that it actually affected my penmanship; the way I signed the initial M's in my first and last names came to share more than a passing resemblance to the M in Mattingly's autograph. Or at least to the M in my best rendition of his autograph.

Between us, we could do pretty much the whole roster. I remember one attendant from the visiting side who could, in a couple of minutes, completely fill a team ball—a ball autographed by everyone on the Yankees roster, with the manager's signature on the ball's sweet spot—all by himself.

Once you got over the shock you felt seeing it done the first few times, it didn't seem too grave a sin. It seemed something of a necessary evil, and to salve my conscience I developed my own code of conduct. Besides autographs destined for my own collection, anything a friend asked me to have signed I got autographed by the player himself. Any autograph requests that had come down to the clubhouse from the front office—for instance, autographed balls to be donated by the Yankees for a charity auction or to a kid in the hospital—I also made sure were legitimately signed.

By the same logic, but at the other end of the moral spectrum, signing your own Mattingly to a ball that was just going to a greenfly was nothing worth beating yourself up over.

. . .

It was unusual to see one of the Guys actually inside the clubhouse. Once Nick saw what the CD Guy was up to, he told security to run him. Nick knew him—the CD Guy had apparently worked for the Yankees in some capacity some years before, which must have been how he got into the Stadium that day— and Nick's disgust with the man was palpable. Nick had less than no interest in free CDs.

"Deals, deals, deals," he muttered derisively, loud enough for his clubhouse staff to hear. "It never stops with the fucking deals."

A half hour later I passed the CD Guy in the hallway outside the visiting clubhouse. He must have seen me eyeing the CDs spilling from his bag when he set it down on the concrete floor outside the door.

I introduced myself as Spider and told him I worked in the Yankees clubhouse.

He told me his name and explained that he did once work for the Yankees, back in the eighties, and now ran a large record store in Lower Manhattan. He was a big guy, paunchy. His fingers were sized and shaped like breakfast sausage links, and when we shook hands, his engulfed mine.

The CD Guy held out a handful of shrink-wrapped albums and fanned them out for me so I could see them. They were good CDs, artists in heavy rotation on the radio and MTV. All CDs I'd have liked to buy. I thought one or two of them maybe hadn't even been released yet.

"Take 'em," the CD Guy said.

"Seriously?"

"Yeah. Take 'em."

I took the CDs and said thanks.

"No problem," he said, clapping me on my shoulder. He

spoke to me like we'd been friends for years. He held out a business card with his name and his store's address and phone number. "Come by sometime next week. I'll show you around and
hit you off with a couple more albums."

"Okay, cool," I said. "Let me know if you need anything
from me."

"If you can get some stuff signed by the players, I'll really
take care of you," he said.

"Yeah?" I said. "What kind of stuff are you looking for?"

"Whatever you're able to pull. Memorabilia. Autographed
balls. Bats. I have a couple of game-worn jerseys in my collection."

"No way I can do a jersey," I said. "And I don't know about
bats. But I can probably get you some balls signed."

Though this was my first "deal," I knew the clubhouse
rules, uncodified but fairly unambiguous, that governed transac-
tions of this type. The rules were implied and not explicit because
no one ever wanted to acknowledge that all this "dealing" was in
fact, even if on a petty scale, stealing and profiteering. But as
clearly as the law distinguishes between felonies and misde-
meanors, in the clubhouse some types of deals—if exposed—
were considered more pardonable than others.

The most important aggravating factor was whether money
changed hands. Selling clubhouse memorabilia—that is, for
cash—was clearly over the line. Nearly as bad was trading it to
someone who you knew was going to turn around and sell it
himself. First of all, selling used equipment or autographs was
greedy; there were other ways to make money, like working
harder for tips (or pyramid schemes). Second, deals involving cash
could come back and bite you in the ass. As big as the sports
memorabilia business was, it had its industry circuit; there were a
finite number of dealers. One guy offers something special for
sale at a baseball card show or in his store—a game-worn jersey,

maybe—and other people start wondering where it came from and how it got there. Word could easily get back to the club-house, or worse, the front office.

Deals that did not involve an exchange of money were somewhat more accepted, or at least tolerated. Let me be clear: you didn't speak of them except to another bat boy you trusted, and certainly not to Nick or Robby. But there was a sense that as long as you kept things on a small scale and weren't greedy or stupid, no one was going to get in hot water over it. Which was why I ruled the jersey out from the get-go. A game-worn jersey was not only worth a great deal of money, but once it left the clubhouse, it had to be replaced. That cost the team money. Scuffed baseballs, old batting gloves, used baseball spikes, cracked bats that were going to be discarded anyway: these things I considered to have negligible value. No one would miss them. Whatever value they had after I got them autographed I considered to have created myself.

The next week I stopped by the store with baseballs genuinely signed by Mattingly, Boggs, Tartabull, Abbott, and Key. The CD Guy seemed pleased and took me back to his office to show me a wall of photos of him with the famous athletes who'd called on him at his store. I paused in front of each one, nodding respectfully.

"Yeah, they're all my boys," he said, or maybe it was "boyz," as if they all hailed from the same 'hood. Then he clapped his hands together and invited me to help myself to some music. I collected a stack of maybe fifteen albums, and he walked me through the beeping theft detector and out the door. I wrote my home telephone number on a scrap of paper and told him he should feel free to call me.

"Thanks, Spider," he said. "Come back and see me whenever you want."

. . .

By the middle of July, Yankees fans and the New York papers had started waking up to the fact that, with the season half over, the Yankees were very much in the thick of a pennant race. New York took three out of four games from the Oakland A's at the Stadium to tie Toronto for first place for the first time in the season. In the last game of the series, Promotional Sock Night, former Yankee Rickey Henderson nearly sparked a brawl by jawing at Rich Monteleone, the pitcher Showalter had just brought into the seventh inning of a game the Yankees were trailing 4–3. After Monteleone retired the next batter, the Yankees exploded for ten hits and ten runs in the bottom of the seventh. When Mike Stanley hit a grand slam to put the Yankees up 11–4, untold pairs of shrink-wrapped athletic socks rained down on the field from the bleachers and upper deck. The umpires stopped the game while the bat boys and grounds crew cleared the diamond. Mattingly ended the game with four hits, including a two-run home run, to lift his season average to .312 and extend a hitting streak to thirteen games; the next day he was named American League Player of the Week for the first time since 1988.

Old Timers' Day, a week later, celebrated the fifteen-year anniversary of the Yankees' last World Championship. The clubhouse was crowded before the game with the stars of the 1978 Yankees team: Reggie Jackson, Sparky Lyle, Catfish Hunter, Ron Guidry, Mickey Rivers, and Willie Randolph. There was a moving ceremony before the game honoring Thurman Munson, the late captain of that Yankees team. Mindful of the eruption I'd sparked from Mantle the year before, I asked for no autographs from the big four—DiMaggio, Mantle, Ford, and Rizzuto—bothering The Mick only for a photo in the dugout before the game.

Also returning to the Stadium for Old Timers' Day were three or four former Yankees bat boys. Nick gave them lockers and uniforms to wear, and they took the field for batting practice with the players who had been on the Yankees roster when they'd had their stints as teenagers in the clubhouse some twenty or thirty years before. To me and the other present-day bat boys, there was something slightly pitiable about seeing these grown men return to the Stadium and relive their teenage years. After the Old Timers' festivities ended and they'd left the clubhouse, we teased each other about who among us wouldn't be able to let go either.

"If I'm still coming back here twenty years from now," I told Bill and Silverio, "shoot me."

Later in the afternoon, I learned via a video clip on the Stadium's DiamondVision that there was another notable Yankees anniversary that could have been celebrated that Old Timers' Day. July 24, 1993, was ten years to the day from the infamous "pine tar game" I'd witnessed as an eight-year-old rookie Yankees fan. Exactly a decade before, I'd been sitting in the upper deck of Yankee Stadium with my dad and little brother. Ten years later, I was sharing the Yankees dugout with two players who had been in New York's lineup that day: Graig Nettles and Don Mattingly. Nettles, who in 1983 was in his last year in a Yankees uniform, was back for Old Timers' Day as a member of the 1978 championship team. Mattingly, who in 1983 was in his rookie season, was suddenly playing as if it might be another decade before he'd even be eligible to become an old-timer.

A few days after Old Timers' Day, I was back at the CD Guy's store, bearing another sanitary sock stuffed with authentically autographed baseballs. Walking the aisles trying to pick out the "ten or twelve" CDs he told me I was welcome to, I had trouble choosing only a dozen from the thousands of albums on display. There was so much good music; I wanted a thirteenth album twice as much as the twelfth album I'd just selected. Even as I wondered how I'd come up with more memorabilia to trade for more music, I told the CD Guy I'd be back again soon. How much would I need to satisfy his appetite, I wondered, so that my appetite would be satisfied in turn?

The next time I visited I delivered another half dozen balls. One or two of these I'd signed myself. I felt guilty handing them over, but not so much that it kept me from accepting more of his merchandise, and I justified that portion of the transaction with a single word: greenfly. It's no different, I told myself, from what somebody else at the Stadium, maybe everybody else, is doing. "What he doesn't know," and so on and so forth.

In time, though, the CD Guy's satisfaction with having cultivated his own Guy, his Inside Guy, began to wane. Signed baseballs weren't really doing it for him anymore, he told me. He halved the number of CDs he'd allowed me on my previous trips and renewed his request for larger-ticket items. I left the store feeling cheated, as if I hadn't received equal value for the baseballs I'd traveled all the way down to Lower Manhattan to deliver to him. Baseballs signed by a Yankees bat boy.

Back at the Stadium, I found lying around the clubhouse a used pair of batting gloves, encrusted with pine tar. These would do. But asking Mattingly to sign a pair of batting gloves that he knew weren't his own was obviously out of the question. I signed Mattingly's signature to them myself. "Game-worn batting gloves," I told the CD Guy the next time I went to see him.

"That's what I'm talking about, Spider," he said. "Get me some more stuff like this."

I left the store that afternoon with the dozen CDs I'd previously become accustomed to receiving. But mulling it over on the 4 train up to the Stadium—the Yankees were playing that night—I still felt wronged. I asked myself: shouldn't signed, game-used batting gloves (albeit fake ones) be worth more CDs than a half dozen signed baseballs (also fake)? Why's this Guy getting so goddamn stingy? What the hell is his problem?

Blinded by greed, I was that certain that I was the one being taken advantage of, the one getting the bum end of the deal. That sure that *he* was taking *me* for a fool.

The Yankees ended July still tied for first place with the Blue Jays. Toronto was scheduled to visit the Bronx for a four-game series the first week of August, and pennant fever had gripped the ballplayers, the New York media, and the City. Playing in his first true pennant race in seven years, Mattingly was in the middle of a fifty-game stretch that saw him hit over .350 with more than fifty RBIs; he hadn't hit like that since the mid-eighties. Bernie Williams had just started a hitting streak that would reach twenty-one games, the Yankees' longest since 1986. Both Paul O'Neill and Wade Boggs were hitting above .300. The stage seemed set not only for an epic series but a run for the division title.

The already significant interest in the Toronto series was further boosted when, on the eve of the first game at the Stadium, the Blue Jays traded for Rickey Henderson, the former Yankee who had nearly incited a New York–Oakland brawl just two weeks before.

As part of his effort to win the Yankees a new municipally funded ballpark in Manhattan or New Jersey, Steinbrenner had loudly complained to the papers all summer about poor attendance at the Stadium. He blamed the low gate on the deteriorating ballpark; on the lousy parking available and the poor public transportation options from the suburbs; on the fact that there weren't enough cops on the streets of the South Bronx. But the problem, apparently, was less the Stadium than it was the losing teams the Yankees had put on the field most of the previous decade. Yankees fans came out in force for all four games against the Blue Jays.

In fact, the fans probably came out too strong: before the first game of the series, many of the forty-three thousand in attendance booed the Canadian national anthem. The boorish behavior dominated the coverage of the game—won by Toronto—in the next day's papers. The Canadian consulate in New York made a statement condemning the disrespect shown to the visiting team; the mayor's office issued an apology on behalf of the City of New York and all New Yorkers.

We weren't sure what to expect the next game. Bob Sheppard, the Yankees PA announcer, read a pregame apology and statement pleading with the fans in attendance not to repeat the previous night's ugly episode.

I was standing next to Abbott on the top step of the dugout when the Yankees position players took the field at the top of the first inning. As we removed our baseball caps, he asked me if I thought the fans would boo again.

"I don't know," I said. "Hopefully not."

But as the first strains of "O Canada" came over the center-field speakers, the boos began again.

The Michigan-born Abbott motioned with his head toward the morons jeering the anthem.

"These are your people," he told me.

After a few moments, though, a chorus of cheers rose to meet the boos and lasted through the end of the song.

"Those are my people," I said.

The Yankees lost the first two games to the Blue Jays, and The Boss showed up in the clubhouse before the third game of the series. I hadn't seen him since I'd been awarded my Yankee Foundation scholarship a few months before, and I wasn't sure I'd get an opportunity to see him again before I left for college at the beginning of September. I hoped his mood hadn't been soured by the fact that the Yankees had dropped two games back in the standings.

"Uh, Mr. Steinbrenner," I said, stepping in front of him as he made his way across the clubhouse. "I'm Matt McGough, I work here in the clubhouse. You gave me a scholarship to go to Williams this fall."

"Oh, sure," The Boss said, extending his hands and grabbing me by both shoulders.

"I just wanted to say thanks," I said.

"Congratulations," he told me, giving me a little shake by my shoulders. "With my grades, I could never have gotten into that school today."

Then he slapped me on the back and continued on his way to the other side of the locker room.

The Yankees won the last two games against the Blue Jays to split the series, and after a brief road trip to Minnesota and Boston, came back to the Stadium and swept three games from the Orioles to move back into a tie for first. The Yankees' pursuit of Toronto seemed positively Sisyphean: on three separate occasions they had moved even with the Blue Jays at the top of the division, but they had yet to pull ahead, even for a day, into sole possession of first place.

I would leave for college in three weeks. Mindful of the shrinking window of time, I couldn't resist the temptation to make one final run on the CD Guy before letting things stand pat for good.

Late that night after the game—another Yankees win—I sat at my locker with a silver ink pen and a pair of my own used baseball spikes, Nikes, the same brand and size that I knew Mattingly himself wore. I was using the pen to add a "23" to each heel and a signature to each tongue when one of the visiting clubhouse bat boys walked past my locker.

"What are you doing, Spider?" he asked.

"Don't worry about it," I said, blowing the ink dry and putting the shoes inside my footlocker.

"Aw, don't pull that shit on me."

I ignored him.

"No, seriously," he persisted. "What's the deal?"

"No, seriously," I mimicked him. "Don't worry about it."

"Spider, you better tell me what's up."

I turned my back to him and started packing my bag to go home for the night.

"Spider, you can either tell me about it, or I tell Nick about it. You think Nick won't worry about it?"

I couldn't tell whether he was joking or not. I didn't appreciate him threatening to bring Nick into it. But given what he'd seen me doing a few moments before, it didn't seem wise trying to stonewall him. On the heels of my recent evolution from being Nick's own dutiful employee to something like a personal squire to the ballplayers, I could sense that Nick may have had it in for me already. Reports of fraudulent dealings with the CD Guy, I thought, just might push him over the edge. Leaving for college in a few weeks, I had enough things on my to-do list already. I wasn't eager to squeeze an ass-kicking from Nick into my schedule.

"It's a CD deal," I told the visiting clubhouse bat boy.

"You've got a CD Guy?" he said with reverence.

"Yeah," I said.

"No shit. Wow."

I recounted the story of how I'd met the CD Guy and how things had escalated over the previous month.

"You got some good CDs?" he asked.

"Oh, man," I said. "Great CDs."

Among the many other errors of judgment I made in dealing with the CD Guy were some highly questionable musical selections. If I'd been thinking straight, I might have pulled together a pretty impressive record collection, a music library that might improve with age, or at least stand the test of time. Say, every Miles Davis or John Coltrane or Thelonious Monk album ever released. The entire oeuvres of Stevie Wonder, Johnny Cash, and Bob Dylan. The Beach Boys, the Beatles, and the Stones. The greatest hits of Beethoven, Bach, and Mozart. A solid collection of blues records. Early A Tribe Called Quest, Gang Starr, Radiohead, or Nirvana.

Here's some of what I selected instead: Wreckx-N-Effect's *Hard or Smooth*; the Jerky Boys' eponymous release; RuPaul's *Supermodel of the World*; Bon Jovi's *Keep the Faith*; Bloods & Crips' *Bangin' on Wax*; Enya's *Shepherd Moons*; TLC's *Oooooooohhh . . . On the TLC Tip*; the soundtrack from *The Bodyguard*; the CD single of Tag Team's *Whoomp! (There It Is)*.

I proudly counted the albums off on my fingers.

"Damn," he said, his voice tinged with awe. "Spider, you've got to cut me in."

"I don't know, man," I said. "I'll have to think it over."

But at that moment, considering what role he might be able to play, an idea popped to mind.

"You can do Tartabull, right?" I asked him.

"I've got a great Tartabull," he answered. "You've seen it, you know."

It was true; I had seen it. His Tartabull might have been better than Tartabull's.

"Can you keep your mouth shut?" I asked him.

"Definitely," he said.

I walked him through my nascent plan. "This Guy's a greenfly, right?" I said.

"Yeah."

"So what he wants more than anything else is to believe that he's down with the players, probably as much as he wants the memorabilia itself."

"Okay."

"So what if I go to the CD Guy and tell him that Tartabull asked me to act as a go-between? That Tartabull himself wants CDs. Like it's a personal thing."

"He'll probably say the sky's the limit."

"And Tartabull doesn't make deals," I said. "There's no way he knows this Guy, no way he'll ever know this guy. It'll never get back to him."

"It's perfect," he said. "We could really bury this Guy," using the clubhouse slang ordinarily employed to describe what green-flies do to clubhouse attendants with their own requests for favors.

"We've got to bury him," I said. "Because after this, it's over. No more CDs."

"Why?"

"I'm sick of this Guy. And I don't want to piss Nick and Rob off just before I go. Nick'll kill me if he sees me asking for one more autographed baseball. It's not worth it. I'll hit the CD Guy up once more, and then I'm done. After that, he's all yours if you want him."

"Are you kidding?" he said. "Hell yeah! I'd love to have a CD Guy. But how many are we going ask him for now?"

"I don't know," I said. "Maybe fifty?"

"Shit, fifty? Really?"

"I think he'll go for it," I said. "We'll go in fifty-fifty. We each make a list of twenty-five CDs, and if he thinks we're burying him we'll just scale back."

He exhaled deeply, speechless at the flawlessness of the plan.

"How's that Wreckx-N-Effect album?" he asked.

I rolled my eyes at him patronizingly.

"You haven't heard it?" I said. "It's sick. A classic."

Down at the CD Guy's store the next morning, I handed over the Nikes and told the CD Guy that Tartabull had asked me to pass a message to him.

"Danny saw me in the clubhouse with some of the music you gave me," I said, "and he asked me to see what you'd want from him for fifty CDs."

"Wow, fifty?" the CD Guy said. "That's a lot."

"Yeah, I know," I ad-libbed. "But that's what he told me to ask you. If you want, I can go back and tell him it's too many."

"No, no," he said quickly, "it's not too many." He thought it over for a minute. "For Danny, I'll do it. Tell him I'll do it for two signed bats."

"Okay," I said. "I'll let him know."

Between innings of that night's game, I met the visiting clubhouse bat boy behind home plate and told him what he needed to come up with as his end of the bargain.

The next day I found two signed Tartabull bats and a list of twenty-five albums—Wreckx-N-Effect at the top—tucked inside my locker. I added his selections to mine and copied the whole list, numbered one to fifty, onto a sheet of lined loose-leaf paper.

A day after that, I dropped a plastic bag of twenty-five CDs, sealed shut with Scotch tape, inside the footlocker in the visiting clubhouse shared by its three bat boys.

I walked back to the Yankees clubhouse feeling buoyant, and only in part because the Tartabull gambit had come off smoothly. I felt relieved to be finished with shady dealmaking, done with the CD Guy, and free from anything that might detract from the week and a half I had remaining in the Yankees clubhouse. The secrecy and deceptions of the CD deal had been thrilling in the beginning, exhilarating in the same way the Network had been when Chris and I first pushed our money across that folding table in the wedding hall in the Bronx. But unlike the Network, I'd come to understand that with the CD Guy, I had put a lot more than just money on the line: certainly my reputation in the clubhouse, and probably also my dream job itself. Sneaking around the clubhouse behind Nick's and Robby's backs? Stealing from the Yankees? The people who'd mentored me and taught me so much, the organization that would pay half my freshman-year tuition? CDs were nice, but not that nice. It made me cringe to think of how easily I'd gotten carried away, how willingly I'd risked tarnishing the best thing in my life. I was ready to chalk up the experience as a phase I'd gone through, one I felt lucky to be over.

There was no one to announce it to, but that day I retired from "dealing." I felt lighter than I had in weeks.

The Yankees had a three-game series scheduled against the Kansas City Royals that weekend. With a night game Friday and a day game Saturday, it would be my last overnight at the Stadium.

Not that any of the guys at work shed any tears over my

fast-approaching departure, or even mentioned it; it would not have been in line with the ethos of the clubhouse. But I had as much fun after we finished work that Friday as any other night in memory. After we finished cleaning the clubhouse and sorting the whites, we walked down to the batting cage in the Columbus Room. I'd grown taller (if not wider) over two seasons at the Stadium, and thanks to all the late-night practice, I'd become a better hitter as well; I stood in against the pitching machine markedly more capable and confident than I'd been a year before. When hitting got boring, we went to the visiting clubhouse, where we played cards and video games until 4:30 in the morning.

Four hours later I peeled myself off the couch in the players' lounge, showered, and was sent up the block by Nick to pick up the morning papers. By the time I returned, a handful of coaches and players had already arrived. It was still too early for any of the ballplayers to send me on a surreptitious food run, so I took a seat at Nick's picnic table in the middle of the clubhouse and opened the newspaper. I was halfway through the crossword when I heard my name from across the room.

I looked up to see Tartabull coming through the door.

"Spider," he said, walking up to where I was sitting. "You know anything about some CDs you were supposed to give me?"

I felt like I'd just been kicked in the stomach. Or was about to be. I thanked God that Nick was out of earshot and that Tartabull seemed confused, not mad.

"No, Bull," I stuttered. "Why?"

"Well, there's some guy upstairs in the parking lot who says he gave you a bunch of CDs for me."

"Yeah?" I asked, trying to visibly furrow my brow.

"Yeah," he said. "I told him I didn't know what he was

talking about. He said, 'You know, Spider.' I said, 'Yeah, I know Spider. But I don't know anything about any CDs.' "

"In the players' parking lot?"

"In the players' lot. I parked my car and he walked right up to me."

"Yeah?" I repeated. It was all I could manage to say. All the moisture had left my mouth.

"Yeah. You better head up there and talk to him," Tartabull counseled me. "He seemed pretty pissed off."

"Okay," I said. "Thanks."

"No problem," Tartabull said, then walked to his locker.

Christ, I thought. What the hell am I going to do?

Not thirty seconds later, the ringing clubhouse phone shattered my anxious daydream. Silverio, standing near the coaches' room, took the call.

"Spider," he shouted from across the clubhouse. "Phone!"

I sprang to my feet and sprinted over, gesturing furiously for him to cover the mouthpiece with his spare hand.

"Who is it?" I stage-whispered.

Silverio shrugged.

"Ask," I implored him.

"Who is it?" he said into the phone, then placed his hand back over the mouthpiece. "Some guy up at the press gate," he said.

"Tell him I'm not here."

"He's not here," Silverio said dispassionately. "No . . . No, I don't know where he is . . . Nope . . . Don't know . . . Okay, I'll give him the message."

"Wow," Silverio said after he hung up the phone. "That guy sounded hot."

"Oh, Jesus," I whimpered.

"What's he so fired up about?"

"Don't worry about it," I said, trying to regain my composure.

Silverio smiled. He definitely wasn't worried about it. I'd guess he was more interested in just watching the color drain from my face. The lofty perch from which I'd been bossing him and Bill around since midseason suddenly seemed much less secure.

I returned to Nick's table and rested my head in the palms of my upturned hands. Oh, Jesus, I thought. What am I going to do? The CD Guy is going to kill me. I thought back to our initial meeting outside the visiting clubhouse and to how shady he'd seemed. How he'd been connected enough to get inside not only the Yankees clubhouse but also the players' parking lot. Good Lord, I thought. I'm fucked. He's going to kill me.

I sat at Nick's table for a full hour without moving from my pitiful pose. I was up to my neck in shit, I realized, and the realization brought forth a torrent of self-pity, a thick layer of which settled on top. Shit and self-pity up to my eyes; it made breathing a labor.

Robby finally came over and nudged my shoulder.

"Hey, Spider," he asked. "You okay?"

I lifted my head to look up at him and felt a tear run down my cheek.

"I don't feel too good," I said.

"Yeah, you don't look too good, either," he said. "Even worse than usual. Why don't you go lie down in the trainers' room? Gino can give you an aspirin or something."

"Ohhhh," I moaned, pushing myself up from the table, pulling myself together.

I'm so sorry, I repeated to myself over and over as I trudged toward Gino's office. As if those genuinely felt sentiments might rescue me from the inevitable cycle of what-goes-around-comes-around.

If I get out of this, I swore, I'll never lie again.

I dressed for the game and told Silverio and Bill that I'd handle balls that afternoon; I left it up to them who did bats and who went down the line. It was one of only a handful of times all season that, exercising my prerogative as head bat boy to decide who did what during the games, I hadn't kept bats for myself.

I didn't know whether or not the CD Guy had stuck around the Stadium for the ballgame and, if so, where he might be sitting. Without knowing that, there was no way I was going to put myself out there for three hours, kneeling in the on-deck circle ten feet from the fans behind home plate, let alone on a stool down the first-base line right up against the right-field seats. Handling balls was ordinarily the least desirable of the three game-time roles played by bat boys, but that afternoon it was exactly what I wanted to be doing: leaving the dugout, head down and running hard, only for brief sprints to the home plate umpire and back.

Just before first pitch, feeling slightly better, I popped back into the clubhouse to call my parents. I'd been sleeping at the Stadium the entire homestand and hadn't seen them in over a week. I'd be coming home after the game that night and I wanted to find out what was for dinner. To be honest, I was also looking for some compassion, something to help me get through the day, a small dose of the unconditional love I imagined would come my way that evening after having been away for so long. There was no way I could confide the circumstances of my dilemma to them, but I knew that a night at home would provide a respite. Time to get my thoughts together. Room to take a breath. I'd slept at Yankee Stadium nine nights in a row with nary a phone call home, but surely even the most prodigal son would be welcomed back to the nest in the last few weeks before he left it forever.

My dad answered the phone.

"Where are you?" he asked me.

"At the Stadium," I said.

"At the Stadium." I could sense his fury through the telephone line. "Well, you're coming straight home after the game tonight," he said. "You hear me?"

"Yes, sir," I said. Never before in my life had I ever addressed my father as "sir." He was that mad, and I was that desperate to get out of the doghouse.

"I don't know what the fuck is going on at the Stadium," he spat into the phone, "but I don't like it one bit."

It's worth noting here that I could count on one hand the number of times I'd ever heard my dad curse. It's not that he didn't have a temper, but he saved the bad words for only the most egregious transgressions of behavior, justice, or mechanical function. The time, halfway through a long car ride, I intentionally put chewing gum in my little brother's hair. The time at the airport when we got bumped from our flight to the beach vacation my parents had waited six months for. The time he cut halfway through his own thumb with a pair of electric hedge clippers.

"What is this," he continued, "about some CDs that you were supposed to give to Danny Tartabull?"

"I don't know," I said. I'd forgotten that I had given the CD Guy my telephone number at home; he'd never used it before.

"You don't know?" my dad said. He was so livid I could picture steam coming out of his ears. "Well, some man called here an hour ago and said he gave you fifty CDs for Danny

Tartabull, and that Tartabull told him this morning that he had no idea what he was talking about."

"Uhhhhh," I said.

"He said he called the clubhouse this morning and you weren't there."

"I don't know."

"None of this rings a bell?"

"No."

"Well, something fishy's going on, and when you get home tonight you're going to tell me exactly what that is. Then you're going to call this man who called, and tell him."

"Okay," I said. But my dad had already hung up the phone.

I made it through the game and took my time with the postgame cleanup routine. I'd never been so grateful to have a pile of filthy baseball spikes to shine or five hundred square feet of carpet to vacuum. It was almost therapeutic.

After the last of the players and coaches left, I sequestered myself in the manager's office and shut the door. I steeled myself and dialed the CD Guy's number at home.

"Hello," he answered.

"It's Spider," I said.

The CD Guy started shouting immediately. "What the fuck is going on? I saw Tartabull today at the Stadium and he didn't know anything about the music I gave you. What the fuck are you trying to pull?"

"Whoa, whoa," I said.

"Whoa, whoa, my ass," he continued, louder every second. "You whoa, whoa, you little shit."

Something inside me snapped.

"Hold on," I said, raising my own voice for the first time. Unrehearsed words poured out of me into the phone. "It's not my problem that Tartabull didn't remember you this morning when you jumped him in the players' parking lot. I gave him those CDs. You think Danny Tartabull's supposed to remember you because you gave him fifty CDs? Are you kidding me? These guys don't pay for anything, ever. You think you're the only guy who ever gave free shit to a Yankee?"

I took a breath. On the other end of the line, the CD Guy was silent.

"Now," I said, "you explain something to me." I had no idea from where I was summoning this audacity. "Why would you call my father at home and tell him what I'm doing down at Yankee Stadium? Don't you know how deep in shit I am at home right now? My dad knows I'm not supposed to be taking stuff out of the clubhouse, and you call him on the telephone and tell him that I'm taking stuff out of the clubhouse? I'm leaving for school in a week, and you just fucked up my last week at home. What the fuck is wrong with you?"

I was nearly in tears from the stress of the conversation, just about hyperventilating into Buck Showalter's telephone.

"I'm sorry," the CD Guy said, suddenly subdued. "I didn't think."

"You're goddamn right you're sorry," I hollered.

"Listen," he said, more conciliatory. "If you want to come down to the store, I can . . ."

"Are you out of your mind?" I cut him off. "I'm done with this shit. D-O-N-E! Done!"

"Okay," he said, and I slammed down the phone.

When I got home that night I told my dad I'd spoken to the CD Guy. It'd been a misunderstanding, I said, but we'd worked it out. Almost eight hours had passed since we'd talked that morning, and my dad's temper had cooled. I'm not sure whether he believed my bare-bones explanation; I think it's more likely that he sensed the anxiety and shame in my voice and just decided to take my word for it that the situation had been resolved. He was displeased with me, I could tell, but disinclined to cross-examine me for details.

Lying in bed that night, I understood not only that I'd dodged a bullet, barely, but that I undoubtedly hadn't deserved to. And neither had the CD Guy deserved the treatment I'd given him on the phone. I imagine that he was as genuinely impassioned a Yankees fan as I. It hadn't been that long since I'd been on the outside of the clubhouse looking in, desperate for autographs myself. In snapping at him on the phone, in using my proximity and connections to celebrity to intimidate and humiliate him, I'd acted in a way that I respected others in the clubhouse—the players, Nick, Robby, the Mule—for never having acted toward me. It was a shameful realization, and I resolved to myself that even if I'd had another two years and not two weeks left as a Yankees bat boy, I'd never play that card again.

After the next day's game, the Yankees left town on a seven-game road trip to Chicago and Cleveland. I used the time to pack up everything I thought I might need for college and figure out how it all might fit inside my parents' car. Freshman orientation would begin Sunday morning, and my dad was planning to drive me up to Massachusetts when the dorms opened Saturday afternoon.

I arranged with Nick for my little brother Damien to fill in for me at the Stadium during the weekday games I would miss once I'd left for school. I promised Nick I'd return to New York from Williams for the two weekend series scheduled at Yankee

Stadium the last month of the season: one against Boston in mid-September, and the season-ending series against Detroit the first three days of October. I knew it'd be hectic getting myself down from school in time for first pitch on those two Fridays and back to Williamstown for Monday morning classes, but the thought that I'd be returning soon made leaving much easier to accept. Especially in the middle of a pennant race.

The Yankees returned from Cleveland once again in first place, still even with Toronto. I had only four games left at the Stadium before leaving home, and it was hard not to get too sentimental thinking that my time with the Yankees was about to come to a close. Without question, these had been the richest two years of my life, and I wondered whether even college life—college!—would measure up to what I'd seen and been through with the Yankees.

There seemed little chance that my learning curve at Williams would be even half as steep as the one I'd scrambled up my first season working in the clubhouse. Yankee Stadium was where I had my first beer and my first fistfight. It was where I was cut my first real paycheck and met my first real boss. There was no telling how many small and large lessons I had learned working in the clubhouse; in hindsight, I'm sure I learned as much about human nature there as I did in the entire course of my formal education.

The job had given me a confidence I hadn't had when, as a sixteen-year-old, I sat down and wrote the fateful letter that would lead me to the Yankees clubhouse. My association with the Yankees probably spared me a good deal of the grief that, as a scrawny bookish kid from the suburbs, I might otherwise have been due from the other kids my age whom I encountered in the City. My job helped me feel comfortable in worlds I'd never had the confidence to move through before, and it made me fear less the unfamiliar worlds I knew I'd encounter down the road. Robby probably put it to me best, after I'd confessed that spring to being nervous about an upcoming college application interview: "Do you know how many people would piss their pants trying to have a normal conversation with Don Mattingly? You talk with Donnie every day. You've got nothing to be nervous about."

I sat next to Jim Abbott in the dugout the night before I left for Williams, and we talked about college life. For weeks leading up to that last game, he'd teased me about leaving and even about my choice of schools.

"Wellesley, right?" he'd asked me more than once.

"Williams," I'd answer. "Wellesley's a girls' school."

"Oh," he'd say, feigning ignorance. "My bad."

Sitting on the bench that last game, Abbott told me about his first week at the University of Michigan, a freshman year that ended with him winning the Sullivan Award. The stories he told me, though, were not of the social rewards that I'd have expected would have followed from his athletic achievements. Abbott spoke instead of how nervous he'd been leaving home for Ann Arbor, and how sure he was that he wouldn't fit in with his new classmates.

"It'll come with time," he told me, putting his hand on my shoulder.

"Yeah?" I said.

"Don't worry about it," he said, smirking, mimicking the line he'd heard me drop on Bill and Silverio so many times that summer.

At the top of the seventh, Abbott stood and nudged me with his elbow. The game wasn't over yet, but he was the starting pitcher the next afternoon and, as was customary, the Yankees were sending him home early for a full night's sleep.

I stood and shook his hand as firmly as I could manage.

"Take care, Spider," he said, looking me straight in the eye. "Be good."

"Thanks," I said. "I will." I meant it.

He brought his hand up and gently cuffed me on the side of the head.

"Don't let the door hit you on the way out," he said, grinning. "And come back soon, okay?"

Retiring from Baseball

I left for college just before noon on the morning of September 4.

The Yankees had a game scheduled later that afternoon at the Stadium against the Cleveland Indians. It'd be the first home game I would miss in nearly two seasons. It would also be my brother Damien's first game as a Yankees bat boy.

It was a three-hour drive from Tarrytown to Williamstown, in northwest Massachusetts, and as my mom, dad, and I drove north from New York, we tuned in to the beginning of the game on the car radio. Abbott walked Cleveland's leadoff batter, Kenny Lofton, then induced a double play and a fly out to end the top of the first inning; the Yankees failed to score in the bottom half of the frame.

Somewhere north of Peekskill, the radio signal from the Bronx started cutting out on us. We heard the Yankees go up 3–0 in the bottom of the third before the broadcast gave way to static. My dad switched the radio off and we made small talk the rest of the way, chatting about where my Regis friends were headed off to school and about the classes for which I'd preregistered that semester. I mentioned that among the other orientation materials I'd received from Williams was a letter breaking down where the other members of the Class of '97 hailed from; all fifty states were represented, with New York near the top of the list.

"I've been thinking," I told my parents. "I'm not going to tell anybody at school about my Yankees connection."

"Yeah?" my dad said.

"Yeah," I said. "I just want to make my own reputation up there. You know, not be 'the bat boy' all the time, like the way it got to be a little in New York."

"I think that's a good idea," he said. "It's a fresh start for you at college."

We pulled onto campus about four o'clock in the afternoon. My dad helped me unload my possessions from the trunk of the car and stack them on the sidewalk outside my dorm. Amidst the piles of boxes and suitcases, I exchanged nervous glances and what's-ups with some of my new classmates. A few freshmen who had already moved in stood outside the dorm's front door, talking about a party someone was throwing later that night.

I was pretty eager for the full-blown college experience to begin, and was pretty sure it wouldn't until my parents had left my side.

"I can take it from here," I told them. My mom nodded, understanding, and I said good-bye to my dad with a handshake and her with a hug. I told them I'd be home for the Red Sox series in two weeks.

It had started to drizzle a little and, notwithstanding my desire to keep my Yankees ties under wraps, the only cap I had within reach was the one I'd packed after coming home from the Stadium the night before.

I was carrying a box up to my third-floor dorm room when one of my new classmates passed me on the staircase. We introduced ourselves. His name was Sam.

"You a Yankees fan?" he asked me, pointing at my hat.

"Yeah," I said.

"You hear about the game today?"

"No," I said. "I know the Yankees were up 3–0. Why?"

"Oh, man," Sam said, shaking his head. "Wow." I was thinking about the pennant race, the fact that the Yankees were two games back of Toronto. Maybe the Indians had evened the score and the Yankees had come back to win it. Maybe they'd picked up a full game on the Blue Jays.

"What happened?" I asked. "They win?"

"No-hitter," Sam said, beaming. "A no-hitter!"

It took a second for the words to sink in.

"You're kidding, right?" I said.

"Seriously," he said. "Abbott threw a no-hitter."

I thought I was going to be sick, simultaneously overcome with pride at what Abbott had accomplished and grief for not having been there to share it. I felt my eyes burning, and I wasn't about to let a wholly inexplicable wave of tears mar my first college friendship.

"Goddammit!" I yelled, and stormed the rest of the way up the stairs to my room. I can't imagine what Sam made of my outburst.

I didn't even have a phone to hook up yet to be able to call the Stadium. A few hours after sullenly unpacking my possessions, I found a pay phone in the dorm's laundry room and called home collect.

"You heard about the game?" my mom asked excitedly. "We got a message from Damien when we got home."

"Yeah," I sulked.

"He was so excited," she said.

"I can't believe I missed it," I said.

"Call back in a couple hours," my mom told me. "I'm sure he'll be happy to tell you all about it."

"It was awesome," my brother told me on the phone after he got home from the Stadium. "Just crazy. They gave Abbott a bottle of champagne in the clubhouse and pulled the pitching rubber out of the mound and gave that to him, too. The crowd made him take like five curtain calls."

I skipped the party that night and spent the evening instead in front of the dorm's communal television, watching highlights of the game on ESPN. After allowing one walk in each of the first two innings, Abbott had settled down, retiring the Indians in order in the third and the fourth. He used a double play to erase a leadoff walk in the top of the fifth inning, and stranded another runner who'd reached on a walk in the top of the sixth. No hits through six innings, and with less than pinpoint control: Abbott walked five batters and had only three strikeouts that day. But he was able to keep the ball low and consistently lured the Indians into groundout after groundout.

As with nearly every no-hitter, a handful of stellar defensive plays made it seem in hindsight as if the no-hitter had been fated to happen from the beginning. Abbott's first close call came in the top of the seventh, when Albert Belle hit a hard grounder in the hole between third base and shortstop. Wade Boggs ranged to his left and dove to stop the ball, then made a strong throw to first to catch Belle by a step. The play put the crowd on notice— Abbott might be able to do it!—and they stood on their feet the rest of the way.

Lofton led off the top of the ninth inning and, on the first pitch, tried to bunt his way on base. The crowd was infuriated, taking the attempt as unsporting, but it didn't seem to bother Abbott; with the next pitch, he retired Lofton on a feeble grounder. With one out, Felix Fermin drove a fly ball 390 feet to left–center field, the deepest part of the Stadium. Bernie Williams chased it down on the warning track for the second out of the inning. Abbott was one out away; the crowd was beside itself. Abbott's first pitch to Carlos Baerga, perhaps the Indians' best hitter, was a called strike. Baerga made contact with the second pitch, but hit it only meekly. The Yankees shortstop, Randy Velarde, charged the ground ball.

As Velarde came up with it, Abbott turned to first base and raised both arms in the air. Velarde's throw settled in Mattingly's glove, and the Stadium erupted. It was the eighth no-hitter in the ninety-year history of the Yankees and the first since Dave Righetti's on the Fourth of July 1983. Watching the highlights of Abbott's no-no, which seemed to repeat every few minutes, I thought back to watching Righetti's game as an eight-year-old on the floor of my parents' living room.

The next morning I used a fistful of quarters to call the Yankees clubhouse.

Silverio answered. I asked for my brother, then kept Damien on the phone only long enough to confirm that Abbott had arrived at the ballpark.

"Lemme speak to him," I said.

I could overhear Damien in the background: "It's my brother."

"Spider," Abbott said when he took the phone.

"Congratulations, Jimmy," I said.

"You should've left for college months ago," he told me. "I hadn't realized what's been holding me back all this time."

"I'm sorry I missed it," I said. "I skipped my first college party to watch the highlights on TV last night."

"I appreciate that, Spider."

"How was it?" I asked. "I mean, how did it feel?"

"Just incredible. It was a great day. I'll never forget it."

"Me neither," I said. I wasn't sure what more to say. "I guess I'll see you in a couple weeks."

"Your brother's keeping your seat warm for you on the bench," he told me.

"Keep an eye on him," I said.

Even in the wake of Abbott's no-hitter, I managed to stick to my word in keeping the Yankees job quiet among my new classmates. I returned to the Stadium the third weekend in September, missing a freshman class semiformal, the first one of the year. All my classmates were going; the week before I left, it seemed to be the only thing people on campus were talking about.

"I've got to go home for the weekend," I told Sam.

"Really?" he said. "Why?"

"There's some stuff I have to take care of."

"It's gonna be a good party," he said.

"I know, I know," I lamented.

It worried me to leave school, even for a weekend, and especially given the party, just as everyone seemed to be getting to know each other; I really thought that my college social life might never recover. But I also knew I'd feel better once I got back to the clubhouse.

In the few weeks I'd been away, the Yankees had lost ground in the standings, falling three games behind the Blue Jays. There was still hope, but with only fourteen games left on the schedule, it was dwindling. On September 5, the day after Abbott's no-hitter, the Yankees had tied Toronto for the division lead for the eighth time that season. And for the eighth time that season, within a couple of days the Yankees had dropped back to second. In the history of baseball, no team had ever spent so many days tied for first place without ever taking sole possession, even for a single day.

The Yankees won both of my first two games back at the Stadium, the second in near-miraculous fashion. Down 3–1 to the Red Sox with a man on first and two outs in the bottom of the ninth inning, Yankees catcher Mike Stanley hit an easy pop fly that should have been the final out of the game. Nearly simultaneously, a fan jumped the low wall along the third-base line and ran out onto the field. I jogged out to home plate from my position near the Yankees on-deck circle to retrieve Stanley's bat. Out of the corner of my eye, even before the ball had descended into the glove of the Red Sox left fielder, I saw the third base umpire throw his hands up in the air, signaling time-out. The four umpires gathered and discussed their ruling while both teams stood around uncertainly, unsure whether the game was over. In light of the potential for fan interference, the umps finally announced, they were nullifying the fly out. Over Red Sox protestations, Stanley would get another chance. I handed his bat back to him and watched from the on-deck circle as he singled on the next pitch. With Yankees now on first and second, Wade Boggs singled as well, scoring a run and cutting the deficit to 3–2. The Red Sox reliever walked the next batter, loading the bases for Don Mattingly. By that point, what happened next had come to seem almost inevitable: Mattingly singled, bringing home two runs and giving the Yankees a 4–3 victory. The win kept New York three games behind Toronto.

Unfortunately, it was the closest the Yankees would be to first place the rest of the season. Beginning the day I traveled back to Williams, New York lost five games in a row, including two to Toronto. I followed the team closely from Williamstown, reading the box scores each morning and tracking Toronto's magic number, the figure representing the total number of Blue Jays wins and Yankees losses that would make a comeback mathematically impossible.

The last weekend in September, with the magic number at five, the Yankees went to Toronto and lost the first two games of a crucial three-game series. With the magic number at one, Abbott shut down the Blue Jays in the final game at the SkyDome, saving the Yankees the indignity of watching Toronto celebrate the division crown in front of them. But even a Yankees win the next night in Baltimore wasn't enough to delay the inevitable; the Blue Jays beat the Brewers in Milwaukee to end the pennant race and New York's inspired run for the playoffs.

There had been a consensus in April that the Yankees had improved their team since the end of the 1992 season. But few people had predicted that they might actually be able to contend for the division title. They'd exceeded all expectations by managing to stay in the race into the last week of September, and the team seemed poised to make an even stronger run at the playoffs the next season.

Mattingly would end the '93 season at .291, with 17 homers and 86 RBIs; a far cry from the numbers he'd put up in the mid-eighties, but still an improvement over his previous three seasons. Jimmy Key, with an 18–6 record and 3.00 ERA, had become the certifiable pitching ace the Yankees had lacked for so long. Paul O'Neill and Wade Boggs had both batted over .300 in their first year with the Yankees; O'Neill in particular had established himself as a fan favorite at the Stadium. Bernie Williams, long heralded as the Yankees center fielder of the future and still only

twenty-five years old, had played his first full season in the majors and secured a place in the Yankees lineup for the foreseeable
future. No one knew it yet, but by the end of the '93 season, the
foundation was in place for the Yankees' extraordinary run of
championships in the late nineties.

I returned to the Bronx for the Yankees' season-ending series against the Detroit Tigers. With the Yankees' win that Friday
night, my first game back, New York clinched second place in the
American League East. Had the wild card been in place, the victory would have given the Yankees their first playoff berth since
1981; but the wild card would not be introduced for another two
seasons. Second place had some symbolic importance, as the beat
writers pointed out in the next morning's papers; for the guys in
the Yankees clubhouse, though, it was nothing to celebrate.

After the game, Nick asked me offhandedly what year of
high school Damien was in.

"He just started his junior year," I told him.

"Is he planning on working here next year?"

"I don't know," I said, surprised at how Nick had phrased
the question. "I mean, I think if you had a spot for him, he'd take
it in a second."

"Tell him I'm holding one for him, okay?"

"Okay," I said.

My last game in pinstripes was Sunday afternoon, October
3. The date held special significance in New York baseball history—it was the anniversary of Bobby Thomson's 1951 game-
and pennant-winning home run for the Giants against the
Brooklyn Dodgers—and the Yankees ended their season in style,
beating the Tigers 2–1 in the bottom of the ninth inning. The
entire Yankees roster emerged from the dugout to greet pinch-
runner Spike Owen at home plate as he scored the winning run

of the game, the final run of the season. The celebration was muted—the team was still disappointed it would not play any more baseball that season—but I was in the thick of the mob, exchanging high fives with the ballplayers as they left the field. It seemed like a pretty good way to end my career in baseball.

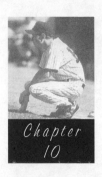

Chapter
10

Extra Innings

Five years later, I was living in Manhattan and a few weeks into my first year of law school when I got a call from the Yankees. The 1998 season had just ended and the postseason was about to begin; for the fourth year in a row, New York had qualified for the playoffs.

Even by Yankees standards, 1998 had been a remarkable season. The team finished its schedule with an American League–record 114 victories, four more than the legendary 1927 Yankees had been able to manage with Lou Gehrig and Babe Ruth. Even prior to the playoffs, the team was being hailed as one of the greatest in baseball history.

With all the media attention, the clubhouse had apparently never been more hectic. Celebrities and reporters from all over the country had flocked to the Stadium, and all of them expected access to the players and the clubhouse. A few weeks earlier, a photographer had been caught leaving the room with a Derek

Jeter jersey tucked into his camera bag. His credential was promptly revoked and he was thrown out of the Stadium, but the thought had occurred that it might be good to have someone around during the postseason who knew the clubhouse routine and could be trusted to keep an eye on things. An extra hand on-deck to help out when the clubhouse got even more chaotic as the Yankees marched through the playoffs.

I gave the offer a great deal of thought.

The first month of law school had hardly been a cakewalk, but comparing my October schedule with the one issued by Major League Baseball, I could see that working the playoffs wouldn't require me to miss any classes. I'd have to do my reading and squeeze homework in among the games being played at the Stadium, but then again, I'd run that drill before.

A larger concern was what it would feel like being back in the clubhouse. I wasn't being asked to bat boy, but I thought back to the last Old Timers' Day I'd worked and how we'd privately disparaged the bat boys who'd returned to the Stadium years after their tenures had ended. I now knew from my own experience that the clubhouse did in fact continue to exert a powerful pull on its former teenage denizens. Even deep in my heart, I couldn't be sure whether it was only because I hadn't been within subway distance that I hadn't made my own return on Old Timers' Day, hat in hand.

But this, I told myself, was a chance to see something I hadn't seen in my two years as a bat boy—playoff baseball at Yankee Stadium, and from a better-than-front-row seat at that—and I couldn't count on the opportunity presenting itself again in the future. In the end, it was too good an offer to pass up.

. . .

I walked back into the Yankees clubhouse the afternoon of the first game of the playoffs. Much there had changed since the fall of 1993.

Don Mattingly had retired in 1995, the same year my brother Damien completed his own two-year stint as a bat boy. Derek Jeter had assumed the mantle of most popular Yankee; it was his photo and not Mattingly's that now adorned school lockers and bedroom walls throughout greater New York. Only two players remained from my last season as bat boy, Paul O'Neill and Bernie Williams. Not counting Jeter, whom I remembered meeting shortly after he'd been drafted by the Yankees six years before, I'd never met any of the ballplayers filling the lockers I still associated with Yankees of the early nineties. It seemed strange to see Jorge Posada dressing at Danny Tartabull's locker and David Cone at Jim Abbott's. Bernie Williams had inherited Mattingly's corner real estate.

Even more remarkable, at least to me, were the changes to the clubhouse staff. Nick had left the Yankees at the end of the '97 season and the team had promoted Robby to take his place. Joe Lee, a former bat boy who had overlapped with Damien, was now Robby's assistant. There were more bat boys—four—than had been there during my days; one of the four did not dress in uniform but, wearing khakis and a Yankees polo shirt, performed clubhouse duties during the game. I was issued a Yankees polo shirt of my own and a pair of sneakers made by Adidas, "the official footwear provider of the New York Yankees."

After batting practice, Robby introduced me to the clubhouse crew.

"Mike, George, Luigi, and Mitch," he'd said, pointing at each one, and then at me. "This is the Spider."

It was pretty clear from the get-go that, besides making sure nothing disappeared from the clubhouse, I had few formal duties to attend to. I set about picking up towels that had been left on the floor, wiping down the tables in the players' lounge, and otherwise just trying to stay out of the way.

The Yankees made quick work of the Texas Rangers in the first round of the playoffs, sweeping the best-of-five series in three games. In the next round, the best-of-seven American League Championship Series, New York defeated the Cleveland Indians four games to two to advance to the World Series.

Game 6, the ALCS-clinching victory, was played at the Stadium, the fifth home game of the postseason. I'd done my best to blend in with the rest of the clubhouse staff, but couldn't shake the sense that I didn't belong. I didn't regret returning—it was thrilling to finally experience a pennant-winning celebration in the Yankees clubhouse, complete with popping corks and gushing bottles of champagne—but after five games I finally understood why it had felt so awkward to see the old-timer bat boys return to the clubhouse. Why, now that I'd made my own return, I felt so out of place and self-conscious myself.

A sixteen- or seventeen-year-old working in a big league clubhouse fits neatly into a nearly century-old role. His well-worn place in the order of things eases his interactions with everyone else in the clubhouse. And though the kid may change and grow older, the role never does. There's no role in the clubhouse, I realized, for a twenty-three-year-old former bat boy, irrespective of how much time he might have logged in the dugout during earlier seasons or how comfortable he might have once felt in that same Yankees clubhouse. No one had stolen anything on my watch and I'd performed every other task asked of me as quickly and diligently as I had in the earliest days of my first season with the team. But that couldn't change what was apparent to me watching the other bat boys now: this was their time, and their stage, not mine. Mine had passed. No wonder I felt adrift.

Games 1 and 2 of the World Series, against the San Diego Padres, were played at the Stadium, and the Yankees won both. I was in the clubhouse after the second game when I crossed paths with one of the team's longtime beat writers. He recognized me and we shook hands warmly.

"You're back," he said.

"Just kind of helping out during the postseason," I said. "I'm actually in law school."

"Law school?" he said. "So what are you still doing here picking up jocks?"

I laughed, but the comment had struck a raw nerve. I couldn't explain to him what I was still doing there; I was still trying to figure it out myself. But the exchange crystallized my conviction that I couldn't return again to the clubhouse.

The World Series moved to San Diego for Games 3 and 4. I watched the first, a come-from-behind Yankees win, on television at my apartment with a few friends. For Game 4, I met a few of the bat boys from the Yankees clubhouse at a cavernous sports bar in Times Square. We staked out a table and watched the Yankees win their twenty-fourth World Championship. People in the bar around us hugged and kissed strangers; we could hear a chorus of car horns outside on Broadway and Seventh Av-

enue. The guys from the clubhouse confessed some disappointment that the Series hadn't ended at the Stadium, but as we tum-
bled out onto the sidewalk and into the citywide street party that
was in full swing, they shook their dejection off pretty quickly.

Mayor Giuliani scheduled a ticker-tape parade for that Friday morning to honor the returning World Champions. I'd
been told that the staging area would be so chaotic with players'
and Yankees employees' families and friends that you might not
need a credential to get on a float. I questioned whether or not
I should go, given my recent realization, but ultimately decided
that if this was my last hurrah, I might as well see it through all
the way to the end. I woke up early and took the subway up to
the Bronx.

By the time I got to the Stadium, a number of the ballplayers had already arrived at the clubhouse, most of them with wives
and children in tow. I was sitting on a couch in the players' lounge
waiting for the buses to leave for Battery Park when Bernie
Williams walked into the room looking for some breakfast.

"Matt?" he said.

"Hey, Bernie," I said, standing up. "What's going on?"

He smiled, shrugging at the dozens of people milling around
waiting for the party to start.

"So what are you up to now?" he asked me.

"You mean here?" I asked.

"No, no. I mean, I saw you around here the last couple of
days. I meant what are you doing with yourself?"

"I just started law school," I said.

Bernie's face lit up.

"Law school!" he said. "Wow. I remember when you were
in high school."

"Yeah," I said, smiling. "I'm done with high school *and*
college."

"So you're gonna be a lawyer?"

"Yeah," I said. "I hope so. Gimme three years."

"I'd always thought it'd be fun to be a lawyer," Bernie told me.

"I never knew that," I said.

"Yeah," he said. "After baseball, and music, it might have been something I'd have liked to try."

Bernie had arrived at Yankee Stadium just about the same time that I had. He'd been the most introverted player in the clubhouse, timid on and off the field, but both he and his career had blossomed in the years since. He'd been named the MVP of the American League Championship Series in 1996, and had been awarded both all-star recognition and a Gold Glove in each of the previous two years. He was coming off a season in which he'd hit .339 and won the American League batting title. He was starting in center field for the New York Yankees and would soon sign a seven-year, $85 million contract that would keep him playing on that hallowed ground for the foreseeable future. He had just won his second World Series ring.

It hadn't occurred to me that a superstar center fielder for the New York Yankees might have been tempted by any other career than the one he had. Six years had passed since we'd met on my first day as a bat boy, a span during which Bernie had become rich, famous, and adored by millions of people. When I was sixteen, he had my dream job. Six years later, I'd come to the understanding that I was suited for different work altogether, and the center fielder for the New York Yankees respected that—and me.

I'd been wrong a few days earlier. It wasn't that I couldn't return to the clubhouse. It was that I no longer needed to. I'd followed my childhood dreams to this point, farther than I might ever have imagined. It was time now to move beyond them.

. . .

The luxury buses the Yankees had rented deposited us—players, coaches, executives, clubhouse staff, and one stow-away—at the base of Manhattan, just north of the Staten Island Ferry terminal. We'd been given a police escort from the Bronx, and as the buses sped down the West Side Highway, tens of thousands of people were visible crowding the streets to the east.

I walked over to where the floats were lined up at the base of lower Broadway. Yankees employees with clipboards directed people onto the platforms above various vehicles. I clambered up onto the least-crowded float I saw, which turned out to be carrying the bulk of the Yankees coaching staff. Once everyone was loaded, the police car at the front of the procession turned on its lights and started moving forward.

When the float I was on made the turn onto Broadway, we were hit by a wall of sound so intense I had to grab hold of the railing next to me to steady myself. Lining both sides of the street, as far as it was possible to see, were hundreds of thousands of people; the crowd was estimated in the next day's papers at three and a half million. Their shouts and cries seemed to bounce off the granite walls of the skyscrapers up and down the Canyon of Heroes; it was deafening.

As the parade crawled up Broadway toward city hall, the noise began to subside a little. The biggest Yankees stars—Jeter, Williams, O'Neill, Cone, Wells, Torre, and Steinbrenner—had already passed by, and back where we were at the tail end of the procession, the fans still packed in against the barricades lining the street were getting a little restless.

Nearing Trinity Church, we inched up alongside a teenager who had climbed up a light post and found a seat on top of the WALK / DON'T WALK signal box. I was standing along the railing on that side of the coaches' float; he couldn't have been more than ten feet away from me. Through the confetti and shredded paper that was still cascading down on us from above, we briefly made eye contact.

"Who are you?" he bellowed at the top of his lungs. "Who are you?"

The fans squeezed in below him looked up at him, then at me, then back at him. He extended his arms out, palms up, and began flapping them toward the sky in the universal sign for more noise.

"Who are you!" he bellowed again, pointing at me.

"Who are you!" they all began to chant in unison. "Who are you?!?"

Acknowledgments

I am indebted to many people for their support and assistance in writing this book. Without their encouragement, I would have found the task both far more arduous and far less satisfying.

First, I am grateful to Bill Thomas, my editor at Doubleday, both for giving me my first chance and, as the manuscript took shape, for guiding me through the process with great enthusiasm and a very sure hand. Also at Doubleday I want to thank Kendra Harpster and Christine Pride. I am tremendously lucky to have Heather Schroder, at International Creative Management, as my agent, counselor, and friend. I can't say whether I'm more grateful to Heather for her confidence in me or for her superb advice, but I don't know where I'd be without the benefit of both. Also at ICM I want to thank Margot Meyers and Chrissy Rikkers.

I could not have hoped for a better teacher, at a more timely moment, than my college writing professor Jim Shepard. His lessons on how to read more closely have made me a much stronger writer, and his early encouragement was instrumental in planting the seed that I might actually be capable of writing a book myself. I might never have completed a first draft of my

first chapter if not for my friend Matt Thomas's close reading of
that initial tentative effort. Game recaps from the *New York
Times*—most written by Jack Curry—proved very helpful in re-
freshing my memory of games played more than ten years ago. I
began this book in earnest while working as a law clerk to Judge
Deborah A. Batts of the United States District Court for the
Southern District of New York, and I am extraordinarily grateful to her, and Bill Delaney, and Sharon Jones, for having allowed
me to do so. Later on, my friends Jeff Alexander, Gist Croft, Cate
Hartley, Dan Ionascu, Marc Johnson, Andrew Miller, Anthony
Qaiyum, and Chris Wiedmann provided particularly thorough
critiques of the complete manuscript, and their comments were
exceedingly helpful. I am especially grateful to Kathy Busby for
her singular role in helping me reach the finish line.

A significant portion of this book was written during a resi-
dency at Yaddo; being granted time to write there was not only an
honor but an added impetus to do my best work, and I am grateful to its staff and to the institution itself. Back in New York City,
I ended enough nights of writing with a late nightcap at West, my
neighborhood bar and home away from home, that I must thank
Patrick Campi and Clay Glad for their hospitality and compan-
ionship. Also in New York, I want to thank the urban storytelling
collective The Moth for inviting me to share a number of my
Yankees stories there. I know of no more exciting and creative lit-
erary scene in New York or anywhere else than that surrounding
The Moth, and I am thankful to Lea Thau, Catherine Burns,
Jenifer Hixson, and Andy Borowitz for welcoming me into it.

Mostly I would like to thank my parents, my brother
Damien, my sister Sarina, and my brother-in-law Jason for their
support and encouragement from day one. For their assistance,
inspiration, and other assorted kindnesses, I would also like to
thank Dan Ambrosio, Tom Bissell, Joan Carvo, Tom Downey,

Brian Eiting, Julie Fendo, Regan Good, Colin Harrison, Liz Hartley, Tovi Kratovil, Joe Lisi, Dunigan O'Keeffe, Jonathan Ryland, John Werwaiss, Chris Wheeler, Derek Williams, and my late friend and high school classmate Greg Trost.

Of course, I am forever indebted to the New York Yankees, and in particular to George Steinbrenner, Dick Kraft, Brian Cashman, Nick Priore, and Rob Cucuzza: for hiring me, for the Yankee Foundation scholarship that allowed me to attend Williams College, and for making possible all the adventures recounted herein. But for the Yankees, I might never have developed a childhood love for baseball, and without that, I might never have crossed paths with most of the people listed above.